THE ABOMINATIONS
OF THE OBAMA-NATION

THE **ABOMINATIONS**
OF THE **OBAMA-NATION**

The Audacity of Ruthless Ambitions vs.
the Hope of God's Assurance

The Anti-Christianity Pro-Shariah
Secular Progressive Revolution
in America

BETTY SUE PROLLOCK
Christian American Patriot

THE ABOMINATIONS OF THE OBAMA-NATION
The Audacity of Ruthless Ambitions vs. the Hope of God's Assurance

Unless otherwise indicated, all Bible quotations are from the New Century Version Bible.

iUniverse books may be ordered through booksellers or by contacting:

iUniverse LLC
1663 Liberty Drive
Bloomington, IN 47403
www.iuniverse.com
1-800-Authors (1-800-288-4677)

ISBN: 978-1-4917-3391-2 (sc)
ISBN: 978-1-4917-3390-5 (hc)
ISBN: 978-1-4917-3389-9 (e)

Library of Congress Control Number: 2014909005

Printed in the United States of America.

iUniverse rev. date: 09/10/2014

All images are from Dreamstime.com except for the image of the author.
Graphic arts on the cover are the work of Margarita Patrova.
Edited by Melody Dareing and iUniverse.
Original coordinator (outside iUniverse) Merisa Davis.

Contents

I want to dedicate this book first and foremost to my Lord and Savior, Jesus Christ. To the One who loves me at the weakest moments of my life. I thank Him for being my constant companion and confidant. I thank Him for His love, His grace, His forgiveness, and His sweet revelation of His Word.

Second, I want to dedicate this book to my wonderful and loving mother, Dorothy Sue Parker. For her nurturing nature, kindness, and gentleness of spirit, and for her contagious sense of humor. I want to thank her for her support and enduring stamina and strength of heart to give me hope and inspiration. I want to thank her for teaching me the bedrock of God's Holy Word and living an example that is true to it. I want to thank her for not giving up on me during the hard lessons of adolescence and teaching me how to forgive. I also want to thank her for her fellowship and companionship, now in the winter of her life, and giving me the opportunity to share our lives together.

I want to dedicate this book to the love of my life, my husband of thirty-five years, Bud. For his helping me to grow into who I have become and teaching me to keep my focus in the right direction, always sprinkling it with humor. For all the beautiful words of encouragement and inspiration, for keeping me and our family grounded, and for being a good instructor about life. For always coming through difficult times with new hope for a better future. For helping me fulfill the never-ending process for the development of this book. And for being the husband I was meant to have and to hold, till death do us part, and being the father who taught our sons the needed virtues to build good character.

I want to dedicate this book to the two apples of my eye. The two people who carry a portion of my heart with them everywhere they go, no matter how far away that might be, Brian Jr. and Benjamin. For their challenges they brought home throughout the years and for the uncanny ability to make me laugh, whether it was at them, at myself, or at something else. For honing my social skills and presenting vigorous debate and helping me develop a stronger character within myself and sharpening my wit. I am grateful for the respect, honor, and love I receive from them both.

I also want to dedicate a portion of the proceeds from this book to There's Hope Ministries in response to God's blessing in making this book a reality. There's Hope America Inc., located in metropolitan Atlanta, Georgia, is comprised of four ministries, each with its own mission and purpose for spreading the message of hope. The kind of hope that frees so many to live by what is really true and not just by our changing circumstances.

I look forward to seeing all of you in paradise someday.

With love,
Betty Sue

Foreword

Yes, we Americans have been asleep. While we were sleeping, fundamental changes have been taking place in this country. Those changes are moving us from our Constitutional government to a bureaucratic government with Shariah-compliant overtones.

This book is about how our God-given rights are being substituted with government-given "equal rights," called social justice, with the intent to make everyone the same or perceivably "equal." Information in this book shows how some see victims of society, such as the poor, minorities, and special interest groups, as needing the government to provide more rights, opportunities, and advantages to them at the expense of the successful, wealthy, white, or Christian citizenry.

They believe this—along with the oppression of the "nonvictims"—will bring about equality.

Betty Sue Prollock has been married for over thirty years and is a mother to two fine grown men, both of whom she is very proud. They bring her joy and inspiration. They also help broaden her insight into the areas of business, sports, cyberspace, humor, and the unique male thought and inclinations.

She is an experienced, skilled laborer in the residential construction field, so she has had an abundance of free time on her hands lately. She is currently the caregiver for her ninety-two-year-old mother, who is blind from macular degeneration.

One of the questions you might be asking yourself right now is, "What qualifies her to write this book?"

She is not sure how to answer that question.

It was almost as if she woke up one day and out of the blue was determined to write a book. It became clear that it was an act of faith because she knows she would not have come up with the idea for a book on her own. She was in unfamiliar territory, but there was a gentle hand that kept moving her forward.

She had recently rededicated her life to Christ and surrendered everything to Him. She prayed for Him to make her an instrument of His peace and grace and for His will to be done in her life.

The next thing she knew, she was writing a book. The irony is she started her research and preparation long before she knew where it would lead.

This is the first time she has ever been at home for a lengthy period of time and not building onto her own home or running a business. She has had several of her own businesses, having worked in various venues including child care, real estate, home improvements, and sales. She has been contract labor and has done volunteer work for churches and the Boy Scouts. Her pursuits into higher education have been limited. This was her choice.

She does not idolize the grand academic world. She believes many very smart people get overlooked because they do not have several letters behind their names and are complaining about enormous student loan debt. For some, it is more about economics than intelligence and knowledge.

Higher education is a great accomplishment, and she applauds those who have achieved it. But experience is educational, too. Life is a good teacher. She believes there are advantages to becoming accomplished through practice. She believes that achievement and knowledge through experience can be applied just as well as those from academia.

She hopes this book proves that.

This book is her view as a well-informed, born-again Christian patriot who has found it impossible to remain silent. She has awakened after a long slumber to find the familiar place where she fell asleep has changed to somewhere she does not recognize.

She hopes to show how our American idea of individuality, self-governance, and national sovereignty of the past is systematically being changed by undermining our foundations. She will also show what we can do to stop this national scale "hope and change" government-sponsored, victim-mentality revolution.

She will expose the thinking behind the agenda using Bible verses, documentation from a variety of sources, and examples from Barack Hussein Obama himself and his book *Dreams from My Father*. Even more examples are from his Obama-nation—a support system spread throughout all departments and government-influenced institutions, including our schools, which also includes organizations such as Gay & Lesbian Alliance Against Defamation (GLAAD) and the Muslim Brotherhood.

The next few years will determine the destiny of this nation. They will determine if our Constitutional rights will be destroyed. Those trying to get rid of those rights have, so far, only managed to bend them.

The silent moral majority needs to arise from its slumber and adorn itself with God's full armor, bear the sword of His word, and remove those scribes of false "hope and change" from positions of authority.

Ephesians 6:11, 14-18 (NIV):

> Put on the full armor of God so that you can fight against the
>   devil's evil tricks.
> It goes on to describe just what that is:
> The belt of truth tied around your waist.
> The protection of right living on your chest.
> On your feet wear the Good News of peace.
> The shield of faith with which you can stop all the burning
>   arrows of the Evil One.
> God's salvation as your helmet.
> The sword of the Spirit, which is the word of God.
> Pray in the Spirit . . . all kinds of prayers
> Always be ready and never give up.
> Always pray for all God's people.[1]

How does that sound? Like many out there, she has past regrets and sometimes forgets to pray and sometimes loses her focus of God's will. But she hopes this book helps to clear up misinformation and help others understand misinformation's subtle—and not so subtle—ways of persuasion and the ideas behind it all that are being used to dismantle and lead this country straight to either God's judgment, secularism, or Shariah (Islamic) law. She is not sure which one would be worse.

"A nation can survive its fools, and even the ambitious. But it cannot survive treason from within. An enemy at the gates is less formidable, for he is known and carries his banner openly. But the traitor moves amongst those within the gate freely, his sly whispers rustling through all the alleys, heard in the very halls of government itself. For the traitor appears not a traitor; he speaks in accents familiar to his victims, and he wears their face and their arguments, he appeals to the baseness that lies deep in the hearts of all men. He rots the soul of a nation, he works secretly and unknown in the night to undermine the pillars of the city, he infects the body politic so that it can no longer resist. A murderer is less to fear. The traitor is the plague."

Marcus Tullius Cicero (c. 106-43 BC)

Introduction

Up until 2008, my political attention was modest at best, and my spiritual attention was not much better. That all changed. "Hope and change" was the cadence of the day, but for some reason, something was amiss. I was in agreement with the need for hope and for some changes, but what was this push to "fundamental change" or "fundamental transform" our country? The fundamentals were not what needed to be changed. They were what we needed to get back to.

The changes were not only rocking the checks and balances and the ideals of achievement in doing business but were changing our perspective. Changes like our responsibilities being exchanged for rights or entitlements and an about-face on our trust in self-reliance and God. The pace at which this was transpiring was staggering. I found myself still reeling over one absurd decision when I would hear of the next one, all of them motivated by an emotional overreaction and not thoughtful deliberation and reason. I could not keep up with them all. This was what prompted the creation of a database that has blossomed into an assemblage that would rival the Affordable Care Act (ACA). Only in volume, that is.

Unlike the ACA, I have actually read everything in my database. Every abominable entry. I named it *The Obamanation's Abominations*. Luckily for the readers of this book, I tried to just glean portions from it to supplement other resources.

One of those other resources was the Bible. It quickly became my inspiration. My focus changed too, among other things. The concepts and fundamentals upon which this country was founded were all right there. Laws of nature, our God-given rights, our sense of reasoning, tolerance, and harmony were all right there. Awareness is wonderful—both in a patriotic sense and in a personal or spiritual one, too.

Awakened to a new respect and love for God's Word and a much broader view of the political landscape than I had ever experienced before, I saw a new purpose or journey had been set before me. There arose a stirring in my soul to listen, read, watch, and learn what was going on underneath the surface of all the political theater. I needed to deliver a message.

The message is to tell about a pattern or a design to remove our Judeo-Christian roots and replace them with something clinical, generic, and cold using deception and coercion on an inattentive society.

My hopes are that a stirring will develop in others to help solidify the importance of standing strong with the principles and values that made this country unique and blessed by God and see the deliberate effort underway to tear us away from those roots. Without roots, an instrument of growth will wither and die and a building without its foundation will crumble and fall. It is very fundamental.

Americans are America. We are America, not the government. And we are the instruments of growth that dictate the direction of prosperity by our moral compass. It is our obligation, our duty, and our right to do just that—dictate the direction of our prosperity.

Come follow me through my findings and revelations of the calculated pattern or design of those who oppose the ideals of Judeo-Christian ethics, moral principles and values, and standards of right and wrong that have been the reality and mindset of America since its inception. And see that it was these ideals that led America to our economic exceptionalism and to become a global inspiration. And it is the moving away from these that is causing our falter.

The first part of this book will unveil my personal journey of discovery, which left me shaken and put on guard. It shows the influence and seduction cast upon the needy and those who are struggling with life's challenges by immoral and power-hungry individuals who have thrown reason and righteousness to the wind.

The focus of the second part is on the character of Barack Hussein Obama through revelations in his book, which I found too numerous and unique to ignore. Chapter 9 is a guided tour through his book, chapter by chapter, giving brief insights, as an average American Christian, of the odd and indirect messages hidden behind a screen of obscurity and double-talk showing Obama's proclivities and tendency for self-justification and resentfulness as I understood it. It continues with examples of his character through his speeches and actions that give the same message and in the same obscure and cryptic way.

Because of the obvious familiarity that Obama has displayed when in the company of Muslims, part 3 of this book concentrates on the data uncovered concerning the activities of certain Muslims and Muslim groups. Obama's exposure to this world, I believe, explains much, if not most, of Obama's slanted views. This part exposes the constant push being pressed upon the practices and procedures in all of America's industries and enterprises to advance Shariah law compliancy, including all the branches of government. At the end of the book, there is a glossary of Arabic words that I found remarkable. Words that I found surprising and some vaguely offensive in regard to their cultural background that could produce such a vocabulary, but also, it is their evaluations and perceptions about "infidels" like myself.

The last but not least part of this book addresses what, I believe, is the fundamental moral drift that has swept across this country, which has left a devastating dearth of morality, logic, and self-restraint. America is the prey of the unjust and the lovers of self who put themselves above all else and are feasting on the bodies, souls, and minds of our children and each other and inviting others to pull a chair up to the table. How long are we going to let them dine and celebrate their immorality?

My conclusion is simple and is the only solution that I consider viable and lasting. I hope for the realization that we need to trust in God and adhere to the laws of nature—God's nature. The nature that we were set upon at the beginning, the nature that has blessed this nation and provided safe haven for so many, and the only nature that will carry us to the end.

A good leader wants to please truth and the laws of nature. A good Christian wants to please God.

I ask you, do you believe that what you believe is really real? Is it just? Is it the truth?

PART 1

The Quest to End the Judeo-Christian Influence

Chapter 1

The Catalyst

St. Paul's Cathedral in New York City

I open my eyes and see daylight streaming in through the blinds of my bedroom window. The first thought rushing into my head is an image of the faces of impatient patrons waiting to be checked out at the retail store where I work followed by the next thought, "Early morning sales meeting; don't be late." These were the last few words of the general manager just before exiting the building late the night before.

Our meetings are constructed by and for a muster of sleepy-eyed employees to perfect our facades of enthusiasm, attitudes, and interest using little play-acting scenarios or skits that we are to practice. We act out pretend encounters with customers so we can practice how to manipulate the situation and their thinking such as only using open-ended questions and such. The other formalities, such as questions and answers and discussions about store policy and logistics concerning the business operations, were more to my liking. These are straightforward. I have never been comfortable with manipulation, even for business purposes, because it seems so disingenuous and deceitful.

I have not been sleeping very well for weeks. The news media and the atmosphere in the general public felt different. A veil of something unidentifiable, something that seems heavy, had been stretched over all of us. The media that I had grown up relying on to keep me abreast of current events and of news in the political arena were showing partiality and prejudice, which seemed to be toward me. Not personally, of course, but of the makeup of my thinking, my sense of right and wrong, acceptability in society, and my feelings of patriotism.

After the meeting, I was able to return home. I was one of the assistant managers, so I worked mostly nights and weekends. Do not misunderstand. I am not complaining. Being general manager has its perks, as it should. I was attending night classes at a campus that was several miles away on the nights I did not work. I was pursuing a residential construction certification, so my interests lay elsewhere. On these occasions of late-night driving, after studying things such as estimating, critical path management, contracts, and blueprint reading, I started listening to talk radio in the car. It quickly became the highlight of the whole day. I started looking forward to listening to Herman Cain and Sean Hannity on late-night talk radio.

I was inspired. They were talking to people who felt the same as I about the political landscape. I felt as if I had some kindred spirits out there. I started sleeping a little better, too.

The unstable climate of my beloved country was causing me to pay attention to it, finally. I call it a climate because it was all around me. It was a subtle attitude of change due to discontent starting to develop. Things to which I never really gave much thought and never considered a problem were the topics of vigorous debate, such as health care and the separation of church and state. I would hear comments and see policy changes at work that I thought were bizarre.

Being totally caught up in work, finances, friends, and family affairs, I had not paid attention to the state of affairs of my country. I was bothered by it, in fleeting moments of thought, but not enough to devote any time to finding out what was going on. That was what was keeping me awake at night.

Longtime friendships I had in the past started to come under pressure. Moral issues were being considered social issues. Principles and standards we stood by together were no longer being held to with the camaraderie we had had previously. I was being accused of being judgmental and hypocritical. I started feeling a chill where there was only warmth before.

I was taught the Bible as a child by my parents but had stopped reading it and going to church except for Christmas and Easter but had always considered myself a Christian. I had just enough knowledge of the Bible to identify the false reasoning I heard on the news. The hair on the back of my neck would bristle. This caused a new focus and new priority in my life. Prayer, church, and Bible study were starting to become my place of refuge and solace. That was just the beginning.

I had a dentist appointment the following week, and, while sitting in the waiting room, I starting listening to the news. Summer was upon us, and an election was coming up. I had not paid too much attention to the candidates. I had always voted Republican and was planning on doing the same this time, too. The talking heads on the newscasts were all abuzz about the Republican and the Democratic candidates.

I lost interest in the news and looked down on the table mounded with magazines. On the table was a booklet with a bust of George Washington on the cover. It looked out of place lying amid the magazines, and I thought it odd for this time of year because his birthday was in February. I figured it must be because the Fourth of July was just around the corner.

Partly through the article, it asked, "What do you know about this little church?" It was a small, humble church building surrounded by huge buildings that reached to the sky. It would probably not be noticed if taking a surround photo of the New York City skyline.

As I was scanning the article, the words "consecrated ground" jumped off of the page. Church? Consecrated? It was talking about St. Paul's Cathedral. St. Paul's Cathedral is where George Washington dedicated this nation to God in his inaugural address on April 30, 1789.

Such being the impressions under which I have, in obedience to the public summons, repaired to the present station, it would be peculiarly improper to omit in this first official act my fervent supplications to that Almighty Being who rules over the universe, who presides in the councils of nations, and whose providential aids can supply every human defect, that His benediction may consecrate to the liberties and happiness of the people of the United States a Government instituted by themselves for these essential purposes, and may enable every instrument employed in its administration to execute with success the functions allotted to his charge.[1]

Washington, DC, was not the capital at the time. New York City was. President Washington was sworn in at Federal Hall on Wall Street, and then they walked to the cathedral to hear Washington make his speech before the members of Congress.

I found out that the ground now known as Ground Zero was once owned by this little church. So Ground Zero was, or is, on consecrated ground? What kind of irony is this, I asked myself? It took just a few seconds to wrap my head around this. That is when they called my name over the intercom. It was time to go get my teeth cleaned.

That is all I could think about on the way home. Is this it? I ended up reading the whole speech. How profound. How eloquent. I marveled over the language and the expressions. It was beautiful. What astonished me was I understood it. This was required reading in school, but I could not understand it back then. Somehow I felt I was supposed to know about this little church. Why? I could not tell you, but I was hungry to know more.

Days pass and I start to feel guidance, a current or a cadence that is leading me to a revelation. The Bible says, "Trust in the Lord with all you heart, and don't depend on your own understanding."[2] What was happening to me?

If through Christ we can come before God with freedom and without fear, wouldn't it be necessary to know who we are and who He is? Is what is happening to this nation and to me the purpose and will of Almighty God? What is that purpose? In order to understand and find out, I first need to know the foundation of this country—what it was founded upon.

Sunlight was beaming in through the window the next day. It was going to be another hot summer day in Georgia. I had the day off and probably should have run some errands, but instead I found myself doing some research.

I start with the concept of a nation dedicated to God . . . the consecration ground. Is that the foundation of this nation, its dedication? Its purpose? Being in the construction industry pretty much all my life, my idea of foundations are concrete or stone. It is the strongest part of the formation necessary to support the full burden of a structure. So, what makes for the strongest foundation of a nation, and why should I be concerned? I have always assumed that America is exceptional and beyond reproach. Are the grumblers against the church and the defamers against America gaining ground? Are they undermining the very ground *they* are standing on? I supposed I was meant to look into it.

I found that our purpose has been a secret buried in the foundation of the United States, which has been hidden since the very first day of George Washington's inauguration. He dedicated this nation to God and consecrated it through God, but there was a caveat. God's judgment will come if we turn away from Him. Does this somehow explain 9/11?

Are we experiencing God's judgment and punishment? Is He angry with us, maybe? With me? Is He trying to wake me up and get me to start paying attention? Is He shaking our world and the ground beneath our feet, and we are ignoring Him? I believe I am starting to wake up.

The next few weeks I made time to listen to the news. It was chaotic in both parties. No one was standing out front, and all of them were cannibalizing each other. It was hard to stay focused. I started watching, listening, and reading the Bible and various news sources more and more. I would stay up late reading and could not pass up any article or commentary that discussed the state of the union. I also took a course on the Constitution online for free from Hillsdale College. It is something I highly recommend everyone to do.

The idea that the Constitution of this country was founded on Judeo-Christian ethics, moral values, and principles apparently is a controversial concept to some. But the more I read about the Constitution's history, the more I realize this concept is absolutely true.

The men that we know as our Founding Fathers based all three of our founding documents on the nature of God. The reality of God shines through His nature and His grace, which results in the willingness to do His will. How is it I am able to understand this and the big thinkers that represent us cannot? This is not hard to find or figure out.

Now wait a moment. I want to think about this. Is it really that simple? I believe it is. I have yet to hear of, know of, or see anyone, ever, with the ability or knowledge to challenge the wisdom of God or His word. I do not care what his or her title is or which Ivy League university gave him or her a diploma. No one is smarter than Jehovah God.

What a great idea for a foundation. It had not ever been tried before, and, while many countries have implemented a form of democracy in their governments since, no one has used this country's specific formula based on the same principles the Founding Fathers established.

So why try to destroy or distort that which is based on perfection?

I am realizing that those who are alien to the nature of God and do not understand the purpose of this nation, from God's perspective, wish to challenge His work, which is evidenced in our Constitution. Worse yet, they are currently occupying offices in our government, our institutions, and the White House.

My lack of attention was resulting in making misinformation and misquotes, deliberate or not, widely accepted as truth. Half-truths, so-called white lies, are where selective facts are being changed or omitted in certain media outlets. These are far worse than outright lies because they are more believable. What still puzzles me, though, is if I can see this, and I just got started, why doesn't anybody else see this, too? Have we all been asleep at the wheel?

These altered facts are being used to exploit the American public. We have become easily manipulated and are led into doing, saying, and feeling whatever pseudo-outrage is being hyped. We do the biddings of those with ulterior motives while thinking it's our own idea. This is scary. How long has this been going on?

If one's intentions were honorable, deceit would not be necessary.

I am finding complacency is very dangerous. The progressive elitists, the statists, whom I now call the Obama-nation, want and need everyone to be complacent in order to retain and gain more power.

But I believe they badly underestimate the silent moral majority, and their folly will be due to their continual disregard of it. At least that is what I am hoping for. I want to awaken this sleeping giant.

This has to stop, or we will wake up one day to a rewritten Constitution, and the Bible, which gives us the principles upon which our Constitution was founded, will be banned as a book of hate and intolerance. It could happen.

Two months have gone by and tension has increased between some of my friends and me. We seem to not be able to find common ground on any given subject. I found Facebook and other social media unsocial and unpleasant due to all the confrontational personalities. I lost interest.

We have a new president, Barack Hussein Obama Jr. I believe Martin Luther King Jr. would have been disappointed, at best, in the results of the 2008 election. I say that, being an admirer of King's dream and his peaceful crusade for America, because King's dream was to become a colorblind nation. His dream was for all people to be judged by their character, not by the color of their skin.

The election of the United States' first African-American president could have been a momentous event for everyone. It could have been the expression of a nation, as a whole, overcoming its dark past. Yet, I fear the only ones who saw the election of Barack Hussein Obama Jr. as momentous were "progressives" and those Americans who saw only his color. They heard his fragrant words but knew little or nothing about Obama or his politics.

It is my goal, as an American, to prevent someone with an agenda of "fundamentally transforming" America from ever seizing the office of president again. We all need to make a move. This book is mine.

There are not enough questions on the important issues being asked by the media. He enamors them. There are too many ideas numbing our instincts, paralyzing our intuitions, compromising our sense of logic, and altering our worldview. These are attempts to persuade us that right is wrong and wrong is right through political correctness. The worshiping media exalt the drama queens and seekers of instant gratification. I find Fox News the only source on cable or noncable news to be sane, which other media sources and Obama-nation demonize.

The Obama-nation did not start this "progressive movement." They have only sped it up and made it worse in an unprecedented way. I am not a scholar, celebrity, or aristocrat. All I have is common sense, logic, and a newfound faith, and even I can see though this. As an average Christian-American woman, I can no longer be silent. The virtue of our nation is disappearing, and we're letting it happen. Only by the grace of God will this nation prevail.

I came dragging myself in one Friday night after work feeling exhausted. That night, I had the pleasure of working with all three of the gay individuals that work at the store. I had the job of trying to manage their time for them. I only did this out of necessity because they do not manage their own time in a productive way, and the general manager will not fire them. Working with them is like trying to herd cats. I grab a quick bite and a small glass of milk and then hit the sack. My last thought and prayer:

> My dear heavenly Father,
>
> I surrender unto You my soul and my service. May my weakness be to You a strength.
>
> May my gullibility and vulnerability be to me my assurance. Cause me to follow the path You prepared for me long before I knew You. Fill me with Your Spirit so that I can fulfill Your purpose.
>
> Guide me. Protect me. Prepare me further with the humbling I need for battle. Bless and keep me. Cause the light of Your favor to shine upon me. Shield my life under the umbrella of Your glory and grace.

I give thanks for Your plan and direction. I give thanks for the whisper in the dark and the shouts in the day proclaiming Your design. I give thanks for Your sacrifice and Your love.

In the name of Your Son and my Savior, who is the whisper and the shout of Your design, Your sacrifice, and may His Light shine through me, dear Lord,

Amen.

Chapter 2

Are We a Christian Nation?

Washington Monument

Laus Deo, **which is Latin for "Praise be to God," is the inscription on the east face of the aluminum capstone of the Washington Monument.**

I open my eyes the next morning, and there is just a dim light coming in through the window. I look out, and everything is wet. I wonder how long it is going to rain. I replay the dream I just had, while staring out the window before the day caused it to disappear. It was a dream that brought a new revelation.

I had ended up sleeping a little longer than I usually did. Rain has that effect on me. What is America? Who are we? That was the prevailing thought. I focused back on the window, a rainy Saturday. I would have to work that night but only a short shift from 5:00 p.m. to 10:00 p.m. This would give me time to do some reading.

Is America still a Christian nation? Is my answer based on my own faith or on public opinion? Is that something of the past? When was the point of transition or is it just being presented that way?

The next morning my husband and I got up to go to church. Bud had been noticing the same things I had in society but has a demanding career that dominates his time. His support for my newfound purpose in life was a godsend for which I am eternally grateful.

He attended a course with me called the Truth Project, which both of us found quite eye-opening. Its theme was, "Do you really believe that what you believe is really real?" It dove into to the question, "What is truth?" It focused on the confession by Jesus to Pilate: "Pilate answered, 'So you are a king!' Jesus answered, 'You are the one saying I am a king. This is why I was born and come into the world: to tell people the truth. And everyone who belongs to the truth listens to me'" (John 18:37).[1]

Here was a pretty clear statement about the reason He came into the world. He came to destroy the works of the devil (1 John 3:8).[2] What is the devil? A liar. He also came to bring a sword, the sword being the Word of God (Ephesians 6:17),[3] and to give His life as a ransom to take away our sins.

We left church, and I started to ponder, again, over the question, "Who are we, we Americans?"

If America isn't a Christian nation, why have a national motto of "In God We Trust"? Why do we have within our Pledge of Allegiance "one nation under God"? Why are the walls of monuments and halls of our government buildings covered with pleas and references to God if America isn't a Christian nation? Were these things put in place against the will or knowledge of the people?

Then it occurred to me; we are "one nation under God." That is who we are. So where does the debate of "separation of church and state" come in? This phrase is not from the Declaration of Independence, the United States Constitution, or the Bill of Rights. I researched the phrase and found it is from a letter to the Danbury Baptist Association written by Thomas Jefferson.[4] It was written to calm the fears and suspicions of government control over their religion, not the other way around.

The reason for the fear: our forefathers' history with the government-controlled Church of England and the Catholic Church-controlled governments in Europe. The First Amendment does not support the interpretation of today's version of the "separation of church and state," because our Founding Fathers believed that churches and church members can and should influence politics. Influence and control are not the same things.

Some argue that the government should have no ties to any one religion—of any kind—and be totally devoid of religious influence. I actually agree. But some proponents of this thought believe government is supposed to promote religious diversity. To quote Ronald Reagan, "There you go again."

The word "diversity" is not in any of our founding documents either. It is a new progressive concept. A person can be misleading depending on his or her viewpoint, political goal, intent, and interpretation of the definition of "an establishment of religion." The principle that is clear is that Congress is not to make any laws that favor the establishment of a religion on a national or government level.

A mandated, totalitarian government religion was what the Founding Fathers wanted to avoid at all costs. So putting this in the First Amendment was a good idea. The Founding Fathers thought it was important enough to put it first in the document. The redefining of this part of the First Amendment is shameful.

This is a touchy subject. Friends of mine who are ignorant on this fact break out in a tirade because they interpret such statements about the Constitution's connection with Christianity as an insinuation the document is a religious one. Others interpret this as saying the Constitution is promoting the establishment of a Christian religion. Both interpretations are wrong. "If you want good fruit, you must make the tree good. If your tree is not good, it will have bad fruit. A tree is known by the kind of fruit it produces" (Matthew 12:33).[5]

This is not referring to a Christian religion but to the premise of Christianity. This is where we get the Judeo-Christian ethic, moral values, and principle, and standards of right and wrong or "laws of nature and of nature's God" or commonly called God's natural law.[6] Right reason. It is not complicated. This is not a religion. Christianity is many things, but it is not a religion. It is, however, *also* found in biblical law. Christianity is our reality. It is the way we validate ourselves and the world around us. It is *how* we think, not just *what* we think. It is a belief system someone can follow that is exhibited by Christians but is not inclusive to them. Virtues of Christianity are not necessarily always exhibited by Christians or by them only. Christianity is also the faith of different branches, or denominations, of Christian religions that practice Christianity. Those denominations are the means to practice this belief system or faith. Another virtue of Christianity, and most important to Christians, is it is the means by which one can have a personal relationship with God and Jesus Christ. This is not complicated. I am a very simple thinker, and this is how I understand it. This is how I think our Founding Father saw it, too. So why all the fuss?

The very first paragraph in the Declaration of Independence affirms that this country's formation was to be declared according to "Nature's God." The very next paragraph begins with "We hold these truths to be self-evident, that all men are created equal, that they are endowed by their Creator with certain unalienable rights, that among these are Life, Liberty and the Pursuit of Happiness."[7]

"Nature's God" and "By Their Creator" clearly establishes that this country was, is, and should continue to be sustained by God's will, not man's will. This reality was the starting point. Mankind is flawed. We always have been and always will be. Progressives, however, believe that mankind is evolving into a more godlike species and sometimes use themselves as examples of this (i.e., intelligence, worldliness, science, technology).

The Truth Project was a nine-week course into the study of truth at our church. Bud and I had just completed building an addition to our house to make room for a new addition to our home. We had decided to bring my, at the time, eighty-nine-year-old blind mother to come live with us, and I would stop working retail and stay home and care for her. Even though the scheduling and distractions were immense, Bud and I did not miss a class.

Our class pointed out how the perspective of contemporary culture, in this country and worldwide, stands in direct opposition to the truth-centered worldview taught in the Bible. If the Bible teaches truth, then are Americans, and the world, following lies that will eventually end up in social insanity?

I believe the reality, upon which the founders relied and knew to be true, simply through history, was the absolute truth that God, His will and nature, is perfect. Therefore, in order to establish the Constitution of the United States and later its amendments, God had to be the only common point of reference. What better premise to have as a fail-safe to "form a more perfect Union" and to draft its documents that would assure the success of this nation?[8] Which would work better, man-made values or those based on the nature of God?

Fischer Ames, coauthor of the First Amendment, said in "The Bible as a School Textbook" speech, "[Why] should not the Bible regain the place it once held as a school book? Its morals are pure, its examples captivating and noble. The reverence for the Sacred Book that is thus early impressed lasts long; and probably if not impressed in infancy, never takes firm hold of the mind."[9]

For 175 years or so it has worked. It should be obvious from the omnipresent fact that mankind is sinful and that "right" and "wrong" are, from the beginning of time and forever more, tethered to the laws of God. That is the basis of Judeo-Christian ethic, moral values, and principle and to the laws of nature. The question is, "Who is he who considers himself wiser and smarter than God?" One doesn't necessarily have to read the Bible to know the answer.

Things in the news have heated up, and we are beginning to get glimpses into President Obama's campaign phrase "fundamentally transform" our nation into something I don't even believe he thought was possible. He knew he had to work fast because his time of no opposition due to the Republican Party minority in both houses of Congress, the judicial branch, and the White House would not last forever.

The machine that was formed to transform this country into something I did not recognize was monstrous. I had to start keeping a database just to retain it all. It was the bailouts, the borrowing of astronomical amounts of money from China, the government takeover of major industries, the pandering to labor unions, the denouncing our Christian heritage, the demonizing the sanctity of life, giving authority to the United Nations over our rights, and all kinds of questionable activity with evil people, and evil religions and organizations, to just name a few. That was just the first three months in office.

I grew up mostly in the '60s and '70s, but I do not remember much of the protesting in the '60s. I graduated in 1975. Protesting was not something I have ever thought about. The Tax Day Tea Party rally in downtown Atlanta in front of the capitol building in 2010 was my first. Bud and I stood there for five hours shouting, singing, laughing, and carrying our homemade signs and finally felt that we were a part of something that could possibly be able to stop our nation's freefall. For me, it was almost a religious experience. Fellowship. Bud was glad he was a part it, too, even though his knees were throbbing. It was good to be there.

My interest in the founding of our nation grew stronger. I started subscribing to numerous media sources and think-tank organizations, such as the Heritage Foundation and Liberty Central. The more I read and researched, the more I believed the solid foundation we have was rooted in Christianity and that there is a brazen movement in play to change that path.

Here are some hard facts. In 1984, two University of Houston political scientists, Donald Lutz and Charles Hyneman, wrote about the sources that most influenced the development of American political thought during our nation's founding era, (1760-1805). Their research paper was called "The Relative Influence of European Writers on Late Eighteenth-Century American Political Thought."[10]

After analyzing some 15,000 items published during that forty-five-year period, Lutz and Hyneman isolated 3,154 direct quotes cited by the founders, identified the source of these quotes, and discovered that 34 percent came directly out of the Bible.

Three-quarters of the biblical citations of this period's guideline came from reprinted sermons, which was one of the most popular types of political writing during these years. Only 9 percent came from secular literature. These statistics undeniably reflect the Bible's impact on the Founding Fathers and on our nation's documents.

One of The Truth Project classes we attended focused on philosophy as "a scientific quest to discover ultimate reality," according to Dr. R. C. Sproul Jr., teaching fellow of Ligonier Ministries and founder of Highlands Ministries. This is the absolute definition of biblical truth. Truth equals reality. That expands our understanding of God.

The dependence on the Bible for guidance and direction in developing this country is the only thing that makes sense knowing all the statements and imploring done by the Founding Fathers to keep God's reality at the core of our nation's laws. Arguments arise when the objective is to manipulate the meaning to serve an individual's self-interest rather than seeing the intent of those writing the original documents.

In discussing the freedom of religion in the First Amendment, the second part of the phrase is totally ignored—"(not) prohibiting the free exercise (of religion) thereof."[11] The Obama-nation does not understand that its strategy and its agenda are as blatantly obvious to some of us as the noses on their faces. The more they meddle in these affairs of God, I believe the more acquainted they will become with God's wrath. I still believe in God's protection. "Respect the Lord your God. You must worship him and make your promises only in his name" (Deuteronomy 6:13).[12]

In 2010, I attended the 8/28 Restoring Honor rally in Washington, DC, that Glenn Beck organized. It was moving. The trip enabled me to generate new friendships and to understand that the forces of fundamental reform of this nation have a mighty opposition. My travel companion was a new citizen to the United States from South Africa, which made the trip just that much more meaningful.

The following October, I attended the Restoring America Conference at my church and heard speeches by Herman Cain, Fred Barnes, Walid Shoebat, and Ann Coulter. This left me feeling like I needed to do something to join the crusade to educate the part of the population that is too busy or too stuck in a rut of daily routines. These are the folks who are clueless to the freedoms and liberties that are being deemed unnecessary for them to have by followers of statism or socialism.

Progressives. I prefer to write, since I am not a speaker with world-renowned distinction or stardom.

One of my conclusions is that I have come to see the 1960s as a time of discord and rebellion that produced a generation that found sticking to a moral and ethical path set forth by God was not as fun or easy as they preferred. So they began the deliberate redefining of the rulebooks. The fail-safes created in the bedrock by the Founding Fathers, which had to remain the prevailing rationale, began to be challenged by progressives who no longer could tolerate God's boundaries of ethics or morals. What they refer to as "social issues."

"Self" became the epicenter of reality. The fact that it was God, in all His perfection, who was and is the ultimate point of origin oppressed them. I ask myself, have things gotten better or worse as a result?

Progressivism is rooted in the philosophy of European thinkers and goes back to the most notable German philosopher, G. W. F. Hegel. It takes its name from "historical progress."[13] According to leading supporters from our past, such as Woodrow Wilson, Theodore Roosevelt, and John Dewey, human nature has evolved beyond the limitations that the founders identified.

They believed that properly enlightened human beings could be entrusted with power and would not abuse it, so, somehow, fearing man's capacity for doing evil would be no longer necessary.

They believe that each period of history is guided by different and unique values and principles that change over time. The "self-evident truths" that the founders upheld in the Declaration of Independence, including natural rights, are no longer applicable. Circumstances, not eternal values and principles, ultimately dictate social justice.

So, if human nature is improving, and fixed values and principles are no longer applicable, then government should be updated according to the "new" reality, right? The Constitution's means of government, with its separation of powers, checks and balances, and federalism, are just obstacles of effective government, according to progressives. They want to replace our Constitutional form of limited government for a more favorable "living Constitution," one which evolves with time.

The 1960s may or may not have been the start of the progressive movement, but it was definitely when they began to speak openly and boldly in public forums. This generation makes up a large portion of the lawmakers, government decision makers, lawyers, teachers, and tax collectors today. The Obama-nation.

The Judeo-Christian ethic, and moral values and principles, and standards of right and wrong are being redefined too by the Obama-nation. The "redefining" is to the cornerstone of this nation established in the Bill of Rights, which was designed to work *only* if God's reality was its base. Godlessness or secularism *cannot* be our base.

Only the most willfully disrespectful person would debate the fact that the generation that founded this great country believed that God had overseen its establishment and continues to protect what has become known as the United States of America. The public expression of this was most common in the past, and the majority of the people appreciated God's laws.

In his first inaugural address, President George Washington said, "No people can be bound to acknowledge and adore the Invisible Hand which conducts the affairs of men more than those of the United States."[14]

In Washington's Thanksgiving address (1789), he said, "That we then may all unite in rendering unto Him our sincere and humble thanks for His kind care and protection of the people of this country previous to their becoming a nation; for the signal and manifold mercies and the favorable interpositions of His providence in the course and conclusion of the late war."[15]

Thomas Jefferson (author of the Declaration of Independence and America's third president) said, "God who gave us life gave us liberty. Can the liberties of a nation be thought secure when we have removed a conviction that these liberties are the Gift of God? Indeed I tremble for my country when I reflect that God is just, that His justice cannot sleep forever"(quote inscribed on the northeast interior wall of the Jefferson Memorial, Washington DC).[16]

I cannot seem to be able to read enough of these historic debates and speeches by such eloquent and uniquely selfless individuals. Conditions of this country would turn around if these were still taught in our schools by teachers who still believe in their message.

Jefferson's warning is as relevant today as it was when he said it. The God who gave and protected our liberties is the same God who can remove and overthrow them according to His wrath and judgment. The question is who do you trust more, God or the government?

Some would say that God is currently judging us now; removing His hand of protection from America and showing us His divine judgment by turning us over to our enemies. I must confess that I have wondered if this is His will before us. Listening to the news can be disheartening, but there are also flashes of hope. I believe the more exposure people have to the "new" reality and the "new" standards of right and wrong behavior and the impact of this false reality, the more their common sense and logic will emerge.

"Lord, guard me from the power of wicked people; protect me from cruel people who plan to trip me up. The proud hid a trap for me. They spread out a net beside the road; they set traps for me. I said to the Lord, 'You are my God.' Lord, listen to my prayer for help. Lord God, my mighty savior, you protect me in battle. Lord, do not give the wicked what they want. Don't let their plans succeed, or they will become proud" (Psalm 140:4-8).[17]

We need to want to avoid judgment and the wrath of God and make America the "shining city on a hill" once again. That way is through knowledge and education of God's natural law and applying it in all that we do. We may think that is too much to do or too hard. Actually, it is no harder than being kind, understanding, humble, forgiving, and thankful, and trying to do the right thing. Does following the Ten Commandments keep us from enjoying our life? Surrendering one's life to Christ or making a commitment to a church are not mandatory, just beneficial for one's soul. Dedication to Christ is a personal decision and cannot be dictated or mandated by an institution or government.

I still have hope even with all the signs that America is fast losing her freedoms and liberties and is falling into the throes of socialism, atheism, humanism, or maybe even fascism or communism. The Obama-nation will come to know the power of God and the covenant this country has with Him the more they try to neglect and abuse the

Constitution and Bill of Rights, documents meant to protect the rights and liberties God gave every American. I will keep the faith.

Freedom is not whatever "Uncle Sam" or "Big Brother" determines freedom to be. We must resist this idea if one of the three branches of the government declares that a God-given liberty is not a God-given liberty but is a temporary and transient "privilege of the state." The fact that our Creator, via natural and revealed law, has endowed us with certain "unalienable rights" and liberties should never be taken for granted. Only God, not governments, can give or take away "rights."

The Obama-nation proclaims that health care or health insurance is a "right" instead of a privilege or responsibility such as a house or car. This is not possible. It is a play on words. They are redefining the meaning of a "right." Their blatant disregard for our Constitution and Bill of Rights exposes their true intentions. They maintain our Constitution is already obsolete, and they believe they have the ability and "right" to change it to accommodate their agenda the same way they alter the meanings and the words in the Bible.

Daniel Webster was right: "God grants liberty only to those who love it and are always ready to guard and defend it."[18]

Some say there is another principle that is equally true: there will always remain a remnant of people who value freedom enough to never surrender it. I guess I fall into that category.

I have come to realize that some believers appear to be Christian in name only. I am not passing judgment on anyone because I have been there myself. I can identify with the behavior. My walk with Christ has had long spans of separation from His grace (the willingness to do God's will in all things) where I turned to self-focus, and my conduct was unbecoming to Christ. Whether it was through guilt or shame, tragedy or despair, or all of the above, I have turned back to the One who sustains me even though my focus is constantly being challenged. Sometimes I feel like a child with a short attention span, but I know that the love and forgiveness of God is overwhelming, and that is why I have hope for this country. *Oh, but by the grace of God, go I.*

Unfortunately, believers not living within God's grace are misleading to the casual observer when we believers do not live our lives in fellowship with God. This forms distrust and disillusionment. It then leads them to the conclusion that it is all fake and is all just for show. If they assume this about God's grace, it is not hard to understand why they discredit the Judeo-Christian ethic, moral values, and principles prescribed by the Creator.

We kind of brought it on ourselves. I know I feel pretty guilty. No wonder they look to other ideologies, like Islam, or turn against everything altogether and conclude that they, themselves, are the best choice to make the laws and rules by which we should all live "to form a more perfect Union, establish justice, insure domestic tranquility."[19]

Hypocrisy does more damage to the church and religion than we culprits realize. I should know; I've been one. However, I believe the church is exactly where these people need to be. It increases the odds of positive influence and change of heart. It helped me. The ironic and sad part is that because they are in the church, the skeptical witness cannot make the distinction between the believers living inside God's grace and those believers living outside of it. They all act the same . . . at church. I believe this is called a catch-22.

It is a good thing that professing a Christian faith is of no consequence in qualifying for citizenship. Profession of faith can only come from personal conviction and not by demand or a condition to achieve some kind of status. That is why being a Christian cannot be mandated by a government entity. It is a matter of the heart or soul. It is a personal thing between you and God. No one can force you to believe in something.

However, the need to understand the premise on which this country was founded—the Judeo-Christian ethic, the moral values and principle or nature's law, and the acknowledgement and acceptance of this law— are necessary for this nation's survival. Fellow patriots are those willing to fight and defend the principals of freedom and liberty expressed in our founding documents.

From the courses on the Constitution, it is my understanding that our Founding Fathers, from studying Aristotle (384-322 BC)[20] and Marcus Tullius Cicero (c. 106-43 BC),[21] learned that the laws of nature implied that a universal standard of morality existed by which our actions and behavior could be measured. They believed that these laws were available to all humans everywhere through reason, and they were eternal. They believed that these were self-evident truths and that constitutional or policy issues that these truths did not directly address should be handled through prudence and practical wisdom learned from a moral education of virtue.

Patriotism and commitment to our country, as a Christian nation, is under a slow attack. The removal of references to God and of Christian symbols, traditions, and practices from the public arena has become common. These are the very things protected by the First Amendment. The more compromises are made, the more emboldened the Obama-nation becomes.

If someone or some other nation were to try to destroy our government, are we not obligated to stand up and let the rest of the country know about it? It shouldn't be any different if it is coming from within the government. To remain silent to such corruption would make us as guilty of betrayal as those attempting the destruction.

Patrick Henry said it best: "Should I keep back my opinion at such a time, through fear of giving offense, I should consider myself as guilty of treason toward my country, and of an act of disloyalty toward the Majesty of Heaven, which I revere above all earthly kings."[22]

Being a proud Texan, I am always quick to try to identify with any and every expression of honor or acts of courage and nobility that comes out of the great lone star state. But sometimes things can be amiss.

In 1954, Lyndon B. Johnson (D-TX), then a senator, put into place what is known as the "Johnson Amendment."[23] This was meant to silence public criticism from religious leaders. This was punishment for the amount of outrage that was voiced over his behavior in Washington while campaigning for reelection. I guess religious leaders expected a higher level of integrity from him than he did for himself. His rule bans ministers from discussing electoral candidates from the pulpit, even though, legally, the First Amendment protects ministers' speech. This needs to be reversed and banned from happening again.

Churches and pastors, right now, live in fear of being punished, being penalized by the government, or being threatened to have the tax-exempt status revoked for what they choose to talk about. Before the amendment, there were no restrictions on what churches could or could not say with regard to speech about government and voting, except only a 1934 law preventing nonprofits from using a substantial part of their resources to lobby for legislation.

As a result, the Alliance Defense Fund sponsors Pulpit Freedom Sunday each year in October. It is an event associated with the Pulpit Initiative, a legal effort designed to secure the free speech rights of pastors in the pulpit. ADF hopes to go to court to have the Johnson Amendment struck down as unconstitutional. Participating pastors have committed to preach sermons that present biblical perspectives on the positions of electoral candidates. More than twelve hundred pastors in all fifty states, the District of Columbia, and Puerto Rico are registered. It has been in practice for over nine years now.

According to *The American Patriot's Bible,* edited by Dr. Richard G. Lee, my former pastor, there are seven principles for Judeo-Christian ethics:

1. The dignity of human life—"unalienable rights" (life, liberty, and the pursuit of happiness); dignity of life and for life, no matter what the status of maturity, is the first principle needed for any civilized society as endowed by their creator (God)

2. The traditional monogamous family—traditional marriage between one man and one woman as the backbone of a healthy society; that matrimony is holy and was created and ordained by God; that children should be produced within the institution of marriage that nature and nature's God dictate; preserving the traditional family is vital to the future of any great nation

3. A national work ethic—referring to almost six hundred references of work in scripture; "an honest day's work for an honest day's pay"; to provide for yourself; independent and free of government encumbrance; to find useful work for our hands; that work is good and should be enjoyed through a sense of fulfillment; does not value laziness; that when we work we use the gifts of God

4. The right to a God-centered education—"the fear of the Lord is the beginning of knowledge" (Proverbs 1:7 NKJV); to understand

creation, you first have to know the Creator; to stand as God's stewards in passing on his truth to our children; how to trust in God; how to diminish the role as teacher when our children mature and need to become fully independent and responsible adults; for the social and national morality to prevail

5. The Abrahamic covenant—the promise between Abraham and God that if Abraham followed God, obeyed His laws and commandments, God would bless Abraham with a generation of children that would outnumber the stars in the heavens (Israel) (Genesis 15:5 NKJV); states that if a person or a nation follows Abraham's lead, that that person or nation will be blessed, but disobedience will bring punishment upon themselves; "Righteousness exalts a nation, but sin is a reproach to any people" (Genesis 14:34 NKJV)

6. Common decency—that a decent nation is made up of decent people; will do the decent, right, and honest thing in time of trouble; will forfeit life and limb under the principle that others should experience freedom; to render aid to others in need

7. Our personal accountability to God—that we will be judged for our actions before God; knowing that there is a penalty for doing wrong and a blessing for doing the right thing[24]

Chapter 3

The Surrender of Sovereignty

What would you do if you came face-to-face with evil? Would you run, stand your ground and fight, surrender, or whip out a violin? We would never want to be in that situation, but then again, maybe we have been and just did not know it. I believe evil has no power except for the power we give it over ourselves personally. If the devil is evil, then he is not omnipotent, omnipresent, or omniscient. Only God is. For the most part, all the devil has is the power of manipulation and deception driven by hate and the knowledge of human nature. He cannot destroy us by his own hand, God does not allow it, but he can convince us to destroy ourselves—or each other.

With that in mind, let us consider the rationale and foundation of the Obama-nation's beloved United Nations and their appetite for world domination. Let's consider the alliances we have created through their "hate speech" agenda, Small Arms Treaty, Responsibility To Protect, global warming, Agenda 21, and the United Nations Convention on the Rights of the Child, to name just a few.

According to the United Nations home page, it is "an international organization founded in 1945 after the Second World War by 51 countries committed to maintaining international peace and security, developing friendly relations among nations and promoting social progress, better living standards and human rights."[1] The website goes on to tell about the four main purposes for the United Nations: peacekeeping, peace-building, conflict prevention, and humanitarian assistance. It also claims the UN works hard on sustainable development, environmental issues, counterterrorism, human rights, disarmament, and nonproliferation.

They all sound harmless—helpful even. Or are these all initiatives of the United Nations to create a "New World Order"?[2] An order, of course, where the UN will be in charge. Since the Obama-nation obtained power, we hear an abundance about entitlements and propaganda for redistribution. Due to the shifting global power to Asia, the UN is glad the United States' current crisis has reduced our previous economic dominance and military superiority. They see the opportunity for progress of their international negotiation process. I see this as the sign of the times.

"Our fight is not against people on earth but against the rulers and authorities and the powers of this world's darkness, against the spiritual powers of evil in the heavenly world" (Ephesians 6:12).[3]

The United Nations is not our friend.

If our Founding Fathers firmly believed God gave them divine inspiration in formulating our nation's foundation, wouldn't you say that turning to the laws and statutes of foreign nations would have been equal to treason in the days of our origin?

With respect to the many who had sacrificed so much to secure our independence and freedom from worldviews such as the Obama-nation's, the UN has repeatedly shown hostility to the sentiment our Founding Fathers stood for and wrote into our governing documents.

"Why are the nations so angry? Why are the people making useless plans? The kings of the earth prepare to fight, and their leaders make plans together against the Lord and his appointed one. They say, 'Let's break the chains that hold us back and throw off the ropes that tie us down'" (Psalm 2: 1-3).[4]

The continual mocking of our governing principles shows itself by the United Nations' pressure to disregard our First Amendment right to free speech with their "hate speech" laws. These laws go so far as to define "hate speech" as preaching the Word of God if it offends someone by revealing his or her sinful nature and behavior.[5]

Why would someone want to silence the revealing of sinful behavior? Such people are part of the campaign that says we are not supposed to judge anything. They say that making a judgment is discrimination. This is a play on words once again. Passing judgment or condemning a person is wrong, but making a judgment about the behavior is not wrong. I repeat, this is not wrong. Discernment is awareness and wisdom. We are supposed to discriminate against bad behavior, not people. Discriminating against and condemning *people* is wrong.

We are to love our fellow man, ourselves, our neighbor, and even our enemies. We are all created equally in God's image. It is the ability to discern our words, actions, and behavior that makes it possible to distinguish between our enemies and our friends. It should be obvious what is at play here.

Growing up in Texas, I was not taught as a child that guns are bad, either, but instead that guns are tools, not toys—tools that are necessary for the job they were meant to do, such as defense, hunting, and recreation. I was taught that inanimate objects do not have bad intentions; only people have those. This is why I will never understand the reason behind the idea that preventing me from defending myself with a proven effective tool for self-defense will make me safer. Could there be another reason they prefer I not be armed?

The UN has pressured the United States to overturn the Second Amendment right to bear arms with its Small Arms Treaty, which I have petitioned against.[6] The purpose of this treaty, and others like it, is to limit and restrict our right to bear most of our sporting, hunting, and small self-defense firearms.

Secretary of State Hilary Clinton and John Kerry have already signed this treaty initiative. Offenders of this treaty could be subjected to the justice of the International Court of Justice if we keep moving in this direction. Informally known as the "World Court," the ICJ is located in The Hague, Netherlands. It is part of the UN, which should tell you all you need to know about its probable attitude toward gun rights and citizen gun ownership.

In April 2010, Chicago's then Mayor Richard Daley held the tenth annual "Richard J. Daley Global Cities Forum," with mayors from around the world. At the event, Daley announced the idea of suing American gun manufacturers in the World Court. Philadelphia Mayor Michael Nutter and Mexico City Mayor Marcelo Ebrard Casaubon endorsed the idea. The World Court can only issue binding decisions in nation versus nation suits right now. I want to keep it this way.

In President Obama's April 2010 address to the nation, he explained the NATO campaign in Libya and cited the Responsibility to Protect doctrine as the main justification for the United States and international community to initiate air strikes against Libya.[7] Responsibility to

Protect, or Responsibility to Act, as cited by President Obama, is a set of principles backed by the UN based on the idea that sovereignty is not a privilege but a responsibility that can be revoked by members of the UN if a country is accused of "war crimes," "genocide," "crimes against humanity," or "ethnic cleansing."

Various United Nations-backed international bodies, including the International Criminal Court, or ICC, have carelessly used the term "war crimes" at times. They can remove a country's sovereignty due to their interpretation of "war crimes" or however else they want to categorize it.

This is also the doctrine that President Obama mentioned when he announced that he was sending American troops into Uganda. The International Crisis Group is the main author of Responsibility to Protect. George Soros sits on the executive board of an influential "crisis management organization" that is responsible for the push to intervene in Uganda.

George Soros's Open Society Institute, founded in 1993, is one of only three nongovernment funders of the Global Centre for Responsibility to Protect and has a uniquely sinister character. Some of the groups to which Soros has contributed, according to an article by "Human Events" on April 2, 2011, are ACORN, Apollo Alliance, National Council of La Raza, Tides Foundation, Huffington Post, Southern Poverty Law Center, Sojourners, People for the American Way, Planned Parenthood, and the National Organization for Women. All are progressive organizations. Soros maintains close ties to oil interests in Uganda's fledgling oil industry, which has the potential of being a two-billion-barrel business. Neither Libya nor Uganda posed a security threat to the United States at the time. This can be a good reason for the lack of drilling for oil on public lands here in America, too, but I wouldn't want to sound like a conspiracy theorist.

The International Crisis Group's retired president, Gareth Evans, and activist Ramesh Thakur are the original authors of the Responsibility to Protect doctrine. George Soros founded the International Crisis Group. This group, in partnership with the World Federalist Movement, is powerful and dangerous.

The World Federalist Movement is a group that promotes democratized global laws with complete constitutional power. It is a main coordinator and member of Responsibility to Protect Center. Thakur recently asked for a "global rebalancing" and international redistribution to create a "New World Order." The article was in the *Ottawa Citizen* newspaper.

When I first started reading this, I had to ask myself if I had been reading too much into this or reading the wrong thing into it. The word "federalist" insinuated the support of a federal constitution or union. If the United States Constitution was the constitution of choice, that would not be such a bad thing. But, alas, my hopes were quickly dashed.

Thakur said, "Toward a new world order, Westerners, (that would be us) must change lifestyles and support international redistribution." This was in reference to the destruction of our Constitution. Then, in referring to some kind of a United Nations-brokered international climate treaty, he said, "Developing countries must reorient growth in cleaner and greener directions." He considered the United States a bully to developing nations due to the expectations we have of those countries because we are the major contributor to their growth.

He continued, saying, "Westerners have lost their previous capacity to set standards and rules of behavior for the world. Unless they recognize this reality, there is little prospect of making significant progress in deadlocked international negotiations . . . the demonstration of the limits to U.S. and NATO power in Iraq and Afghanistan has left many less fearful of 'superior' Western power."

I find a glimmer of hope even with a powerful statement like this. It seems if the United States is not on board with their agenda 100 percent, "there is little prospect of making significant progress in deadlocked international negotiations." This could explain why we Westerners are being pushed to adopt watered down or ungodly ethical standards.

Thakur is considerably premature in his evaluation of our loss of "capacity to set standards and rules of behavior for the world," also. I do not believe that for now, but they are pressing for it very hard.

The UN has pressured the United States to have its military serve and swear allegiance to the UN instead of allegiance to the United States Constitution. They want our military serving under the United Nations' peacekeeping forces and wearing UN insignias on their uniforms. One thing is certain; they are persistent in their search for the chinks in our armor of sovereignty.

My son was stationed in Balad, Iraq, in a joint compound while he was serving in the army. He was not there but a few months but I prayed for his safety constantly. This was also another motivator to watch and listen to the news concerning foreign affairs. It angers me when I think of him being over there, and then I read something like this.

The appetite for power by greedy people knows no bounds. The UN also wants a world tax imposed on all financial transactions to fund a global model of social services providing "needy people" with a basic income, free health care, education, and housing. This sounds like a Muslim jizya tax. This is a tax that the Quran (9:29) specifies must be levied on Jews, Christians, and some other non-Muslim faiths as a sign of their defeat and enslavement under the Islamic social order. I will address this later in part 3 of this book.

The drive is part of the UN's aim to create a so-called "social protection floor" under the authority of the Commission of Social Development. The "social protection floor" will become the UN's primary focus from 2015 onward when the Millennium Development Goals project concludes.

"The money to fund these services may come from a new world tax," reports the *Deseret News*, quoting Jens Wandel, deputy director of the United Nations Development Program, who said that a long-term funding plan for the project would center around "a minimal financial transaction tax (of .005%). This will create $40 billion in revenue."[8]

"No one should live below a certain income level," stated Milos Koterec, president of the Economic and Social Council of the United Nations. "Everyone should be able to access at least basic health services, primary education, housing, water, sanitation, and other essential services."

This line of thinking goes against the reality of freedom and of self-responsibility, self-accountability, and the ability to make one's own decisions about one's own welfare and the welfare of his/her family. It also goes against the ethics, values, and principles taught in the Bible. The needy should depend on the charity of others not the mandated taxes of their neighbors. Gifts from charities are acts of love and compassion. Tax collection in the name of "hope and change" is socialism.

True charity offers help needed to get someone back to a self-reliant state and not dependency on others. We are not to just give a man a fish, because we only feed him for a day, but to teach a man to fish, so he can feed himself for a lifetime. Besides, we are to be dependent on God, not world governments, for our daily bread.

According to the report, the new global tax is designed to be on a progressive scale, with higher earners paying more to help provide "all needy people with a basic income, healthcare, education and housing." "The rich should pay their fair share" is a term I have heard recently over and over. This is proof of the on-going attempt by the Obama-nation and UN to con Western taxpayers to pay for their goals for a global government. It also explains the push by the Obama-nation to shift the thinking of Americans to look to government as the supplier for all of their basic needs here in our own country right now. How else could they justify providing for the basic needs for the entire world if they haven't implemented it here first?

The question is why would anyone trust the world leaders of socialist or Marxist governments, or worse, with a slush fund under its control under the pretense of solving the plight of the world's poor as its justification? I ask again, who considers himself wiser and smarter than God? This would be a diabolic downgrade. The UN showed its true colors when it used money meant to go to relief projects but went instead to enrich its own bank accounts, including the $732.4 million budget for earthquake-shattered Haiti. I saw a recent video of Haiti, and it doesn't look much different from the pictures we saw on the news just after the disaster.

A UN report entitled "Resilient People, Resilient Planet; A Future Worth Choosing" calls for punishing economies deemed not "sustainable" by establishing, "natural resource and external pricing instruments, including carbon pricing, through mechanisms such as taxation, regulation and emissions trading systems, by 2020."

A 2010 UN blueprint for putting it back at the forefront of a global government includes the idea to rebrand global warming as "overpopulation," as a means of dismantling the middle classes while using "global redistribution of wealth" and increased immigration to reinvigorate the pursuit of a one-world government.

The UN is also using the discredited man-made global warming to up the ante on industrially developed countries, such as America, through the imposition of carbon taxes. This is the "cap-and-trade" system, which is the American version of the same tactic used by the Obama-nation.

The conspiracy behind the anthropogenic (caused by humans) global warming myth was exposed by the University of East Anglia's Climate Research Unit (a.k.a. Hadley CRU), which released 61 megabytes of confidential files onto the Internet.

The Obama-nation did not even skip a beat or look over its shoulder once as Obama hustled off to Copenhagen for the Global Warming Summit with the United Nations Climate Change Conference (UNCCC) so he could push for his cap and trade agenda.

The scary thing is that this could have been the first step in achieving a one-world government with the UN as the ultimate center of our earthly universe. Maybe getting right with God right now doesn't seem as far-fetched and unpopular as it was previously. We have everything already in place to prevent all of these bad things, but only if we make a stand to preserve them. I hope we do because it gets worse.

The United Nations Climate Change Conference held in Durban, South Africa, in 2011, provided an opportunity for global progressives to make their argument that ordinary people should surrender their freedom and hand all money from taxes and power over to unelected, unaccountable "experts" like, well, the people at the conference.

The issue that had been called "global warming" for years was then rebranded as "climate change" due to the last decade's worth of data that proved "uncooperative." The term "overpopulation" was not found as popular either for obvious reasons. They also presented a plan under which the West (that would be us) would be mandated to respect "the rights of Mother Earth" by paying what they referred to as a "climate debt." Mother Earth?

I heard an alarm going off, and I don't think it is the one next to my bed. It was in my head, but I am hoping I was not the only one that heard it. Actually, everyone should have an alarm go off in his/her heads because it does not stop there, as far as the UN goes.

Another document I ran across is called "Agenda 21," which they adopted in 1992.[9] I had to sit down and read about this one over and over. It is a comprehensive plan of extreme environmental worship, social engineering, and global political control, and regrettably, the Obama-nation seems to be on board with it. This radical socialist plot is completely at odds with American liberty and values.

Agenda 21 attributes:

- put a cap on the number of people that they believe this planet can have by implementing population-control measures such as: forced abortions, promotion of antiprocreation behavior such as homosexuality, reduced or selective health-care accommodation for the elderly, and eliminating the ability of civilian self-defense
- limit energy consumption and minimizing the human "carbon footprint" on earth from fossil fuels
- force so-called "sustainable development" on the people of the world
- limit consumption of meat
- limit the use of electricity in our homes and at work, such as air-conditioning
- eliminate single-family suburban housing
- eliminate property ownership
- eliminate private car ownership
- limit Individuals' choice of travel
- regulate privately-owned farms and home gardens
- advocate social justice: "the right and opportunity of all people to benefit equally from the resources afforded by society and the environment"
- relinquish national independent sovereignty

Sounds great, does it not? The United Nations' agenda is being secretly pushed into local communities by a global organization known as ICLEI (formally called the International Council of Local Environmental Initiatives). This plan is usually disguised by innocent-sounding terms such as "Smart Growth," "Wildlands Project," "Resilient Cities," "Regional Visioning Projects," and various "green" or "alternative" projects.

The Republican National Committee and the Tennessee House of Representatives each have presented a resolution ruling, both of which are very similar, that addresses the destructive nature of this agenda. The liberty-minded John Birch Society also has taken action on this matter that, in addition to the other two, stops the state and local governments from using or spending money on any Agenda 21—related programs, or from working with ICLEI. However, pieces of this agenda have already been started without the approval of the Senate and without the knowledge of the American people.

Various extreme progressive groups, including People for the American Way and the largely discredited Southern Poverty Law Center, have attempted to demonize those who fight against Agenda 21. So far, their statements and defense of the UN's plan have mostly fallen on deaf ears, thankfully.

The Democratic Party in Tennessee issued a press release inaccurately claiming the UN scheme was "non-controversial." It cited support by other "democratic nations" as evidence, even while ignoring the plan's backing by dozens of mass-murdering regimes and assorted dictatorships.

New Hampshire and Georgia have also introduced similar measures opposing the plan. Others are expected to join the battle as pressure continues to build. Also, a growing number of local governments have been dropping their controversial membership in ICLEI, saving taxpayer money and ensuring that the United Nations "sustainability" schemes do not take root in their communities. More local governments are expected to join the fight.

Back on May 17, 2010, the United States Supreme Court gave its decision in the Graham V. Florida case citing a 1989 United Nations Treaty (Article 37(a) of the United Nations Convention on the Rights of the Child) that was *never* approved of or agreed to by the United States, as part of the basis for its ruling.[10]

Basically, in doing so, the Supreme Court was using foreign laws to better define our own Constitution.

More specifically the Eighth Amendment to the Constitution, which determines fair treatment for juveniles, was not clear enough for their legal decision. Why would the court consider this, knowing the obvious intentions of the United Nations to destroy our nation's sovereignty and Constitution and replace it with a secular authority in its place?

I know how all of this sounds. Sorry for the information overload. I have to trust that someone will read and act upon knowing these things in ways that will secure our way of life. I believe all of this is true. I see the actions and reactions; I hear the echoes resounding over and over from voices in the media and from the mouth of our president. My sources are all over the place—radio, Internet, websites, news stations on TV, books, magazines, newspapers, etc. I was getting the same information about the same topics. It was random. It answered my questions. I am now someone who watches news and reads newspaper articles—and not just the liberal or just the conservative rags, although I find the liberal media offensive and tend to keep it at a minimum. I make notes of new laws and regulations that have been put in place lately. The question is this: are you seeing the pattern through your own eyes? No matter what anyone thinks, keep reading. I believe the truth will stick once we have heard it.

Chapter 4

The New United States Constitution

The Constitution of the United States

Christmas came and went, and it is now a new year and facing all new trials and tribulations in the world. My mother and I have fallen into a routine that involves going to church on Sundays and going to the YMCA once or twice a week. She is proving to be a true inspiration and joy to me and others. No more days and nights of going to work and being offended by having my beliefs and principles trampled on, leaving me to pretend not to notice or understand what was being done. It was always a challenge to keep my mouth shut.

One day I ran across an NRANews.com article exposing a movement to torch the United States Constitution.[1] I had read other articles before on a push to make our Constitution and Bill of Rights unrecognizable. But those only included moves to make them more secular, more socialistic, and Shariah-compliant.

This article talked about the "Democratic Constitutionalism Movement." Harvard law professor Mark Tushnet perhaps offered best expression of this movement's intentions when he said, "For 30 years, conservatives have hijacked the Constitution, and we're taking it back."

Woodrow Wilson wrote, "For it is very clear that in fundamental theory socialism and democracy are almost if not quite one and the same. They both rest at bottom upon the absolute right of the community to determine its own destiny and that of its members."

I believe Woodrow Wilson to be a progressive.

The movement first showed itself in a 2005 American Constitution Society conference at Yale University Law School called "The Constitution in 2020." It has had another conference since, in 2009, and had a book published with the same name. The *New York Times Magazine* described its purpose in an article: "The organizers set out to gather together a group of scholars to define a progressive constitutional agenda for the coming century. The democratic constitutionalists see courts and political movements as partners, influencing each other and society as a whole."

Even Justice Ruth Bader Ginsburg made statements discrediting our Constitution during an Egyptian television interview on January 30, 2012. She lamented and dissuaded the newly-forming Egyptian government not to use the US Constitution as a model and urged them to look to other countries with newer constitutions for guidance as they craft their own. Her suggestion was South Africa's Constitution, which she called a "really great piece of work."

One major player at the core of the destruction of our founding documents and the one person instrumental in political activism, along with modifying our nation's direction, is the billionaire globalist George Soros. I will be mentioning him often, as his influence and multiplex of overlapping organizations and foundations is systemic. I believe him to be a mentor to President Obama.

Two other key people that initially became associates in the Obama Campaign and later heavily involved in the transition into the White House were among the participants of the conferences: John Podesta and Cass Sunstein.

John Podesta is chairman of perhaps the most successful organization of the Soros policy-influencing machine, the Center for American Progress. I also believe that most of the challenges to our liberties and freedoms and the change of our national direction as a democratic republic have come from this group and been turned into policy by the Obama-nation.

Cass Sunstein was a natural fit for the conferences, as his 2004 book, *The Second Bill of Rights: FDR's Unfinished Revolution and Why We Need It More Than Ever*, proposed a radical new document to replace America's traditional Bill of Rights.

1 Timothy 1:4-7 says,

> Tell them not to spend their time on stories that are not true and on long lists of names in family histories. These things only bring arguments; they do not help God's work, which is done in faith.
>
> The purpose of this command is for people to have love, a love that comes from a pure heart and a good conscience and a true faith. Some people have missed these things and turned to useless talk. They want to be teachers of the law, but they do not understand either what they are talking about or what they are sure about.[2]

It was starting to warm up outside, and I heard about another Tax Day Tea Party rally in downtown Atlanta at the courthouse. I was excited. Bud was not quite as excited as I due to some pain he started having in his knees, but being the trooper that he is, he went with me and was glad for it. It was the same atmosphere and the feeling I had before. This time, I got to shake Herman Cain's hand. I had been listening to his radio broadcast on AM radio and had become a fan.

As I have mentioned before, the undermining of our Constitution and the God-given principles and values at the heart of it can be subtle. The radicals who would deface the current Constitution plan to do so by stealth, by the details written below the surface or created by alternative means, such as administrative law or international treaties and agreements. This is the real threat.

A lead-off speaker during the follow-up 2009 Constitution in 2020 Conference, Professor Aziz Huq of the University of Chicago Law School, laid out the need for a deep political masquerade to accomplish real change. He directs the Brennan Center for Justice, which litigates voting rights, redistricting and campaign finance reforms, and policy work on presidential power and congressional oversight.

"We'll start with the problem of candor," Huq said. "No constitutional movement ever got very far by admitting that it sought innovation in the founding document. Or by admitting that it was enabled by the particularly social/historical or doctrinal circumstances of the change that it urged. Yet to be a credible movement for constitutional change—a credible social movement—that movement has to deny, in a sense, its ultimate goal."

Obviously all of their deceit and misinformation have been applied.

And the "deniable" goal clearly is to change what we see as our rights. The rights that gave us our unique reputation as the freest people in the world. Their plan is to make a new set of government-granted privileges masked as "rights." It's a kind of cultural "affirmative action" creating a constitutional caste system within the American populace—the haves and the have-nots. This is currently reflected in the Obama-nation's widespread culture war.

The last lesson of the Truth Project that Bud and I took was on "The State: Whose Law?" It pointed out the design, structure, and role of the state in God's plan for human society and the rightful extent and limits of its power. It showed that the state has to operate within proper boundaries, or it can become horrendously pathological and abusive if not kept in check.

One of my favorite, frequently quoted passages, was by Alexis De Tocqueville, a French jurist who visited the United States in 1831. He said this:

> I sought for the greatness and genius of America in her commodious harbors and her ample rivers, and it was not there; in her fertile fields and boundless prairies, and it was not there, in her rich mines and her vast world commerce, and it was not there. Not until I went to the churches of

America and heard her pulpits aflame with righteousness did I understand the secret of her genius and power. America is great because she is good, and if America ever ceases to be good, America will cease to be great.

God, Family, Country: Our Three Great Loyalties

Amen.[3]

The state has to be strictly subordinate to God's sovereign dominion and control. Why? Human governments are capable of error and transgressions. They have to be held to a higher ethical law to prevent them from wreaking havoc in the lives of the citizens.

To use the progressive definition of the Constitution as a "living organism," we have to understand that these people see themselves in the same light as genetic engineers. Cultural engineers, if you will. They are trying to alter the DNA or ethics encoded in our value system that guides us in the development and functioning of all that we do and how we think. Changing our freedoms and principles into something entirely unrecognizable—something most Americans, like myself, would consider a form of cancer.

If you were to suspect this is a key part of the Obama-nation's program for "fundamentally changing America," you would likely be right. President Obama has been quite up-front about his intentions. I have finally heard what it is he is saying. In fact, his "change" is a move in direct conflict with the individual liberties protected and guaranteed by the US Constitution as we know it.

The progressive movement has a dictionary being used by the Obama-nation to rewrite America's founding document to a global model. That work, I'm guessing based on South African ideas, states the guarantees the founders recognized as preexisting God-given rights—among them free speech, freedom to assemble, the right to be protected against undue search and seizure—are, according to progressives, all considered "negative rights."

I have actually heard President Obama use the term "negative rights" in reference to our Constitution in one of his many interviews.

These people are not talking about replacing the US Constitution outright. They seek to embed key viral elements of the proposed document, in a bit-by-bit replacement that will ultimately transform the whole nature of the Constitution's meaning. What is it that these people find so attractive in the South African Constitution? In a phrase, the answer is something they call "positive rights."

This is a play on words and their attempt to redefine everything. Progressives base their idea of what is a "positive right" and a "negative right" on how these rights relate to government. One restricts government, which they see as "negative," and one restricts the governed (that would be us) under the disguise of taking care of us, which they perceive as "positive."

The problem with this is that our "rights" are granted to us from God not governments. Our "rights" are the blessings of the natural laws mandated by God's perspective or His nature for continuity and a sustaining, moral people. With good reason they are "rights," for they are not privileges or responsibilities for individuals to achieve or acquire for themselves. History may have proven time and time again that what is too easily gotten is not appreciated. But history has also proven time and time over to beware of he who comes bearing gifts.

Among the "positive rights":

- access to adequate housing
- access to health-care services
- sufficient food
- appropriate social assistance

We already have public housing, social medicine, food stamps, and welfare for the poor and vulnerable. Is this what everyone is supposed to want from the government and be grateful to the government for it?

I suddenly had a moment of pause. Courts must consider international law in rendering decisions in this "new America," and may also consider foreign law. One of the "negative rights" we will have to surrender is our sovereignty. Shariah law will be one of the constructs in their judicial decisions. This is already in play as I have previously mentioned and will address further in chapter 14.

Even if we consider giving up our liberties and our current rights due to some implanted disillusionment that the present system isn't working, just like the way they convinced us our medical system was broken and needed them to fix it, consider this: none of these "positive rights" are even slightly attainable by the tens of millions of South Africans who live in unthinkable conditions of poverty. They also suffer from a murder rate nearly seven times higher than ours in the United States. Why trade liberty, freedom, and opportunity for this?

And the justification: Placing socio-economic rights in a constitution does not mean that every individual is entitled to assistance on demand. The state must take reasonable legislative and other measures, within its available resources, to achieve the progressive realization of each of these rights. Under a "limitations clause" on the socio-economic rights, the court's overall responsibility is to determine whether the infringement on the right is proportional to the resulting societal benefit.

Are these "rights" or are they entitlements, or better yet, privileges? I believe they are privileges or entitlements doled out under a deeply over reaching system of state rationing. With perhaps as many as seven million South African citizens that have died of HIV and AIDS, the constitution's guarantee of the "right" to "have access to health care services" was pointless under the regime of President Thabo Mbeki.

He denied the epidemic existed and kept Western life-saving medicine at bay while his people died. How could this framework of activists and professors alter the United States Constitution to take on elements of the South African model? Obviously not by any means provided in Article V of the Constitution, where the founders intentionally made things like this extraordinarily difficult to do. So what do they want? By what means do they purpose to alter the foundation of our nation? By what means do "positive rights" creep into constitutional law?

Those questions were actually at the very core of the second Yale conference. Among the backdoor approaches discussed:

- Enacting "landmark" laws that are too big and too complicated and that bring dramatic fundamental change. These laws take on the force of the Constitution (Obamacare).
- Enacting international treaties that have the force of law. As one speaker put it, "Once you have an Article II (ratified by the US

Senate) treaty in place, it can undo state law that's contrary, and undo federal law that's contrary" (Small Arms Treaty).

- Creating administrative law that the speaker claimed would be beyond the normal scope of judicial review (i.e., Environmental Protection Agency, Internal Revenue Service).

The Obama-nation has already done or has tried to do all of these things addressed at the second conference. Attendees also discussed a grassroots political effort to force the United States Senate to get rid of the filibuster with its sixty-vote requirement to close down debate, making all sorts of simple majority legislative mischief possible.

Conservative champions like Jim DeMint and Tom Coburn have used the "filibuster rule" with great effect, using it to stop all manner of outrageous legislation. The truth is the Founding Fathers wanted the Senate to be a deliberative body and to ensure that the voice and rights of the minority were always heard.

What the Soros-funded groups propose is a melding of their scheme to replace the Constitution with administrative orders, landmark laws, such as Obamacare, treaties, and the like, along with raw propaganda and a long-term, grassroots activist agenda. They want to mobilize for change on the streets—if you will, like Occupy Wall Street.

Yale law professor Jack Balkin, among the leaders of the "Constitution in 2020" movement, said grassroots politics is the key under "democratic constitutionalism": "The basic way that the Constitution changes over time is that people persuade each other that the way they thought about the Constitution and what it means is not the right way of thinking about it. That's why you just can't focus on elections, judicial appointments and the constitutional culture. That's why you have to focus on the peoples' arguments about norms."

Keep in mind that "norms"—"international norms"—are at the heart of the gun-ban movement worldwide.

It is a well-recognized "norm" that the UN pointedly refuses to recognize armed self-defense as a human "right." It is certainly that way for many in the "democratic constitutionalism" movement, for the kind of laws that have left South African citizens at the mercy of brutal murderers, and criminal violence is the vision they want for America's "constitutional norm" in our unforeseen future.

Thomas Jefferson, who I believe to be one of the most inspiring Founding Fathers, said it best to Thomas Cooper on November 29, 1802: "If we can but prevent the government from wasting the labours of the people, under the pretence of taking care of them, they must become happy."[4]

The endeavor to deliberately manipulate thoughts and what people will accept as "norms" in a given society to achieve a desired ideology is absolutely sinister. This prevents and interrupts the natural process of change caused by the consequences and reflection of our actions.

The midterm elections were just around the corner, and I was sending out e-mails to everyone I knew. This was my attempt to strengthen their resolve as mine had been.

Perhaps the most direct explanation of the goals the "Constitution in 2020" had were penned in a blog by Emily Zackin, now an assistant professor at Hunter College. "These 'positive rights' or 'welfarist policies' obligate government to intervene in social and economic life, promoting equality rather than simply procedural fairness," she wrote.

So, the term "fairness" is used, the very basis of real blind justice in America. This is to be replaced with social or cultural favoritism decided by a team of law school radicals. Dr. Zackin, who won top honors from Princeton for her PhD dissertation, was one of them.

"Positive Constitutional Rights in the United States" cited South Africa's constitution as an example:

"(The) South African Constitution includes the right to medical care. The text of the U. S. Constitution contains no such explicit guarantees, and the Supreme Court has consistently declined to interpret the Constitution to include them," she wrote.

These privileges or entitlements, disguised as "positive rights," are the key elements that make the South African constitution so attractive to welfare statists who would control every element of American life. These entitlements dump fairness in favor of drastically skewing the playing field to the advantage of select groups of citizens.

With this stealthy Soros-backed effort, the new, radical US Constitution that would emerge in the future will likely include as "positive rights" many government-granted privileges and collective rewards centered around endless names of "justice," such as "social justice" or "economic justice" or "green justice."

In a spot-on *Canada Free Press* analysis of the effect of "positive rights" versus "negative rights," Daniel Greenfield characterized the combined "positive rights" pressed by the so-called progressive establishment as "the right to be taken care of in every way possible."

"Positive rights" offers only one thing—a privilege that is overseen by the government and universal benefits at the cost of individual liberties. Yet privileges, unlike actual "rights" that we receive by God, can be withheld at the whim of those who hold the power of government. As for the sixty-one-thousand-word South African Constitution, perhaps Mark S. Kende, now head of the Constitutional Law Center at Drake University Law School, spelled out the best view of what US proponents are really striving for in a 2003 law review article.

The title of the article was clear: "Why the South African Constitution Is Better Than the United States.'" Giving meaning to Sunstein's delirious "most admirable constitution in the history of the world" opine, Kende says the description fits because "It contains a lengthy list of socio-economic rights, which the drafters hoped would protect and assist those . . . who are poor and vulnerable."

"Conversely," he says, "the United States Supreme Court has been unwilling to find socio-economic rights in the United States Constitution."

Their unwillingness to misconstrue the intent of the articles in the Constitution needs to remain a permanent condition.

One thing that I picked up from the Truth Project was that when ruling entities throughout world history overstep their bounds—deny the sovereignty of the constituents, seek to control every area of human life—tyranny, oppression, and violence usually follow.

Chapter 5

Misinformation or Misdirection

The reflecting pool in front of the Lincoln Memorial

I have made so many discoveries that I sometimes have to step away and find solace wherever I can. That includes things such as finding a good movie or television show; something neutral and without a forced acknowledgement or acceptance of a non-Christian view or assumption. It is getting harder and harder to do. I guess I had not realized how pronounced this drift had become. This is especially true for movies. They are pushing political statements in not-so-subtle ways, too. The only true promise of inspiration is when I read the Bible.

I have always believed that truthfulness and honesty are inseparable parts of good character. Telling lies can become a habit. It's a habit that can become engrained in one's very lifestyle to the point that one's conscience can be destroyed and rendered insensitive. A lie can become the consensus if told often enough.

It's still a lie, whether it is fostered on the movie screen, in the news media portrayed as common knowledge, or to promote one's ideological agenda. Lying to cover your tracks or to avoid having to acknowledge blame or guilt seems to have become standard operating procedure. People are flawed and make mistakes, and lying about it does not erase the mistake; it just means another mistake was made. A lie. In a world with no accountability, lies are completely acceptable, and truth becomes relative.

I believe a perfect example of this was the attempt to cut back on what was considered a waste of fresh water in the Lincoln Memorial Reflecting Pool. The solution resulted in the pool now being under constant attack from green slime.

The National Park Service reported in its December 2009 Environmental Assessment Report that something like this was expected after the completion of an almost two year, $34 million renovation with stimulus money to make the pool "sustainable" and "improve the quality and appearance of the water."[1]

The newly renovated pool is now filled with recirculated, non-potable water that is filtered and pumped in from the nearby Tidal Basin. When the pool needs to be cleaned—bird droppings are a major problem—the water can be "returned to the Tidal Basin," NPS said.

The old pool, completed in 1924, held about seven-million gallons of potable (drinking) water, much of which evaporated or continually leaked out. The leaks forced regular purchases of drinking water from the District of Columbia, but it was not a problem to keep it clear.

It is questionable whether their expensive remedy has reduced operating costs. This is a result of acting in haste and not thoroughly thinking their ideas through. So, was it really a waste of fresh water? This was an attempt to implement the "green initiative" to conserve and recycle the water with no regard to the cost. Sustainable? Maybe until the District of Columbia cannot afford it anymore. Haste makes waste, and in this case, green slime. They were not being honest about it, either. In my opinion, the whole project was based on the lie that the renovation was justified, and the consequences of that lie are still being felt today. Sometimes recycling is not a good idea.

"The republican principle demands that the deliberate sense of community should govern the conduct of those to whom they entrust the management of their affairs; but it does not require an unqualified complaisance to every sudden breeze of passion, or to every transient impulse which the people may receive from the arts of men, who flatter their prejudices to betray their interests" (Alexander Hamilton, Federalist 71).[2]

On a national scale, the Obama-nation is seeking to render our Constitution meaningless along with this effort of equal offense to rewrite or redefine true history as it relates to Judeo-Christian influence as I mentioned before.

Christian chaplain Pastor Todd DuBord submitted a letter to officials at the nation's historic Independence Hall in Philadelphia asking them to provide a more truthful and better experience for visitors after the pastor heard a tour guide make several statements discounting the Christian beliefs of the Founding Fathers while DuBord was on a guided tour.[3]

DuBord previously exposed tour guides at the United States Supreme Court building that were denying the multiple representations there of the Ten Commandments. He also exposed the agenda at work in the District of Columbia when the replica of the Washington Monument capstone, which is engraved with *Laus Deo*, or "Praise be to God," was positioned in the visitor's center so observers were not able to see the inscription. A coincidence, perhaps, but most likely not. It was "fixed" shortly after. In the very house in which they adopted a Creator-filled Declaration of Independence, not one positive comment was made about any one of the Founding Fathers' Christian faiths.

Various others have found a series of other efforts to remove mentions of God and references to the Christian faith and influences on the Founding Fathers from government grounds. In 2008, an "oversight" at the nation's $600-million-plus Capitol Visitor Center in Washington, DC, left the national motto "In God We Trust" absent from the historical displays. It took 109 members of Congress to get that changed.

DuBord also expressed how disturbed he was by what appeared to be revisionism in the presentations given to visitors at the Supreme Court. The marble frieze directly above the justices' bench was presented as the images of the people depicting the Majesty of the Law and Power of Government and that a table with ten Roman numerals, the first five down the left side and the last five down the right, were representative of the first ten amendments of the Bill of Rights, which is not true.

Those ten Roman numerals represent the Ten Commandments. In 1988, the Supreme Court had just become a National Historic Landmark and came under control of the United States Department of the Interior, which rewrote the handbook to leave out the reference to the Ten Commandments completely. The handbook from 1999 just said that the frieze "symbolizes early written laws" and referred to the depiction as the "Ten Amendments to the Bill of Rights."

I have so wanted to return to Washington, DC, and stay long enough to visit all the historical buildings and try to be imprinted by the majesty and magnum opus that our Founding Fathers instituted and memorialized there. The trip I made for the 8/28 Restoring Honor Conference was much too short. My fear, even now, is, will I be lied to? Will the things that I hold most dear about my country be omitted or redefined?

A resolution was passed reaffirming "In God We Trust" as the national motto of the United States, in an effort to encourage its display in public buildings and send a message to those who seek to remove God from the public domain.

Rep. J. Randy Forbes (R-VA), chairman of the Congressional Prayer Caucus and sponsor of the measure, said the resolution serves to clear up confusion over a speech President Obama gave in 2011 in Jakarta, Indonesia, where he stated that the motto was instead *E Pluribus Unum*, Latin for "Out of many, one." The blunder was quite telling.

"For the President of the United States to incorrectly state something as foundational as our national motto in another country is unacceptable," Forbes said. "The President is the primary representative of our nation to the world, and whether mistake or intention, his actions cast aside an integral part of American society.

"We need to make clear to the people in this country that our motto is 'In God We Trust' and encourage them to proudly display that motto," Forbes said.[4]

I could not agree more.

It was shortly after this inaccuracy that the Forsyth County Department of Transportation consented to a non-mandatory sticker of our motto that anyone registered in Forsyth County can have free of charge to display on his or her Georgia State license plate. Needless to say, I got several and gave them out to friends and family residing in Forsyth County.

Rep. Dan Lungren (R-CA) said the reaffirming is also important because the word "God" has been challenged in the courts when used on public buildings, such as the new United States Capitol Visitor Center, and in the Pledge of Allegiance when it's recited in public schools.

"This is an important message that we need to affirm. It is under attack, and we are not wasting time. How could we waste time making sure 'In God We Trust' is enshrined in our national motto?" Lungren said, after hearing murmuring from a condescending Jerrold Nadler (D-NY). Nadler said that the resolution is simply words that do nothing.

Rep. Jeff Miller (R-FL) said the United States has relied on its faith in God since its inception and then quoted Ronald Reagan: "If we ever forget that we're one nation under God, then we will be a nation gone under."

A black minister, the Reverend Wayne Perryman, filed suit against the Obama-nation for racial discrimination against white people. The lawsuit (case C11-1503) began because he was fed up with all the rhetoric coming from the Obama-nation blaming all of Obama's failures on white Republican racists.[5]

Perryman and journalist Robert Parks began researching the Democrat Party and became enraged when they noticed the Democrat Party, via its website, was whitewashing its own history. On the archived Democrat.org site, which has since been scrubbed, they gave a brief acknowledgment that their party was formed over two hundred years ago. The statement said that over two hundred years ago, the Democratic Party's founders decided that wealth and social status were not entitlements to rule. That was it. There was no mention of any of their mistakes or indiscretions. No mention of the fact that also over two hundred years ago, the Democrat Party blocked all efforts by Republicans to abolish slavery. When challenged, they added the following paragraph to the history portion of the website:

> Change is the inescapable driver of history in the US. Our party's founders believed then, just as we do now, that being a Democrat means meeting the challenges of changing times so that all America can prosper. That's why the people of this country have always turned to Democrats when times got tough. (In addition to trying to rewrite history regarding Democrats and slavery, they are also trying to hypnotize people into believing the Democrats were instrumental in civil rights—not mentioning anything about all the efforts they made to *block* all of the Republican efforts toward civil rights.) Democrats are unwavering in our support of equal opportunity for all Americans. That's why we've worked to pass every one of our nation's Civil Rights laws, and every law that protects workers. Most recently, Democrats stood together to reauthorize the Voting Rights Act. On every civil rights issue, Democrats have led the fight. We support vigorous enforcement of existing laws and remain committed to protecting fundamental civil rights in America.

According to Perryman and Robert Parks, this was a blatant lie, and they have called them on it. According to Parks's legal brief to the courts, the Reverend Al Sharpton said, "We never got our '40 acres and a mule.'"

"Yes, we did, and they were taken away by a Democrat," Parks said.

This is from Parks's legal brief:

> On January 12, 1865, General Sherman and Secretary of War Edwin M. Stanton went to meet with twenty Black community leaders in Savannah, GA to discuss freedom and reparations for former Black slaves By June 1865, over 40,000 former slaves were settled on 40-acre tracts of land. Over 400,000 acres were allocated. In September of 1865, Democrat President Andrew Johnson reversed Field Order No. 15, issued special pardons, and returned the land to former slave owners.

> The Republicans gave, yet a Democrat took it away.

Part of the lawsuit is to ensure the Democrat Party is portraying its history truthfully and factually. The Reverend Perryman writes:

Modern-day Democrats must stop preaching that they are the compassionate party of black people and confess that it was their predecessors who started many of the racist practices that we are now trying to eradicate. History clearly shows two things: (1) that the roots of racism grew deep in the hearts and souls of the Democrats and (2) without the past efforts of the Radical Republicans and the Abolitionists, the Civil Rights Legislation of the '60s would not have been possible. Republicans laid the foundation for civil rights by passing legislation and instituting programs that Democrats were adamantly opposed to, such as:

1. The Thirteenth Amendment in 1865 to abolish slavery.
2. The Civil Rights Act of 1966 to give Negroes citizenship and protect freed men from Black Codes (The term originated from "negro leaders and the Republicans" according to some historians) and other repressive legislation.
3. The First Reconstruction Act of 1867 to provide more efficient government of the Rebel—Democrat—controlled states.
4. The Fourteenth Amendment in 1868 to make all persons born in the U.S. citizens. Part of this Amendment specifically states "No State shall deprive any person of life, liberty, or property without due process of law; or deny any person within its jurisdiction the equal protection of the laws."
5. The Fifteenth Amendment of 1870 to give the right to vote to every citizen.
6. The Ku Klux Klan Act of 1875 to stop Klan terrorists from terrorizing black voters, Republicans, white teachers who taught blacks, and abolitionists.
7. The Civil Rights Act of 1875 to protect all citizens in their civil and legal rights and to prohibit racial discrimination in places of public accommodation.

8. Freedmen's Bureau was a social program established by Republicans to feed, protect, and educate the former slaves.
9. The 1957 Civil Rights Act and the 1960 Civil Rights Act were signed into law by President Eisenhower who also established the U.S. Civil Rights Commission in 1958, a commission that was rejected by Truman during his administration.
10. The 1964 Civil Rights Act where Republicans pushed law through while the Southern Democrats like Al Gore Sr. debated against its passage. More Republicans (in percentages) voted for this law than Democrats.

Parks believes shame of their past is why Democrats do not want blacks to know their history. One of their heroes, President Woodrow Wilson, Parks explained, had a racist-driven presidency that he "didn't learn in college." He pointed out that Wilson allowed various officials to segregate the toilets, cafeterias, and work areas of their departments. One justification involved health. Wilson's administration felt that government workers had to be protected from contagious diseases, especially venereal diseases, which they imagined that blacks were spreading. In extreme cases, federal officials built separate structures to house black workers.

During Wilson's reign, whites replaced most black diplomats. Numerous black federal officials in the South were removed from their posts, and the local Washington police force and fire department stopped hiring blacks. Wilson's own view, as he expressed it, was that federal segregation was an act of kindness.

Suppose a Republican president had done all of these things? Black Americans would have justification for calling Republicans racists, but they do not. You can Google "Woodrow Wilson Segregationist." According to Parks, black Democrats do not have much of an excuse for being deceived because of the Internet, which can give people access to truth. No matter what, the Democratic Party owns its racist history and needs to admit the truth to black Americans.

Does this kind of deceit arouse God's anger or judgment? The void of His presence is becoming visible in the lives of our executives and our governing authorities. The idea of God's anger is sometimes hard to grasp. It is easy to imagine that God is like an angry parent or friend, but God's nature and actions should not be judged by our human experience with human emotions. God's anger is not an uncontrollable emotion like ours. His is a determined expression of His will against sin and His righteousness is always at work. For people who try to do His will, His righteousness is experienced as salvation and grace. For those who do not, His righteousness is experienced as discipline. God's anger can be experienced by a separation from Him, too, and can be understood as Him giving people the very thing they seek.

"Because they did these things, God left them and let them go their sinful way, wanting only to do evil. As a result, they became full of sexual sin, using their bodies wrongly with each other. They traded the truth of God for a lie. They worshiped and served what had been created instead of the God who created those things, who should be praised forever. Amen" (Romans 1:24-25).[6]

God's anger is evident in allowing those who resist his way to have their own way. According to the book of Revelation, evil leads to more evil, so that evil ends up destroying itself. This is a message of hope also I believe. Evil will diminish itself by its own activity. This means that when people identify it in themselves and turn away from their own evil ways to embrace the ways of God, they no longer experience his anger and once again can experience His presence. I believe this to also be God's grace. This means that there is a distinction between those who follow God and those who do not.

I am not trying to pick on Democrats. I believe the Democratic Party is a necessity, along with the Republican Party, to achieve balance in a free nation. The United States of America is a Democratic Republic, not just a democracy and not just a republic. They are both essentials needed to accomplish the proper checks and balances needed and to keep accountability for both. However, I believe the progressive movement has infiltrated the Democratic Party much more than the Republican Party, but there are signs of their influence in both parties. They have managed to deceive more Democrats, though, both black and white. Here are some statistics that could explain the vast chasm occurring between the two parties with some revelations that have made the Democratic Party so vulnerable and showing the disenchantment in the principles to which this country has tried to adhere to for decades.

Results from Gallup's daily tracking polls conducted between June 1 and August 31 of 2012, are as follows:[7]

	Democrats	Republicans	Typical American
Those who seldom/never attend church	52%	38%	46%
Those who attend nearly weekly/monthly	20%	21%	20%
Those who attend every week	27%	40%	33%
No religious affiliation	19%	9%	15%

Gallup defines "Democrats" in its polling analysis as those who either identify themselves as Democrats or who identify themselves as independents that lean toward the Democratic Party, and defines "Republicans" the same way.

All in all, these statistics may show the likelihood of why the Democratic Party has been an easy target for the progressive movement. They have let their "shield of faith" down and have made themselves vulnerable to the "burning arrows of the Evil One" (Ephesians 6:16).[8]

The Supreme Court upheld the New York City school district practice of releasing students during school hours for religious instruction in the 1952 case *Zorach v. Clauson*. That isn't the significant point here, but this is what was written in its defense:

> The First Amendment ... does not say in every respect there shall be a "separation of Church and State." Rather ... there shall be no concert or union or dependency one on the other. That is the common sense of the matter. Otherwise the state and religion would be aliens to each other.
>
> Municipalities would not be permitted to render police or fire protection to religious groups ... Prayers in our legislative halls; the appeals to the Almighty in the messages of the Chief Executive; the proclamation making Thanksgiving Day a holiday; "so help me God" in our courtroom oaths—these and all other references to the Almighty that run through our laws, our public rituals, or ceremonies, would be flouting the First Amendment.

When the state . . . cooperates with religious authorities by adjusting the schedule of public events . . . it follows the best of our traditions. For it then respects the religious nature of our people and accommodates the public service to their spiritual needs.

To hold that it may not would be to find in the Constitution a requirement that the government show a callous indifference to religious groups. That would be preferring those who believe in no religion over those who do believe. We cannot read into the Bill of Rights such a philosophy of hostility to religion.[9]

Chapter 6

The Animus to Christianity

The Holy Bible

I think almost all Americans, especially Christians, would see as peculiar that President Obama delivered a Thanksgiving speech entitled "One Thanksgiving, Grateful for the Men and Women Who Defend Our Country."[1] In it, he referred to Thanksgiving as a "celebration of community." What were absent were any religious references, even though Thanksgiving is a holiday based on giving thanks or praise to God. He just said his family was "reflecting on how truly lucky we truly are."

I do not believe luck had anything to do with it. I, too, am deeply grateful for our men and women who sacrifice so much in the defense of our country and Constitution. As I have mentioned prior, my son was in the military and my husband's father retired as Col. Jack D. Prollock in the United States Air Force. But I also hold a deep gratitude to God for the opportunities and blessings He has given to us in this noble experiment, known as the United States of America, which we have come to love.

"All you nations, praise the Lord. All you people, praise him because the Lord loves us very much, and his truth is everlasting" (Psalm 117).[2]

For most Americans, Thanksgiving is a time to reflect on all these blessings, including the blessing of our military. His speech, in my opinion, fell flat and empty. A couple of old adages come to mind here: "What comes out of one's mouth says more about the person saying it than what he is saying it about," and "You can only fool some of the people some of the time, but you can't fool all the people all the time." Conservative sneers were met with ridicule and mockery.

"They knew God, but they did not give glory to God or thank him. Their thinking became useless. Their foolish minds were filled with darkness" (Romans 1:21).[3]

The truth is the Obama-nation always reacts surprised and angered when someone points out what is to some, obvious. They hate it when others make examples of repeated displays of President Obama's lack of godly conviction and reverence. They prefer it be ignored.

For what I believe is most of America, hearing the Word of God from true men of God is healing, comforting, reassuring, and provides biblical knowledge and meaning, but most of all, we receive immense joy from being able to worship, give thanks, and sing praise to Him with fellow worshipers.

In the book of Romans, Paul writes that everyone knows that God exists. Some just do not attempt to acknowledge Him. He felt that the difference between Christians and non-Christians was not that the Christian knows God and the non-Christian does not but that non-Christians just choose to ignore God.

I have always known about the need to worship God, but I did not always feel the joy. Even then, when my heart was not fully in it, I still absorbed the teachings from His Word—sometimes more than others. What limited knowledge I have gained from the Word of God, though, has helped me identify misquotes and misinformation that are predominately used in the Obama-nation.

This made the speech given by President Obama at the 2012 National Day of Prayer breakfast equally peculiar.[4] Most of the speech had overtones of scorn and sounded more like a scolding. At one juncture he said, "I know that far too many neighbors in our country have been hurt and treated unfairly over the last few years, and I believe in God's command to 'love thy neighbor as thyself.'"

It was as if he were accusing the audience filled with ministers of being guilty of doing this or allowing it to happen. He then went on to say that the same Golden Rule is found in other religions, too, pointing out that this concept wasn't unique to Christianity. He was trying to make the point not to discriminate. I can only speculate as to what kind of discrimination and assume he was referring to racial discrimination. It is as if he is living in a time warp that is stuck in the 1940s or '50s. God's will and nature has moved the window of acceptability, insight, and justice so much farther down His path of revelation since then. Obama is stuck in the past, and I hear resentment and not inspiration in his words.

The Bible goes much deeper into the subject. The second chapter of James implores everyone not to treat anyone differently, no matter what his or her status or birthright and to love your enemies. However, progressives see discrimination of any kind as bigotry and unfairness. They believe being indiscriminate, accepting everything, is a moral imperative. They do not want their actions to be judged. This extreme ideology makes insight, discernment, judgment of character flaws, and the need to distinguish between right and wrong unnecessary.

President Obama, while still addressing his audience, tried to use scripture to promote a political agenda by using it completely out of context for his convenience. Not being a biblical scholar, I still had a chuckle escape when he talked about "Jesus's teaching that 'for unto whom much is given, much shall be required.'" This verse isn't about giving more to the poor or paying more taxes so the government can do it, as President Obama alluded. Jesus spoke these words to the apostles. The "much" that Jesus is relating to was the knowledge of salvation through Him and the "requirement" was to go out into the world and share it. The humor in this was that the president's audience was mostly all ministers who know the Bible very well, much better than I. Again, his speech fell flat and empty but this time with a touch more splash.

President Obama, as a candidate, made one of the most shameful speeches I have ever had the misfortune to hear. It was made on June 28, 2006.[5] This sad display of irreverence and haughtiness toward Christianity and the Word of God was very revealing on the condition of his heart. He specifically referred to the books of Leviticus and

Deuteronomy, and the Sermon on the Mount, as examples that he considered to be unachievable expectations of the Bible. He then tried to apply scripture as the inspiration for Obamacare and the redistribution of other people's money. The absence of clarity is clear, and the mixed-message speaks volumes.

Attitude can reveal itself in many ways, even unintentionally. On September 15, 2011, while addressing a meeting of the Congressional Hispanic Caucus, President Obama misquoted the Gettysburg address by dropping "under God" and rearranging the verbage from the original text.[6] The message was very clear in this example, too. Whether this was intentional or just carelessness is suspect.

Atlanta is pulling out of another hot summer. There was another Restoring America Conference that I attended, and I did not miss any of the speakers. I was truly captivated by the two conferences before, and this one promised to be just as inspiring. One of the speakers at this one was Dinesh D'Souza, who talked about a documentary film he was producing in the near future called *2016*. Another speaker was David Barton. He was a historian and the founder of Wall-Builders, an organization dedicated to presenting America's forgotten moral, religious, and constitutional history, heritage, and heroes.

After hearing what these men had to say, I found out about Rev. Jim Wallis. He was a member of President Obama's "faith council" and was a spiritual adviser to the president. The reverend of what, I am not sure, has some uniquely unsavory views concerning our country. He once labeled the United States "the great captor and destroyer of human life" and championed communist causes and thinks all churches should promote "social justice."[7]

He believes and proclaims that Jesus was a socialist and that the Bible teaches socialism. He is the founder of the Washington-based social justice group Sojourners, which describes itself as a "biblical call to social justice, inspiring hope and building a movement to transform individuals, communities, the church and the world."

He openly supported the Occupy Wall Street movement. Wallis made some startling statements about America's history and heritage in an interview aired nationwide at a weekly, coffee shop-like series, "Lifetree Café."

He said, "It's not a Christian nation. It's never been a Christian nation. We set this up so that it would not be a Christian nation for any religious framework."

What he said would be true if you want to portray Christianity as a religion established by the government. Actually reading the *Federalist Papers* and our founding documents could give him pause. The only way for this kind of misdirection to be exposed is for more of us to find out the truth. I want to encourage everyone to seek the truth. Read all of our founding documents, including the *Federalist Papers*. Especially read the Declaration of Independence and the Constitution for yourself.

One of Rev. Jim Wallis's associates, David Gushee, a columnist for the Huffington Post and founder of the Evangelical Partnership for the Common Good, which identifies adherents as "Progressive Christians," targeted the Tea Party movement as not having Christian values because it does not advocate socialism and social justice as being biblical.

Being a Tea Party movement patriot myself, the Tea Party charter is not necessarily a Christian one, but I would say most of the patrons do appreciate the laws of nature and the original intent of our founding documents. The Obama-nation fails to realize that their constant tongue-lashing is essential not only to the growing success, but the actual survival, of the Tea Party movement. We welcome it with open arms.

Chapter 7

The National Council of Churches

Washington National Cathedral

The Protestant Episcopal Cathedral Foundation was chartered by Congress on January 6, 1893, and oversees the Washington National Cathedral and its sister institutions. The bishop of Washington serves as chief executive officer.

This church is now performing same-sex marriages. The Reverend Gary Hall, acting dean of the Washington National Cathedral, made the announcement that the church would host same-sex weddings and then proceeded on with a message about gun violence and the need for gun control.[1] The appeal fell on the ears of what was an obvious progressive audience when his oration was met with a standing ovation. I would have left in tears.

"There used to be false prophets among God's people, just as you will have some false teachers in your group. They will secretly teach things that are wrong—teachings that will cause people to be lost. They will even refuse to accept the Master, Jesus, who bought their freedom. So they will bring quick ruin on themselves" (2 Peter 2:1).[2]

Apparently Hall was an antiwar activist back in the 1960s and has tried to put a religious spin on his unique interpretation of biblical right and wrong. The Bible does not support his rhetoric. It rejects it. The message of progressive religion and activism that he exercised in the 1960s is one he hopes to flame up today.

"Be careful for yourselves and for all the people the Holy Spirit has given to you to care for. You must be like shepherds to the church of God, which he bought with the death of his own son" (Acts 20:28).[3]

It took eighty-three years to complete the cathedral beginning in 1907 and ending in 1990. The foundation stone was laid in the presence of President Theodore Roosevelt, and the last finial was placed in the presence of President George H. W. Bush. Decorative work, such as carvings and statuary, was ongoing as of 2011.

Congress has designated the Washington National Cathedral as the "National House of Prayer." During World War II, monthly services were held there "on behalf of a united people in a time of emergency." Before and since, the building has hosted other major events, both religious and secular, that have drawn the attention of the American people.

The cathedral was only slightly damaged during the 2011 Virginia earthquake. Initial inspection revealed minor exterior damage and even less damage to the inside, and it was deemed to be sound. More shaking of consecrated ground, perhaps? The 5.8 earthquake, the largest the East Coast of the United States had seen since 1944, was felt very strongly in Washington, DC, and damaged several buildings along with the cathedral. Repairs are expected to cost millions and take several years to complete.

The high altar, the Jerusalem Altar, is made from stones quarried at Solomon's Quarry near Jerusalem, which is said to be where the stones for Solomon's Temple were quarried. In the floor directly in front of that altar are set ten stones from the Chapel of Moses on Mount Sinai, representing the Ten Commandments as a foundation for the Jerusalem Altar.

Now this is the really interesting part. Across the United States, it has more than fourteen thousand members, more than 88 percent of whom live outside the Washington area, and who are divided into committees by state. Every year, each state has a state day at the cathedral, on which day that state is recognized by name in the prayers. Over a span of about four years, each state is further recognized at a Major State Day, at which time those who live in the state are encouraged to make a pilgrimage to the cathedral, and dignitaries from the state are invited to speak.

Make a pilgrimage?

My question to them is this: Did Jesus work to establish a vast entity we know as the institutional national or international church, or was it the kingdom of God? The kingdom of God is what Jesus refers to as the church; the two are the same. I do not believe these folks understand the difference between a building or an institutionalized religion and the kingdom of God.

Jesus uses the expression "kingdom" much more than He uses "church" to describe the object of His mission. The word "church" can be used in reference to a gathering of people for a central purpose, like an army for battle, political proceedings, or religious services.

"So I tell you, you are Peter. On this rock I will build my church, and the power of death will not be able to defeat it" (Matthew 16:18).[4]

Is Jesus referring to a building, property, or highly organized groups that join together to form large organizations? Or is He referring to a new relationship with God founded on the content of Peter's confession that Jesus is Christ? A community. The two are related but are not the same thing. Those in God's kingdom are the church. The church is just the visible manifestation of that kingdom. However, the Obama-nation wants to use it for its own ends.

I believe they are exploiting the cathedral for a national or one world social religion concept to pacify certain groups of people's sensitivities. This would be a good kicking-off point to try to instigate it by getting Christian moderates to believe that the Obama-nation is in solidarity with those of us who prefer to "cling to their religion." Unfortunately, this could be used for something much more sinister.

Some refer to the Obama-nation's godfather, Antonio Gramsci, the prominent Italian Marxist who developed the theory of "Cultural Marxism."[5] This is a two-part system. One is to bring the violent revolution "through the barrel of a gun," which would not be an effective method in advanced industrial societies such as ours where average citizens possess guns in their homes and carry them around on their person.

The second part, and the more "contemporary" revolutionary tool, was to capture the "mind of a society." Gramsci deemed this a more important doctrine. This is far more palatable and seductive, for it is based on nonviolent, persistent, and "quiet" transformation of traditions, families, education, media, and day-by-day organized support.

Can we all remember the term "fundamental transformation?" Has this ideology not been seen in all the aspects of our communities, our schools, and our entertainment, and in the actions of the Obama-nation? They are strategic. They periodically insert a new DNA sequence into America's "cultural code," adding malignant systemic elements into the cultural bloodstream to reform our sense of reason, bit by bit, day by day.

Entering into every civil, cultural, and political activity in America will not work unless they can successfully target their greatest enemy: the Judeo-Christian ethic—moral values and principles and standards of right and wrong that created and still prevail in American culture in all its forums, activities, and expressions. They are going to have to "change the residually Christian mind . . . so that it would become not merely a non-Christian mind but an anti-Christian mind" (Martin, *The Keys of This Blood*, 250).

"I know that after I leave, some people will come like wild wolves and try to destroy the flock. Also, some from your own group will rise up and twist the truth and will lead away followers after them" (Acts 20:29-30).[6]

This is where the National Council of Churches enters. The following are some highlights demonstrating how Gramsci's theory is targeting Christian religion in America. *The Christian Century*, a progressive, ecumenical magazine based in Chicago, stated in 1946 that it "informs mainline Christianity." It argued Protestantism could not win America until it rids "itself of the illusion that the American mentality is still individualistic and that the churches are gaining because they are recruiting individuals into their membership. The American mind is not predominantly collectivism in its structure."

That is a great observation on their part. The problem is they see the reality of the "American mind" as something that is not set firmly in a concrete formation and something that can be dissuaded. They truly underestimate the power of God as they proceed to do battle with the Holy Spirit. Their remedy for what they consider a weakness was to lure us to the demands of a "collectivist church" and push for cooperating groups to disconnect from established religions to form a universal or world church. In my opinion, this is the sole purpose of the National Council of Churches.

I believe the diverse institutions of the kingdom of God, or the Christian church, that make up all the different denominations, and unique characteristics of religious practice is a safety net. What has evolved over time since the establishment of the early church is no accident. Being believers in Christ makes us members of the kingdom and that is what holds us together while we exercise the different aspects of Christianity as a means to practice our faith.

The NCC has assumed what could become a position in harmony with political entities represented by socialism. Following Gramsci's theory, changing American life would mean the "secularization" of religion—"the distinction between the secular and the sacred" would be "removed from the thinking of the American church."

Charles Gregg Singer reported that their message was the social gospel "without mention of sin and its punishment or the redeeming work of Christ upon the Cross."[7] This is redefining our Christian religions.

"Formerly public supporters of communism, the NCC recast itself as a leader of the 'religious left.'" While America was fighting the Cold War, the NCC funded communist regimes in Yugoslavia and Poland and guerrillas in Zimbabwe, Angola, Nicaragua, and Cuba. The NCC considers the United States "an oppressor, both at home and abroad."[8]

Today the NCC inserts the political correctness gene into presidential politics, as it called on "candidates to tone down their rhetoric about one another's faith and avoid sowing religious discord. Candidates should feel comfortable explaining their religious convictions to voters."

The statement warned against placing public attention on religion, as "there is a point when an emphasis on religion becomes inappropriate and even unsettling in a religiously diverse society such as ours."

Note the new value-connoting terms of "inappropriate" and "unsettling" that the media frequently uses. They are following their new mandate quite effectively.

Current NCC task forces include eco-justice, immigration, justice for women, health, racial justice, and living wages. The NCC preaches, "It's Time to Occupy for the Minimum Wage: The Occupy Wall Street movement has brought the growing issue of income inequality to the forefront of public discourse in hundreds of cities and towns across the country." The year of the "Ethics of Energy" was 2011, according to the NCC.

"Supporters can take a huge first step. One that wouldn't cost taxpayers, rich or poor, a penny by rallying around an increase in the federal minimum wage," according to the NCC.[9] Revealing another layer in its structure, the NCC joined the Institute for Policy Studies to influence United States and foreign defense policies.

We had been anticipating the new movie coming out by Dinesh D'Souza, *2016*. Bud and I went to see it the first day it came out. It was not a packed house, but there was a fairly good-sized crowd waiting to see it. We waited and waited. Finally, they let us in with an explanation that they had to clean the theater. The movie was everything I had hoped for. The truth was now going to be heard about Obama. However, during the movie the lights would come on and then go off, and by the end of it, we could all tell that they had turned off the air-conditioning. To finish it up, they did not turn on the lights to ensure a safe exit when the movie was over. I was really glad we did not bring my mother.

The behavior of the theater personnel was a disappointment, but it was taken in stride by all attendees. It was addressed with humor and eye-rolling amazement. I felt good to be a part of a group of random individuals assembled together for a common sense of apprehension. This is what I felt at the Tea Party rallies, too.

Even though the movie did not address the spiritual aspects of Obama directly, it did show his philosophical association of Christianity, capitalism, and white people as all-inclusive and the disassociation he wants with all three.

Chapter 8

Liberation Theology or Ideology?

The Statue of Liberty

Jesus said, "I am the good shepherd. I know my sheep, as the Father knows me. And my sheep know me, as I know the Father. I give my life for the sheep" (John 10:14-15).[1]

Jesus used parables or stories through His life to help everyone to understand His message. The story He used to help His people discern between false teachings and the truth was about sheep. He often refers to His people as sheep or "the flock" because of the characteristics of sheep. They need a shepherd to guide and protect them so they will not fall prey to those who wish to devour them.

In John chapter 10, He warns them to beware of those who do not enter through the door but enter "the sheepfold" in other ways or means. The real shepherd will be the one entering through the door. Jesus refers to all others as thieves and robbers. The people who know Him and read His Word, "the flock," follow Him because they know His voice and know not to follow a stranger.

Jesus said, "I am the door, and the person who enters through me will be saved and will be able to come in and go out and find pasture" (John 10:9).[2]

So hearing about liberation theology was baffling to me. I found it to be poisonous doctrine. It appeared in Latin America during the 1950s and 1960s and helped spearhead the second wave of "Progressive Marxist Christians."[3] It claims that the New Testament can be understood only as a call for social activism, class struggle, and revolution aimed at overturning the existing practices of capitalism and implementing a social utopia where the poor will unseat their rich oppressors. Resentfulness, blame, and pride are perfect tools. Could this be why the Obama-nation wants the poor to see all wealthy people as undeserving of their riches? This doctrine bestows this envy uniquely to white people. The overtones of the Obama-nation have been riddled with this theology using the media and Hollywood as a megaphone to disperse the seeds of discontent.

I define evil as anything that brings sorrow, distress, or calamity, including moral wrongdoing, where human beings choose to do what hurts other human beings, or any part of creation just for the sake of hurting it. I believe evil works against the life-giving power of God and seeks to thwart God's will.

"The wrong things the sinful self does are clear: being sexually unfaithful, not being pure, taking part in sexual sins, worshiping gods, doing witchcraft, hating, making trouble, being jealous, being angry, being selfish, making people angry with each other, causing divisions among people, feeling envy, being drunk, having wild and wasteful parties, and doing other things like these. I warn you now as I warned you before: Those who do these things will not inherit God's kingdom" (Galatians 5:19-21).[3]

Before Benedict XVI became pope, he addressed liberation theology in 1984 in "Instruction on Certain Aspects of 'Theology of Liberation.'" In his critique, he noted that liberation for Christians is first and foremost liberation from the radical slavery of sin. While it is important for Christians to become involved in struggles for justice, freedom, and human dignity, certain forms of liberation theology are "damaging to the faith and to Christian living," and it uses "in an insufficiently critical manner and concept borrowed from various currents of Marxism."

Marxism is the ideology and socioeconomic theory developed by Karl Marx and Friedrich Engels. It is the fundamentals of communism. It's the idea that political, economic, and social principles and policies of socialism are the best practices for social justice. It is a driving force against capitalism. It has a nasty historical reputation but seems to still be a favorite tune sung by those critical of what our Founding Fathers found to be the most fair.

The "Black Manifesto" is a repeat of the liberation theology concentrating on the African American community.[4] The difference is that this movement claims to have characteristics based in the Bible. Student Nonviolent Coordinating Committee member James Forman presented it to the National Black Economic Development Conference in Detroit in 1969.

"The manifesto is a call to arms for blacks in the United States to overthrow the current government, which it characterized as capitalist, racist, and imperialist, and to set up a black-led socialist government," he said.[5]

That doesn't sound biblical to me, although, I do see its presence in our government today.

Malcolm X rejected Christianity, but his criticisms were adopted by the founders of the black-power movement—Stokely Carmichael, of the Black Panthers, and Ron Karenga. The black power movement seduced James Cone, who was a devout follower of Martin Luther King Jr. prior to his induction.

Cone is considered the founder of black liberation theology, and his goal was to reconcile black power with Christianity. Jeremiah Wright, the controversial minister of the Barack Hussein Obama family, named Cone as *the* preeminent influence on Wright's own theology. The problem is this is not Cone's theology. This is Marxist ideology based on skin color rather than economic classes or anything else.

James Cone did not learn Martin Luther King Jr.'s most fundamental lesson:

> If you have weapons, take them home; if you do not have them, please do not seek to get them. We cannot solve this problem through retaliatory violence. We must meet violence with nonviolence. Remember the words of Jesus: 'He who lives by the sword will perish by the sword'. We must love our white brothers, no matter what they do to us. We must make them know that we love them. Jesus still cries out in words that echo across the centuries: 'Love your enemies; bless them that curse you; pray for them that despitefully use you'. This is what we must live by. We must meet hate with love. Remember, if I am stopped, this movement will not stop, because God is with the movement. Go home with this glowing faith and this radiant assurance.[6]

Martin Luther King Jr. was a forgiving man of noble character.

President Obama's attendance at the Reverend Wright's church is not the only key link of his progressive leanings. The key link is his involvement with the 1998 Black Radical Congress in Chicago. Reverend Wright shared on a panel with Cornel West and Michael Dyson of the Democratic Socialists of America (DSA) and Socialism Commission. The title of the panel was "Faith as a Weapon: Spirituality and the Role of the Church in the Radical Movement."[7]

It is clear that the "Progressive Christian" movement has penetrated organized religion for decades. Feeding the public with disinformation, those in the movement seem to ignore the fact that Abraham Lincoln and many white Americans fought a civil war that resulted in the end of slavery. They ignore the Civil Rights Act of 1964. The Obama-nation is now attempting to use "faith as a weapon" to destroy the Christian religion in America.

Abraham Lincoln (on June 16, 1858, then a candidate running for the Senate, at the Republican State Convention, to the Republican Senate and House of Representatives) said, "A house divided against itself cannot stand. I believe this government cannot endure, permanently half slave and half free. I do not expect the Union to be dissolved—I do not expect the house to fall—but I do expect it will cease to be divided. It will become all one thing, or all the other."[8]

I had mentioned previously that the "Cultural Marxism" theory was a two-part system, and the first part was "through the barrel of a gun." What do you think is going to happen in this country if they try to start phase two?

Why do you think the Obama-nation wants to take away your Second Amendment rights? They will not start phase two if they are looking down the barrel of a gun themselves. This will be a topic in a later chapter.

John Adams wrote this in a letter to Thomas Jefferson on June 28, 1813:

> The general principles, on which the Fathers achieved independence, gentlemen could unite . . . And what were these general principles? I answer, the general principles of Christianity, in which all these sects were united: And the general principles of English and American liberty, in which all those young men united, and which had united all parties in America, in majorities sufficient to assert and maintain her independence. Now I will avow, that I then believed, and now believe, that those general principles of Christianity, are as eternal and immutable, as the existence and attributes of God; and those principles of liberty, are as unalterable as human nature and our terrestrial, mundane system.[9]

Psalm 23 (text in parentheses added by author):

> The Lord is my shepherd; (Relationship)
> I shall not want. (Guarantee)
> He makes me to lie down in green pastures; (Comfort)
> He leads me beside the still waters. (Peace)
> He restores my soul; (Healing)
> He leads me in the paths of righteousness (Guidance)
> For His name's sake. (Purpose)
> Yea, though I walk through the valley of the shadow of death,
>   (Testing)
> I will fear no evil; (Security)
> For You are with me; (Faithfulness)

Your rod and Your staff, they comfort me. (Discipline)
You prepare a table before me in the presence of my
enemies; (Revelation)
You anoint my head with oil; (Consecration)
My cup runs over. (Joy)
Surely goodness and mercy shall follow me all the days of my
life; (Blessings)
And I will dwell in the house of the Lord, (Worship)
Forever. (Eternity)[10]

PART 2

The Odyssey of Barack Hussein Obama

The Guided Tour Of Obama's book:
Dreams from My Father

Books

The midterm elections came, and, for the first time in my life, I was encouraging everyone to go vote. My church was giving out voting record lists so everyone would have a clear picture for whom they were voting. A candidate's voting record speaks much louder than his or her words. I had not voted in a midterm election before. I never took the time to research the voting record of the candidates. I obviously was not the only one who had failed in these measures, or our country would not have had to suffer through the thralls of being "fundamentally transformed."

After hearing Dinesh D'Souza's lecture about his journey of discovery about Obama and his travels to Kenya, and then later going to the theater to see his movie *2016,* I decided it was time to read Obama's book for myself. I found his book to be repugnant and inconsistent with Christian rationale. He had a euphuistic way of expressing himself, which I found cagey and indirect. Was there a reason for this, or was it just due to the lingo that was used, and he had grown accustomed to in Indonesia? For whatever the reason, he did not sound like an average American. I was ashamed for him at the confessions and thoughts that he shamelessly expressed.

Due to the unclear way he spoke, the average person would probably find it hard to read and understand his book. I know I did. Most of my difficulty was that I just did not want to believe that what was jumping off the pages was the revelation of someone so openly spiritually blind. I did not want to believe that what I was reading was straight from the mind of someone I was suppose to admire, the leader of my country. But with dictionary, thesaurus, Bible, and Wikipedia at hand, I was able to decipher the colorful and flowery language that he used to fashion his life's story and maybe help give a more enlightening "Western" insight into his mindset than he did.

Chapter 9 is my attempt to do just that—to give you a guided tour of his book through my eyes or my perspective as an average, nonacademic American Christian. I will now escort you through the different parts of Barack Hussein Obama's book, *Dreams from My Father.* This is not a narrative about the events in his life, but of his evaluations and reactions *to* events that contributed to his state of being and his perceptions.

This is not an attempt to judge or condemn Obama. Only God knows the condition of his heart completely. But I can judge his actions, behavior, and words to determine whether he is following the standards of right and wrong that we are all subject to as fellow Christians. I do not hate Obama. The only thing I am allowed to hate as a Christian are things—things that lead to sin in God's eyes. I do, however, think he is headed in the wrong direction, and he is taking us with him. I pray his relationship with Christ will grow.

"You have heard that it was said, 'Love you neighbor and hate your enemies.' But I say to you, love your enemies. Pray for those who hurt you" (Matthew 5:43-44).[1]

Chapter 9

His Book: Preface to the 2004 Edition

I was not far into reading Obama's book, *Dreams from My Father,* when I became aware of the over-shadowing haze of misperception and the void that existed in his life. A void he was compelled and desperate to fill at an early age and is obviously still searching to fill today. Left to develop and create his own conclusions and rules of right and wrong, the companionship he chose formed by easy acceptance, and a burning desire for belonging—all based on feelings and impressions with no guidance or instruction. It was, and I suspect is, an awkward, abstract, unpredictable world in which he lives. No absolutes. No top or bottom. He is the epitome of a soul that wanders and observes the behavior of the spiritually void and self-indulgent to set his own boundaries and moral aptitude—the unintentional mentors throughout his life that have established the foundation of who he is and why he is. I emerged with a sense of pity and regret.

Obama said his book was the result of being elected president of the *Harvard Law Review* (para. 1, p. vii). I never made the connection from the context and content of his book. I am guessing, but I believe that perhaps Obama wanted to document a history for himself for future endeavors.

He believes his experiences are reflective of the black American experience, in general, and all mixed-race families suffer from identity crisis, which Obama also admits (para. 1, p. vii). Since the majority of people in America are of mixed ancestry and cultures, I will speculate that he believes any other ancestry, culture, or race mixed with the black race is particularly extraordinary and unique. I suppose it is. If he were to step away from looking through the scope of only the black race, wouldn't a racial or cultural mix make all of us unique?

Barack Hussein Obama had a big year in 1992. He ran a voter registration project, began a civil rights practice, and started lecturing on constitutional law at the University of Chicago. He later won a seat in the state legislature but considered it boring and mundane and kept an eye open for something else (para. 1, p. viii). Due to an extremely negative view of white people, he was surprised their votes resulted in the United States Senate nomination. This, however, did nothing to dissuade his mistrust and cynical regard for white people (para. 1, p. ix).

I can see his point of view, but I have a different vantage point regarding the hurtful nature of prejudice. I can understand the hunger to rush transforming unacceptability to acceptability. However, changing the hearts and minds of those swallowing a bitter pill of conscience and shame at the time of the first Reconstruction was not easy. It is hard for people to accept when they are wrong. Their conscience and God's voice of right reason had been kept silent for a long time. Time was the healer here for both the offenders and the offended. Each generation after Reconstruction has and will, if allowed to, prove this. Hostility, violence, hatred, and revenge are tools to make things worse on both sides. Obama does not see that these things embedded in bitterness are the enemy. The negative connotations and lack of vision—both hindsight and foresight—of Obama and his lack of understanding propelling his point of view are radical and vengeful. He doesn't see that the wounds are healing—just that they are there.

Oddly, the only regret Obama appears to have is for refinement to his manner of delivery. He appears to have no remorse for any of his speeches' content or for life choices, which were absent of self-analysis or reflection. Feeling justified of his resentfulness, he deems them only, and I quote, "inconvenient politically, the grist of pundit commentary and opposition research" (para. 2, p. ix). My view is his regret should be reversed. It's the content that shows a lack of good judgment.

His moments of thought exposure are compelling. In the account of what he calls "Clinton's Third Way," he insinuates that President Bill Clinton gave in to the "compassionate conservatism" of George W. Bush's first campaign. He describes Clinton's decision as, "a scaled-back welfare state without grand ambition but without sharp edges." Grammatically speaking, it would be without grand ambition or sharp edges or with grand ambition but without sharp edges. His incorrect or peculiar way of phrasing things gives way to confusion and misunderstanding, granted. But what comes through loud and clear is this; he sounds completely at odds with President Clinton's compromise and shows anxiety for Clinton's not pushing more forcefully to socialize or nationalize our medical system. His scornful mention of the "compassionate conservatism" was heard loud and clear also (para. 3, p. ix). I think he believes white conservative Republicans are incapable of compassion.

His distorted view of compassion falls more in line with vengeance when you consider his actions as president rather than his words. Compassion is love. It is the love in, "Love your neighbor as you love yourself" (Matthew 22:36-39).[1]

In my opinion, Obama's compassion is a type of self-centered love or self-pity, with the purpose of gaining something in exchange for love or sympathy, which is disturbing given his position.

He even goes on a tirade of disgust and in agreement with international liberal writers, which are not named, in this passage, "the end of history, the ascendance of free markets and liberal democracy, the replacement of old hatreds and wars between nations with virtual communities and battles for market share" (para. 1, p. x). He thinks all of these are bad.

Stepping away from his book for a moment, Obama's lack of commitment or interest in a higher power or God showed itself when he made no reference of God in the statement he made about the terrorist attack on the United States on September 11, 2001. He did express disbelief and inability to understand people who would be driven to carry out such murderous acts. Fear and hate are powerful tools when they are used to warp the minds and hearts of the ignorant and needy—the utility of fundamental, violent theology, for example.

Back on his book, I found Obama's lament disingenuous based on his overall tone of sarcastic mockery. He makes accusations that somehow his name is "an irresistible target of mocking websites from overzealous Republican operatives" (para. 4, p. x). He believes it was because he has a Middle Eastern name and not because of his displays of reverence and familiarity to Islamic states and statesmen. He grew up around Muslims. He exhibits their value system.

Obama is consumed with the idea of struggle. Entering struggle, conflict, or crisis is a constant. He takes great measures to seek them out, especially if they are indiscriminate or farfetched. Due to crisis and conflict being where he is most comfortable, he sows discord nationally, globally, and individually. With these things, he does not discriminate.

That seems to be his default status. Perhaps they are articles or elements for exploitation?

His observations of struggles here in American are between (para. 4, p. x):

- "worlds of plenty and worlds of want"—he believes the wealthy (which he sees as the white race) are wealthy because they exploit the labors of the poor (which he sees as the black race) by oppressing them to keep them poor. He believes that "success" is synonymous for "greed" or "power," whether it is an individual or a nation. The idea that not all "power" is bad is not a consideration for Obama, not unless it is his. He believes the poor will always be poor and the wealthy will always be wealthy unless he can do something, anything, to change it. There is no consideration for good decisions, motivation, inspiration, opportunity, creativity, will power, or hard work.

- "modern and the ancient"—he believes technology and modernization cause strife, and that is unfair to those who prefer not to or can't stay up-to-date with the latest innovations. He means to slow down the prosperous and engage in a large-scale expansion and mass development of the diminished. Enemy or friend, foreign or domestic, large or small is not a matter of concern.

- "those who embrace our teeming, colliding, irksome diversity while still insisting on a set of values that binds us together"—Is he referring to the Judeo-Christian ethics, moral values and principles that the Word of God, law of nature, and our Constitution are based on and are planted deeply within? Again, he is looking for conflict and strife, and this struggle, I can only hope, will land him on his knees at the foot of the One who sits at the right hand of God. In the meantime, say "hello" to the Holy Spirit.

- "those who would seek, under whatever flag or slogan or sacred text, a certainty and simplification that justifies cruelty toward those not like us"—This statement of his exposes his disregard and misinterpretation of the Bible. Among all the other documents, countries, and governments that support them, it would also include our own over two-hundred-year-old Constitution. My concern, though, is his blindness toward the Word of God.

I associate blindness with unbelief. It is the quality of the foolish rather than the wise. The wise see; the foolish are constantly running into obstacles they cannot see. Spiritual blindness is the inability to see God's discipline and correction, too. Opponents of Jesus are referred to as "blind leaders." It also gives us the term "the blind leading the blind."

"They are blind leaders. And if a blind person leads a blind person, both will fall into a ditch" (Matthew 15:14).[2]

Opponents and the ones they lead are bound to fall into a pit due to their spiritual blindness because they focus on the lesser rather than on the greater aspects of the law.

"How terrible for you! You guide the people, but you are blind. You say, 'If people swear by the Temple when they make a promise, that means nothing. But if you swear by the gold that is in the Temple, they must keep that promise'" (Matthew 23:16-22).[3]

The "gold" is representative of Christ and the "Temple" is representative of religion in this parable.

I conclude, as a critic of this first part of Obama's book, that he fails to identify corruption as the culprit in this quote, "desperation and disorder of the powerless" (para. 5, p. x). He sees corruption as the rule instead of the deviation from the rule of law. He identifies and empathizes with the twisted lives of children on the streets of Jakarta, Nairobi, and the streets of Chicago's South Side. He sees our justice system as inconsistent and unfair. Again, he sees this as the rule instead of the corruption caused by the departure of it that he says uses "a steady, unthinking application of force" for those he sees as the powerless (para. 1, p. xi).

He rejects a strong arm of law in the determination of right and wrong and the enforcement therein as the "embrace of fundamentalism and tribe" (para. 1, p. xi). Instead of seeing the need for the uncorrupted rule of law and its enforcement, he believes the system we follow, the rule of law that is based on God's natural law or laws of nature, will be our doom.

His Book: The Introduction

I understand that writing a book, even one about someone or something other than oneself, tells more about the author than what he or she is writing about. I believe even a fictional book with nothing but imaginary places, figures, or events will show the author's character in one way or another. Writing a book can be a means of total exposure of what lies within. I question if Obama recognized this phenomenon at the time he wrote his book.

Obama first refers to his election as president of the *Harvard Law Review* in his book's introduction. He noted the burst of publicity that followed was about the "peculiar place in the American mythology" because he was a black man, and his election was somehow forcing recognition of that fact. He felt the attention was more due to the change in legacy rather than being an accomplishment or achievement of someone deserving. He preferred to see it as "America's hunger for any optimistic sign from the racial front—a morsel of proof that, after all, some progress has been made." This comes from the heart of an antagonist or community organizer of mutineers. He talks as if he is living fifty years earlier (para. 1, p. xiii).

Obama took a year off after graduation to write distorted book components such as (para. 2, p. xiii):

"an essay on the limits of civil rights litigation in bringing about racial equality"
"thoughts on the meaning of community and the restoration of public life through grassroots organizing" (ACORN)
"musings on affirmative action and Afrocentrism"

The last one is particularly disturbing concerning the revisionists approach to history called Afrocentrism. This can be seen as African Americans' desperation to assert themselves in what they see as a Eurocentric-dominated society. Concentrating on their heritage and customs as distinctly African, non-European origins, it often denies or minimizes European cultural influences while accenting historical African civilizations that independently accomplished a significant level of cultural and technological development.

Afrocentrism generally places blame for all atrocities directly or indirectly on the Europeans and denies any serious culpability of wrongdoing on the part of the black African. Examples of extreme Afrocentrism are supremacist groups including the New Black Panther Party or the Nation of Islam. It focuses on African American culture and the history of Africa, and reconstructs history and culture to tell only the achievements and development of Africans and African Americans. Proponents believe that the white Eurocentric-dominated society downplays or discredits contributions of various African people and, in the attempt to avoid guilt and shame accompanied with the enslavement of Africans, that those contributions and the significance of the African race are being written out of our history.

This is so not true. This is turning black achievement and accomplishment on its head. White people take pride in the fact that we saw slavery as an evil activity and acted accordingly. African Americans have made tremendous contributions to American society in every way, and all this will do is destroy that. This is heartbreaking, not just for America, but for the black community as a whole.

Obama reveres himself as wise to the world and noncynical. That may be true toward black people, but the cynicism toward white people is paramount. As for his being "wise to the world," I am sure he has learned an abundance of things in all his travels. However, Jesus said this world is worth nothing if people lose their souls to gain it (para. 3, p. xiv).

"It is worth nothing for them to have the whole world if they lose their souls. They could never pay enough to buy back their souls" (Matthew 16:26).[4]

Adopting the values of the sinful social order is the meaning of worldliness in the most negative sense of the term. It is this sense that we live in the world but not of the world.

"Do not change yourselves to be like the people of this world, but be changed within by a new way of thinking" (Romans 12:2).[5]

Obama fears exposing things about himself that expose decisions he considers contradictory to his world now (para. 3, p. xiv). I find this puzzling. For most of us this is the maturing process and is not an aspect of betrayal of some sort. He mentioned that he is careful not to expect too much from society. I actually agree with him about this but for different reasons, I am sure.

Losing one's innocence to bigotry is a hurtful and eye-opening experience and can generate a plethora of negative feelings if not put into perspective. Like any other vile deed, racism and bigotry are devices of the ignorant with foul views. Everyone will have to deal with it in one way or another. I know I have. This is not unique to black people. I am not sure Obama is aware of this. Angry or hateful people say and do hateful things. It is not a bad reflection of the one on the receiving end; it is only a bad reflection on those dishing it out, and it is apparently a fact that Obama was never taught and has let affect his entire outlook on life.

His overall perception of white people is negative, as I read, to the point that he even withheld the fact that he had a white mother at certain times in his life, around the age of twelve or thirteen, in order to remove the idea of being "ingratiated" to white people (para. 2, p. xv).

His dissention was attached to Americans, mostly. He resents how others perceived him due to his mixed heritage. Because he was so preoccupied and focused on how he should categorize himself, he assumed everyone else was trying to do the same thing to him. Thinking that everyone in the room was thinking about him and that the world revolved around him is fairly normal for an adolescent. Most adolescents think the same thing about themselves, though. The problem is I believe Obama still thinks everything is about him (para. 2, p. xv).

Another problem is Obama imagines that some may guess he has a troubled heart due to the, and I quote, "mixed blood, the divided soul, the ghostly image of the tragic mulatto trapped between two worlds." He attributes everything associated with racism and the tragedy of it to the "sons and daughters of Plymouth Rock and Ellis Island, . . . children of Africa." He considers it naive to be, as he puts it, "wedded to lost hopes" for a racially blind society (para. 2, p. xv). It seems he is doing everything he can to prevent hope of a society with blindness toward class or race from happening.

With much less flair for the dramatic, Obama confesses that he does not rely on the stories of his childhood and wants to stop trying to make sense of it all. He sees it as "plugging up holes in the narrative" and "accommodating unwelcome details." For some reason, he prefers to avoid life choices that are in opposition to his past. I would find this statement commendable if he were not headed in the wrong direction (para. 1, p. xvi).

Obama considers his book a testament to his attempt to identify with his father as a black American and nothing more. At the time it was written, he had not accomplished any great feats worthy of record and knows his experience is not the average black American experience. However, he apparently thinks his childhood experiences were not much different from those of other black people in America or Africa. He also, apparently, thinks the events shared in his book show him in good favor, and so he deliberately left out things that did not accomplish that goal (para. 2, p. xvi).

Some of the dialog is approximated and some characters are composites. Some events are out of order, and some of the names— except for family members and a handful of public figures—were changed. I believe that out of all the stories, believable or not, actual or not, his perceptions of the events are insightful, and so that is my focus (para. 1, p. xvii).

Origins

Chapter 1

The first story told by Obama is of him and his roommate sitting on the fire escape smoking cigarettes and shouting down at "white people from better neighborhoods" to "scoop the poop" as they passed by walking their dogs, saying "you bastards" and then laughing at the expressions on the white people's faces. I am sure the eloquent proclamations and stellar behavior of these two young gentlemen are of apparent noble distinction and would make any mother proud. The destiny of the one to whom the presidency of the United States of America awaits is self-explanatory, at least to all who do not read his book (para. 1, p. 4).

This kind of banter seems to be the only thing he feels comfortable partaking in because of his discomfort talking about personal things and divulging feelings and thoughts. He was suspicious and distrusted everyone and kept everyone, black or white, at a distance.

When he heard the news of his father's death, Obama was uncertain how to react because his father was more a myth than a real memory. Frequent stories and select memories were told by his mother and grandparents; his father left Hawaii in 1963 when Obama was two years old, in an effort to stymie any and all resentment toward his father. The stories glorified his father's life and justified everything he did, both good and bad.

This is probably why Obama finds this such an easy fallback for himself now as president. They assert that his father had "a fearsome vision of justice," in reference to an event over the accidental loss of a pipe by a friend that he dealt with harshly. His mother engineered a mental image of his father having uncompromising honesty and confidence (para. 3, p. 7).

I can relate to an image of a father that can stand the test of time. My father has done that very thing in my mind. My memories of my father are somewhat faded but the feelings of contentment, safety, security, and love are still there. I lost my father went I was eighteen years old, just five months after I graduated from high school. It was a time when I was full of myself, spit and vinegar, and I had all the answers to all of life's questions. Of course, that was not true, but someone would have had a tough time convincing me of that. If only I could have seen what was coming, maybe I could have made a few more memories with him. I was truly blessed to have had loving Christian parents.

Obama's father was from Kenya, of the Luo tribe near Lake Victoria in a place called Alego. His paternal grandfather was a prominent farmer, a tribe elder, and a medicine man with healing powers. His father grew up herding goats and attended a school set up by the British colonial administration. Obama's father won a scholarship to Nairobi and, on the eve of Kenya's independence, his father was selected by Kenyan leaders and American sponsors to attend a United States university. This is how he came to be a student in Hawaii and meet Obama's mother. They married in 1960, and Obama was born in 1961. His father shortly afterward went to Harvard to pursue his PhD, leaving Obama and his mother in Hawaii. They divorced when he left to go back to Kenya.

It would probably be fair to say Obama needed to ask questions about all the issues surrounding his life but was afraid to ask. His mother picked up on this, and her remedy was to buy him books to introduce a general knowledge of things outside his and her sphere of influence. One book was significant, *Origins*. This was a book on different theologies and their genesis; Mythology, Hinduism, the Bible, etc. The only comment he makes about the Bible was why "an omnipotent God would let a snake cause such grief." Obviously there is no substitute for the real thing. I believe the book *Origins* just caused more confusion rather than gave answers (para. 2, p. 10).

One of the questions Obama needed answered was about the interracial marriage issue existing here in the United States at the time his parents were married, rendering their marriage illegal. In his book, he refers to the issue as miscegenation. I am not sure why he uses this term due to its offensive overtones, which he mentions. Today, scholars avoid the word because it suggests a concrete, diverse, biological phenomenon rather than a categorization imposed on certain relationships. Perhaps he is not an advocate of interracial marriage due to his conclusions of being the product of one?

His resentment seemed to be directed more toward Americans who, while professing to be a Christian nation, practiced antimiscegenation in the first place. Not having any scriptural reinforcement on this racial issue, there is no wonder he has such disgust for American Christians, or at least the white ones, and the slow turn from sin and its practices. His confusion and mistrust of his white maternal grandparents still remained, even though they openly accepted his parents' marriage and their grandson.

Laws banning race mixing were enforced in certain American states from 1691 until 1967 when the US Supreme Court unanimously ruled in *Loving v. Virginia* that antimiscegenation laws were unconstitutional. It was banned in Germany from 1935 until 1945 and in South Africa during the early part of the apartheid era from 1949 to 1985. Sexual relations between such individuals were banned also in all three examples. Although an "Anti-Miscegenation Amendment" to the Constitution was proposed in 1871, in 1912-13, and in 1928, thankfully no nationwide law against racially mixed marriages was ever enacted.

Obama's assessment of American character is that they are feckless. His definition: "Men who embraced the notion of freedom and individualism and the open road without always knowing its price, and whose enthusiasms could as easily lead to cowardice of McCarthyism as to the heroics of World War II. Men who were both dangerous and promising precisely because of their fundamental innocence; men prone, in the end, to disappointment" (para. 3, p. 16).

McCarthyism is the practice of making accusations of disloyalty, subversion, or treason without proper regard for evidence. According to Wikipedia, it also means "the practice of making unfair allegations or using unfair investigative techniques, especially in order to restrict dissent or political criticism." He repeatedly makes insinuations that white people have an innate feeling of superiority over black people and believes people in the Deep South, in particular Texas, are all bigots. Being someone who has lived in various southern states and hails from Texas, I found this especially offensive and shortsighted.

This conclusion came on the heels of an episode he had with some Texas racists. Being a proud Texan myself, I can testify that not all Texans are racists or bigots. Out of all the Texans I know or to whom I am related, I do not know of one who fits that stereotype. If they are of those mindsets, they do not profess it openly, with good reason.

Like Americans in general, he sees his white grandfather as "an American character, one typical of men of his generation . . . because of their fundamental innocence; men prone, in the end, to disappointment" (para. 3, p. 16). Due to his grandfather's perception of himself as a freethinker, he enrolled the family in the local Unitarian Universalist congregation, the First Unitarian Church of Honolulu. Obama attended Sunday school, where he was taught a New Age religious doctrine that encompassed different aspects of several religions. This explains his faultfinding with Christianity.

While doing some research on the church, I found an article on a website that I like. It was very revealing. This particular church was well known for its far-left politics and served as a sanctuary for draft dodgers from the Students for a Democratic Society at a time when Bill Ayers was a leader in that organization.[6]

The pastor since 1995, the Reverend Mike Young, affirmed this during an interview with WND where he proclaimed that his church has "always" been involved in political activism even before his pastoral service began there.

"We are involved in community organizing, helping churches in foreign countries . . . social justice issues . . . like making sure inmates get dinner," said Young. I am assuming he was alluding to foreign prisons, for American prisons do not have that kind of problem.

While Obama's membership as an adult in the controversial Trinity United Church of Christ has received minimal media attention, almost nothing has been reported about his membership to and his Sunday school attendance at First Unitarian. Its far-left activism may have helped provide his initial political education and the connection to Bill Ayers through the Students for a Democratic Society adds interest. I am sure this was just a coincidence because there are no parallels or predispositions between the two ideologies, now are there?

The church notoriously granted sanctuary to United States military deserters recruited by the SDS. The deserters' exploits at the church were front-page news for months in 1969, including articles in the *New York Times*. Eventually, the police raided the church as well as another nearby Honolulu worship house, Crossroads, which was also providing sanctuary to draft dodgers.

This knowledge of his early religious upbringing shines a new light on Obama's 2008 statement: "This is a guy (Ayers) who lives in my neighborhood . . . the notion that somehow as a coincidence me knowing somebody who engaged in detestable acts forty years ago— when I was eight years old—somehow reflects on me and my values doesn't make much sense."

Ayers might not have been Obama's mentor, but he could have been his hero.

When Obama's maternal grandmother died in November 2008, the memorial service, attended by the then-presidential candidate, was held in Honolulu's First Unitarian Church.

Getting back to his book comes with one declaration Obama made about mainstream America, "the seeming triumph of universalism over parochialism and narrow-mindedness, a bright new world where differences of race or culture would instruct and amuse and perhaps even ennoble" (para. 3, p. 25).

I have no problem with the concept where differences of race and culture would be shared, but I do have a problem with his triumphant view of universalism over parochialism.

Since there are so many denominations in America, I wonder if unity is important? The lack of unity, I believe to a certain extent, protects us from a world-dominating religion. Unity based on organization, rather than doctrine, can be dangerous. Those who seek organizational unity are either looking for levels of authority to wield or be subject to, or they are just wanting a broad acceptance of doctrinal generalities. These, by nature, reject the doctrine of Christ. I believe the development of different branches of the Christian faith here in America is a safeguard that arose from our exercise of religious freedom and individualism. I believe everything happens for a reason.

His reference to "narrow-mindedness" is more a reflection of his mind because of his lack of willingness to be open-minded to God and the Judeo-Christian ethic, moral values, and principles. His vision is obviously one that has us moving away from "parochialism" or the teachings of the Bible and God's will and moving toward universalism and the acceptance of diversity and multiculturalism as our new nondenominational and generic religion of nonfaith.

Chapter 2

It started to sound like Obama finally got the dad he needed when his mother married an Indonesian named Lolo at the beginning of this chapter. Life was simplistic—or at least leaned toward primitive but civilized—when they moved to Indonesia.

Lolo met Obama's mother while attending the University of Hawaii. Lolo taught Obama a form of Islam mixed with Hindu and that "a man took on the powers of whatever he ate" (para. 1, p. 37). This belief brought on some pretty strange culinary delights, such as tiger, dog, snake, and grasshopper.

Similar cultural distinctions exist right here in this country, too. Customs, nomenclature, and habits can differ greatly from state to state and city to city. The influences can weigh heavily in a variety

THE ABOMINATIONS OF THE OBAMA-NATION

of directions. It can be fun and educational, but it can be scary and intimidating at the same time.

Obama received most of his guidance and instruction from his stepfather. He once stopped Obama from giving his money to beggars and told him to "save your money and make sure you don't end up on the street yourself" (para. 3, p. 39). Since there wasn't much detail about the situation, this sounded like good advice. Yet, Obama told it with negative overtones.

Obama's stepfather exhibited coarseness and a lack of forgiveness or tolerance toward servants that made mistakes or cost him money because of his Islamic-Hindu value system. However, he was tolerant of the cross-dresser who cooked in their home. Apparently he was a good cook.

He told Obama that he should be tough and tried to teach him that strong men kill weak men simply for being weak. He also taught his young stepson that a strong man will take a weak man's lands and then make the weak man work in his fields. And if the weak man's woman is pretty, the strong man will take her, too. Teaching Obama this manner of survival of the fittest seemed barbaric to me. This may have been a lesson necessary and unique to the reality of life in Indonesia. But does this give explanation for the strategies and tactics being implemented by the Obama-nation? I see influences but changed to those they perceive as the weak overtaking those they perceive as the strong.

This "Indonesian reality" is the nature of man at its worst not the nature of law or God's natural law upon which America was founded. But if this is what Obama was taught as a child, that this is the way of the world, this could explain why Obama sees the rich and prosperous, be it individuals or countries, as the bullies or "strong men" that prey upon the weak. Does this also explain his pursuits of riches and power? Does this explain his ideas of minorities, or nonwhite individuals, as the weak that are taken advantage of by white people? This possibly is the mind-set behind the idea that the way to prevent this from happening is to take from the evil rich and redistribute the wealth to the poor on a global scale (pp. 40, 41).

In America, however, the right to acquire property is sacred. Justice George Sutherland of the United States Supreme Court, in an annual address to the New York State Bar Association on January 21, 1921, said this: "It is not the right of property that is protected, but the right to property. Property, *per se*, has no rights; but the individual—the man—has three great rights, equally sacred from arbitrary interference: the right to his life, the right to his liberty, and the right to his property . . . the three rights are so bound together as to be essentially one right. To give a man his life but deny him his liberty, is to take from him all that makes his life worth living. To give him his liberty but take from him his property, which is the fruit and badge of his liberty, is to still leave him a slave."[7]

Obama's mother worked at the United States embassy teaching English to Indonesian businessmen. Visiting Americans would make passes at her, which helped fuel Obama's mother's and his unfavorable view of Americans. He referred to some of them as "caricatures of the ugly American, prone to making jokes about Indonesians until they found out that she was married to one, and then they would try to play it off" (para. 3, p. 43).

This reinforces his notion that power is evil instead of snobs being discourteous or rude. His mother identified both power and corruption as the same thing and being evil. She concluded that Lolo had given in to this evil power after he landed a job in the government relations office of an American oil company where he began to achieve some success. She considered him a sellout and did not want power to take her son. She loathed the wealthy American oil businessmen and their wives because of their complaints about the quality of Indonesian help. Even though she tried to teach Obama to disdain the blend of ignorance and arrogance that characterized what she saw as the typical American, she decided America was where she wanted Obama to be (para. 3, p. 47).

Obama became skeptical and cynical toward white Americans and about the world where poverty, corruption, and the constant scramble for security were always at the forefront. He saw his mother pushing her virtues onto him, which were independent from faith in a higher power, and Obama stated she failed to instill them in him. Personally, I see her success.

In her refusal to identify with Christian influence, she had the belief her faith was of a rational, thoughtful person that shapes her own destiny. Her belief was one that is basically anti-Christian and, in some cases, sacrilegious. Obama describes her as a lonely witness for secular humanism, a soldier for the New Deal, Peace Corps, and position-paper liberalism. She decided to instill in Obama her values, which she considered purer than Christian values, devoid of religion, and through the memory of his biological father (para. 1, p. 50).

And so the process began. She pushed him to embrace black people—learn about the civil rights movement (I am guessing focusing on authors with a liberal bias only), listen to the recordings of Mahalia Jackson, and read the speeches of Dr. Martin Luther King Jr. She had him listen to stories of schoolchildren in the South who were forced to read books handed down from wealthier white schools (probably because they were given to them and were glad to have them), but who went on the become doctors, lawyers, and scientists.

Obama's mother tried to instill the belief that to be black was to be the beneficiary of a great inheritance, a special destiny, and that these glorious burdens are those only black people are strong enough to bear. Her attempt to build his self-esteem could have been great, but she was doing it in a demeaning way toward white people and all other nonblack people, too. Instilling a sense of higher value based on skin color made Obama guilty of the same thought process that he now abhors in white people. He resents other people for not seeing black people—especially children—the way he sees them. He believes black children should be protected from experiencing self-doubt because Obama is afraid they would eventually believe that it would be better to be white. I can see protecting them from bigotry, but not self-doubt. How else will they achieve self-confidence and develop a good self-image?

He does not understand the natural growing and maturing process that every young man and woman goes though no matter the skin color. One of them is self-doubt. A person must face many challenges in life, and self-doubt is one that everyone needs to resolve. I think it's an impossible one to avoid. Thankfully, Obama had to consider that his mother's account of how the world is and why, and his father's place in it, was "incomplete" (para. 3, p. 52). He would not consider the possibility that his mother might be misinformed or incorrect. It is clear that his skepticism of his mother's views was based on her being white. She had already shot herself in the foot.

Chapter 3

Obama's mother ended what she considered his stepfather's capitalistic influence by shipping her young son off to his maternal grandparents in Hawaii. What was an obvious negative impression of his stepfather's way of engaging in business also was a humbling experience for him, because his grandfather no longer had a successful business, and his grandmother was now working. They were not as well off as they were before. He made an observation of tension always floating around the house because his grandmother had landed a well-paying job and was making more money than his grandfather. Obama's assessment of the situation was that "they had decided to cut their losses and settle for hanging on. They saw no more destinations to hope for" (para. 1, p. 58).

His grandparents, even though they were financially struggling, managed to get him into prep school. His grandfather attributed it to pulling some stings with his boss, who was an alumnus. However, Obama had suspicions that interest in him was related more to affirmative action policies rather than favors from his grandfather's white boss.

Like anyone that moves to a new and unfamiliar place without familiar faces, Obama felt like a fish out of water and felt he had nothing in common with anyone. After living in a country with minimal varieties of people or Americans with character quality issues, he viewed Americans as overindulgent and the American culture as centered on consumption. It's tragic that Obama was only exposed to the worst aspects of our culture and had no one to shine a light on its better attributes.

Obama had told his prep school classmates a slew of lies glamorizing his life and his heritage, so he was somewhat apprehensive when his father came back to Hawaii for a Christmas visit and scheduled a presentation for Obama's class. He referred to his feelings surrounding his father as "something volatile and vaguely threatening" (para. 6, p. 63). To someone like myself, that would be having a guilty conscience. But feeling shame requires an admission of guilt for doing something wrong. Truthfulness is not something to which he seems to strictly adhere. It is just an option, no better, no worse.

Since it was Christmastime, his mother was to visit at the same time as his father. Obama tells of one incident where the tensions rose to a very high pitch. His father was a Muslim and didn't have any understanding of Christmas, or our American traditions, spiritual or secular. Obama's father found all the hubbub unnecessary and felt it inconvenienced Obama's academic pursuits. Apparently he said some hurtful things that caused Obama to have ill feelings toward the concept of Christmas instead of toward his father. As he puts it "I saw it for what it *was:* a lie" (para. 3, p. 68). This made a big impression on our future president.

Chapter 4

Because of his ingrained perceptions of white people, Obama migrated toward other black people for solace at school. His grandfather would take him to shady bars and to brothels, so his grandfather could have a few drinks and play pool, poker, or bridge. Again, these were not exactly the role models needed for a growing boy. One of his grandfather's drinking buddies is believed to be the communist Frank Marshall Davis. Obama, referring to him as just "Frank," said Davis became one of his childhood mentors. Obama calls him a poet of black theme poetry (para. 4, p. 76).

Resentments and frustrations gained additional momentum after his mother moved him and his little sister into a small apartment near his prep school and lived on a government student grant obtained by his mother while pursuing a master's degree in anthropology. After trying to identify with characters on TV, the radio, movies, and pop culture, Obama found refuge in sports. He learned how to conduct himself in competition.

He was greatly influenced by the other black guys that trickled into the islands and whose confusion and anger would help shape his own. He felt like the only common ground he had with white guys was on the basketball court because his "blackness couldn't be a disadvantage," (para. 1, p. 80) assuming that his blackness was a disadvantage at all other times.

Due to all the bad experiences with bigots that he encountered, Obama concluded that all white people thought themselves superior to black people. He states, "It was as if whites didn't know they were being cruel in the first place. Or at least thought you deserving of their scorn" (para.

3, p. 80). The only exceptions to this rule were his grandparents and his mother, of course.

He was conflicted about his conclusions about white people, but the field had already been plowed, sowed, and toiled over, and this is what was being reaped. The mentality and mind-set of the ungodly was all that he was being exposed to, and that was the basis of his evaluations. Individuals that held integrity, honor, honesty, nobility, and love for neighbor were avoided. Never once does he mention going to a church or being subjected to Christian ethics, values, and principles and it having a positive effect.

Obama sees everything through a microscope of race. He expressed rage over a sincere statement from a white friend made after attending a party where his friends were the only white people there. The friend said he understood what Obama might feel like when he was the only black guy at a school party. Rage is all he felt (paras. 6, 7, p. 84). What a missed opportunity. It is times like these when the skin color disappears and hearts can have true fellowship. That is not what he felt compelled to do then and possibly not what he feels compelled to do now.

His evaluation of the rules is that they are the white man's rules (para. 1, p. 85):

- white people have the power and black people cannot get it
- white people perceive all that black people have is from them— their manliness, their protection, their language, their clothes, their books, their ambitions and desires, everything
- everything is according to whatever the white man wants
- that the fundamental power white people think they have over black people and have always had will outlast the black man's individual motive and inclinations; that any distinction between good and bad white people should be held negligible
- that nothing belongs to black people, including their humor, their songs, etc.
- believes that choices a black person makes are not really their choices because he thinks that the only choices available for refuge is a trap
- feels the only thing that is his as a black man is the withdrawal into a smaller and smaller coil of rage—the knowledge of your own powerlessness and defeat

- believes the refusal of the black man to acknowledge defeat by the white man, and the subsequent lashing out of blacks against the white man's system, would be labeled paranoid, militant, violent, or "nigger"

This was so disturbing that I hardly know how to address it other than to say I am astounded at how full of hate a person could be. How can anyone argue that this person is not a product of his environment? How can someone argue a child is not affected when he is left to grow up without guidance and nurturing necessary to develop a stable mind and be an asset to himself and to society as a whole?

Problems we have in life can be perspective-lifters, if what we are looking to achieve is to be lifted up. Obama tends to sleepwalk through his days until he bumps into an obstacle that stymies him. He does not realize that when you encounter a problem with no immediate solution, your response to that situation will either take you up or down. You can lash out at the difficulty, at some imaginary or perceived culprit, with resentment and feeling sorry for yourself, but that will take you down into a pit of self-pity.

Alternatively, the problem can be a ladder, enabling you to climb up above it, look down on it, and see the problem from higher ground. Once your perspective has been heightened, you can see around it for a solution, see ahead to where it leads, or behind from whence the problem came. Better yet, you can look away from it altogether. Viewed from above, the obstacle that frustrated him would be only a light and momentary problem. This is the perspective that God has.

"So we do not give up. Our physical body is becoming older and weaker, but our spirit inside us is made new every day. We have small troubles for a while now, but they are helping us gain an eternal glory that is much greater than the troubles. We set our eyes not on what we see but on what we cannot see. What we see will last only a short time, but what we cannot see will last forever" (2 Corinthians 4:16-18).[8]

Obama was in the ideal frame of mind to find Malcolm X's autobiography appealing. Obama ascended him to superhero status for his self-recreation, his insistence on respect, his uncompromising message of order, his martial-like discipline, and his force of will. One aspect Obama did not give much credence to was Malcolm X's theology.

Obama considered that religious baggage. It was not the conditions or foundation of his religion for which Obama had disregard; it was Malcolm X's consideration of it in the first place.

The most disturbing condition of the mind and heart of Barack Hussein Obama Jr. is his considering as a path to self-respect, feeling the need to "recede into mere abstraction" the white blood in him (para. 2, p. 86).

Chapter 5

This chapter begins when Obama is a little older, and he mentions a "great party" that he and his roommate hosted. A philosophical discussion must have occurred with a female at the party who was not a liberal thinker like himself. The conversation itself was not given in his book, but her exiting statement was revealed.

"You always think it's about you," the woman said.

Obama's justification was, "Like I was somehow responsible of the fate of the entire black race" (para. 2, p. 92).

Consider if he had a different stance, and it was one with a more positive approach. If he could have known that he would someday be in such a position of power as president, the inspiration and means of unity of a whole nation could have been epic.

Instead, young Obama considered her statement to be "high-horse, holier-than-thou, you-let-me-down" (para. 1, p. 93) because she was not of the same mindset. She was the one who did not understand where he was coming from. I am assuming she was black, too, for he failed to make note of it. Due to prior history, he surely would have made that distinction. Like most "progressives" I have met, not seeing things from their point of view—or disagreeing with it—is always because we do not understand.

His prep school years were spent only half-awake; he lost interest in school; correspondence ceased between him and his father; he indulged in pot smoking, drinking, and "a little blow" (para. 4, p. 93). I am not surprised his recall of his life during this phase produced no real remarkable activities. This is the result of a mind numbed by alcohol and drugs and seeking out companionship of like-minded dimwits. He thought pot would "help you laugh at the world's ongoing folly and see through all the hypocrisy and bull . . . and cheap moralism" (para. 1, p. 94).

His mother, aware of the element to which he was drawn, tried to give motherly advice about destiny and not relying on luck or fate, but it fell flat. In his words, "her faith in justice and rationality was misplaced, that we couldn't overcome after all, that all the education and good intentions in the world couldn't help plug up the holes in the universe or give you the power to change its blind, mindless course" (para. 2, p. 96). I just consider this the philosophical ravings of someone who had smoked way too much pot. The two of them settled on a college in Los Angeles.

The idea that all college can get you is "an advanced degree in compromise" (para. 1, p. 97) is what he picked up from his communist poet mentor, Frank. Obama said that really stuck with him as he was "as indifferent to college as toward most everything else" (para. 4, p. 96). Frank also told him, "You're not going to college to get educated. You're going there to get trained. They'll train you to want what you don't need. They'll train you to manipulate words so they don't mean anything anymore. They'll train you to forget what it is that you already know. They'll train you so good, you'll start believing what they tell you about equal opportunity and the American way and all that. They'll give you a corner office and invite you to fancy dinners, and tell you you're a credit to your race. Until you want to actually start running things, and then they'll yank on your chain and let you know that you may be a well-trained, well-paid nigger, but you're a nigger just the same" (para. 4, p. 97). This added more fuel to the fire growing inside.

Frank Marshall Davis, lovely fellow. He lived in Honolulu, Hawaii, where he ran a small business and was fairly active in the black labor rights movement to the point where the FBI tracked him in the 1940s because it considered him dangerous. He wrote poetry and articles for newspapers in Chicago and Atlanta. He died in 1987 in Hawaii but not before having had a big influence on our future president.

The majority of black people in mainland America proved to be more positive and forward thinking. Unfortunately, this did not dissuade Obama's negativity or victim mentality. The black people were focused on trying to make something with their lives and were not spending all their time being angry or trying to guess what white people were thinking about them. One black girl pointed out, "it's the black people that make everything racial and wanting me to choose . . . they're the ones who are telling me that I can't be who I am" (para. 3, p. 99). He totally rejected this premise.

Obama thinks integration is not a matter of conscious choice. He believes in keeping to one's own race or culture. He wants blacks to be vigilant about separation and diversity. He sees the white population of America as a hole in time and space that sweeps other races or cultures into it as an assimilation of minorities into a dominant culture. White power is a matter of gravitational pull and one of which there is no retreat.

He does not consider that America has its own culture. He does not consider American culture as one that is evolving through time and events unique to our country and which encompasses different peoples, their experiences and deeds. I believe what he is referencing in "a dominant culture" (para. 1, p. 100) is the nonpagan, non-African, noneverything else, Judeo-Christian ethic, moral values, and principles that comprise the dominant rationale of individual, freedom-loving Americans. An antireligious, totally secular vision is the only thing he considers acceptable.

He sarcastically states, "Don't you know who I am? I'm an individual!" He concludes, in a resentful manner, that black people are forced to believe that "only white culture could be neutral and objective . . . nonracial . . . willing to adopt the occasional exotic into its ranks" (paras. 1, 2, p. 100). Thankfully, this is not true.

In total avoidance of looking into his own heart, challenging his perception and trying to see things from a different viewpoint, which includes views expressed to him from people of black heritage, Obama still thinks black people who do not think about everything through the prism of race have mixed-up hearts. He thinks they are frightened at the ability to identify with that precept, and Obama finds it crucial not to compromise on this. Anything short of his viewpoint he refers to as falling asleep, not "still awake," and a sellout (para. 3, p. 100).

I am so grateful the philosophical premise was instilled in me at an early age to never be afraid to give up what I am for what I could be; to be bold, step out on faith, and pursue things higher or greater than what I thought possible. Barack Hussein Obama's achievement as president of the United States of America could have been so much greater if he had only learned this at an early age, too. Faith in God yields hope and encouragement.

Instead, he migrated toward the misled, the spiritually blind, and sought out emotional distraction. He identified with politically active black students, foreign students, Marxist professors, structural feminists, and punk-rock performance poets. He filled his head with far-fetched questionable constructs such as neocolonialism or puppet governments—Franz Fanon and his theories of decolonialization—Eurocentrism, and with the thinking that white people have the inability to respect other cultures and that they engage in unprovoked aggression toward distant peoples . . . and patriarchy (para. 4, p. 100). His radical cohorts and he would ground out cigarettes in the hallway carpet of the dormitory and play their music so loud that the walls began to shake in their own microrebellions. Hoping to be seen as smug, they were resistance-elites and in a class of their own distinct superiority. That stands true today.

The following passage is from a book, *Heart of Darkness*, Obama had read where the author, Conrad, sees in Africa "the cesspool of the world, black folks are savages, and any contact with them breeds infection." Judging from the content of this statement, if I may speculate, this comes from a much worse, warped mind than the subject of this book. This is a book I will never read.

Unfortunately, Obama thinks he can come to know the mind-set of white people from the book, "what makes white people so afraid . . . their demons" (para. 7, p. 103). He thinks the book would help him figure out the way white people's ideas get twisted around and would help him understand how they learn to hate black people.

So we learned to hate black people? Obama has previously stated our disregard—now hatred—was innate or in our DNA.

He later admitted to becoming so wrapped up in his perceived injuries and imagined traps by white people that he realized his thinking had stunted and narrowed his growth socially. But I do not believe that he came full circle because he still finds means to keep his racial diverseness and radical ideas. He has just managed to ascend to a level of coexistence and tolerance after having a humbling confrontation with a friend. I am skeptical that one confrontation with one friend could wipe out a lifetime of orchestrated resentment and animosity in one fell swoop without involving the revelation of a higher power. Possible but not probable. His current directives and reactions demonstrate no such change in his convictions. But the result of that confrontation did produce some self-reflection. He did not give any detail (para. 5, p. 111).

He revealed in a conversation with a fellow student that his grandfather was a Muslim. He did not confess to being a Muslim himself or if his father was. I found this very interesting because it is common knowledge that the Muslim religion is possessive and lays claim to the offspring of its followers (para. 6, p. 104).

Chapter 6

Obama was in the mood to change things after spending four years in the pit of an identity crisis. After four years of no correspondence with his father, Obama wrote to him to request a visit to Kenya. He received a positive response back from his father. The response was "You know your people, and that you know where you belong" (para. 2, p. 114). He also applied for transfer to Columbia University so he would be "in the heart of a true city, with black neighborhoods in close proximity" (para. 4, p. 115).

Obama went to New York and moved in with a friend, who was a Pakistani from London. He had overstayed his tourist visa, so he was here illegally with no intentions of leaving. Even with all the distractions presented by New York City, Obama still focused on the glimpses of racism and aligned himself with the black cultural vision.

His mother and half sister visited shortly after he settled into his new digs. His mother told a story involving a nasty letter from Obama's paternal grandfather from Kenya stating he did not want the Obama blood sullied by a white woman. The letter stated that Obama's father may have still been married, which was proven true, to his first wife from the village when he met and dated Obama's mother.

Obama's parents married anyway. After Obama was born, his paternal grandfather threatened to have Obama's father's student visa revoked, forcing the family to return to Kenya. Due to the Mau-Mau rebellion going on at the time in Kenya, Obama's maternal white grandmother was insistent that her daughter and baby Obama stay in America out of fear of them being killed. This was the reason he gave for their separation.

Obama, after listening to his mother tell about her and his father's first date, concludes that the love shared between them was unique. I believe that is good, but he goes on to say he suspects most Americans think that kind of love cannot exist between black and white people. I found that a very sad and untrue statement (para. 2, p. 127).

With stories of his father told by a woman who idolized him, Obama's father was always lingering in his subconscious, causing him to have many dreams of him. But Obama never got to go visit his father in Kenya before he died.

Chicago

Chapter 7

What were the odds that Obama would seek out one of the most notorious cities in American history for corruption, Chicago, to settle in?

It was 1983 when he made the decision to become a community organizer, which was no surprise. In my opinion, a community organizer alias is community antagonist or intimidator. A rebel. It is his or her goal to try to effect change not necessarily pursuant to a permanent solution based on thoughtful evaluation, analysis, and practicality, just a change. His ambition was to organize black "folks" to bring about a revolution that he labeled as "change" (para. 2, p. 133). He considered this a perfect direction to take based on his father, his mother, and her parents, and their Marxist ideology. The fuel he used to pursue this path was Indonesian beggars and farmers; his stepfather, who he concluded was lost to capitalistic power; his black racist and vengeful friends in college and high school; his experience around white people in New York; and his father's death.

He seems to have this unwavering belief that he needs to cling to his experiences of antagonism and assumptions. Obama seems to believe that those things make him who he is, and he settles into a state of apathy about changing that part of his life, stating, "That is how it should be, that to assert otherwise is to chase after a sorry sort of freedom" (para. 1, p. 143). He infers that black people have never had an identity in this country and believes the only solution was organizing black people into a community in order to give them the platform to demand that white people redeem themselves or pay their debt to black people. I happen to know that not all black Americans feel this way, and I'm confident Obama knows that as well. That does not dissuade him, though, in his quest for his kind of change and leaving chaos in his wake.

Obama resisted good advice from black people who told him to give up organizing and get a real job and make something of himself. They said things such as, "You can't help folks that ain't gonna make it no how, and they won't appreciate you trying. Folks that wanna make it, they gonna find a way to do it on they own" (para. 1, p. 136).

These were my kind of people. However, they underestimated the effects of giving free stuff to people. Giving free phones, free food, free lodging, money for education, and free health care to people will make them your new, loyal, best friend. Unfortunately, buying friendship is not a good idea. These same best friends will turn on you when you stop giving them handouts or start expecting them to earn these things for themselves. Those who want to make it in life, no matter the pigmentation of their skin, must find a way do it on their own. Expectations are the same for everyone. That is the only way we will appreciate our blessings and learn self-reliance and self-respect.

Obama went to a lecture at Columbia University "for inspiration" after turning down a position with a New York civil rights organization that was facilitating dialogue and organizing conferences on issues facing black people, such as drugs, unemployment, and housing. The lecture speaker was Kwame Toure', formerly Stokely Carmichael of Students for Nonviolent Coordinating Committee. He was also the honorary prime minister of the Black Panther Party in the 1960s (para. 4, p. 139; para. 1, p. 140).

Carmichael's lecture was very productive in motivating Obama in the ways of community organizing. The techniques Carmichael used increased the number of registered black voters from seventy to twenty-six hundred in 1965. Even though Carmichael was coined as saying, "It is a call for black people in this country to unite, to recognize their heritage, to build a sense of community. It is a call for black people to define their own goals, to lead their own organizations." The heavy influence from Frantz Fanon and Malcolm X made Carmichael more radical and focused on Black Power.

Carmichael also became critical of civil rights leaders who simply called for the integration of African Americans into existing institutions of the middle-class mainstream. He changed his commitment of nonviolence, too. Witnessing police brutality prompted Carmichael to change tactics to condone violence, which led to the creation of the militant social group known as "The Black Panthers."

Carmichael was a big fan of Che Guevara, a Marxist revolutionary. Carmichael stated, "The death of Che Guevara places a responsibility on all revolutionaries of the world to redouble their decision to fight on to the final defeat of Imperialism. That is why in essence Che Guevara is not dead; his ideas are with us."

Carmichael is noted for saying,

> Now, several people have been upset because we've said that integration was irrelevant when initiated by blacks, and that in fact it was a subterfuge, an insidious subterfuge, for the maintenance of white supremacy. Now we maintain that in the past six years or so, this country has been feeding us a thalidomide drug of integration, and that some Negroes have been walking down a dream street talking about sitting next to white people; and that that does not begin to solve the problem; that when we went to Mississippi we did not go to sit next to Ross Barnett; we did not go to sit next to Jim Clark; we went to get them out of our way; and that people ought to understand that; that we were never fighting for the right to integrate, we were fighting against white supremacy. Now, then, in order to understand white supremacy we must dismiss the fallacious notion that white people can give anybody their freedom. No man can give anybody his freedom. A man is born free. You may enslave a man after he is born free, and that is in fact what this country does. It enslaves black people after they're born, so that the only acts

that white people can do is to stop denying black people their freedom; that is, they must stop denying freedom. They never give it to anyone.[9]

Actually, Obama and Stokely Carmichael share a common legacy. They are cut from the same cloth. Both have become consumed with hatred, discontent, and vengeance. They both, among all the other racists that carry out their frustrations in acts of vengeance bent on force, disorder, or disruption, remind me of all the tiny air bubbles that get caught up in a torrid undertow fighting gravity and the force of the current.

They waste their energy and intellect focused on imagined evil forces in the illusion of conflict and oppression. They fight against the forces of nature that do what they do best and carry the bubbles of truth to the surface.

Committing evil deeds to combat evil intentions, even imaginary ones, will only result in one thing: the triumph of evil. I believe the natural consequences of our actions, the pursuit to do good, self-reflection and corrections made from that reflection; if left unmolested or forced by mortals in unnatural directions, will result in goodness prevailing. So, like the bubbles that just let nature (that is the nature of God not man) take its course, the ones fighting evil with evil end up as bubbles floating to the surface with everyone else. We all end up in the same place: in front of the throne of God on Judgment Day.

When has fighting hatred with hatred ever ended well? One can harbor different kinds of hatred. One kind can cause someone to be rejected or spurned but without the malicious intent to kill. Another is one so deeply seeded that it results in murder. Another is a hatred toward someone that is reflected in an attitude of indifference or disregard. No one wears hatred well. It can turn a person's heart cold and bitter even while the person mistakes it for righteous indignation.

Righteous indignation is anger. It is to be rightfully angry with someone or something that is disrespectful or demeaning to God or the things of God—such as Jesus. That is the same as anger toward evil deeds and evildoers. That kind is a holy anger because it has no malicious intent. It is not retaliatory, or personal, nor is it based upon a fleeting emotion or a perceived personal injustice. It is a settled condition of the mind and stands opposed to anyone or any action that defies God and His ways.

Psalm 139, which many believe was authored by David, states with great intensity that the author feels hate toward the enemies of God. This passage does not necessarily contradict Jesus's command to love one's enemies. It is seen as David's fierce loyalty and jealousy of God's honor. It is a hatred that expresses itself not in wishing harm to God's enemies, but in seeking their repentance. It is their deeds that are the enemies of God.

"I do not really want the wicked to die, says the Lord God. I want them to stop their bad ways and live" (Ezekiel 18:23).[10]

It was shortly after this potent mental induction from Carmichael that Obama got a call to come to Chicago as a trainee for an organizing drive. He was asked what made him angry because being angry was a requirement for the job. He did not divulge his answer. He was told the churches had much influence, so he would have to work with them as an institutional base to build power. He was told that churches just gave lip service concerning the plight of the poor and homeless but would not work with him just out of the goodness of their hearts.

He was told all this by his new boss, Jerry Kellman, a.k.a. Marty Kaufman, as identified by *New York Times* columnist Maureen Dowd. Kellman also told Obama that Chicago was the most segregated city in the country and that the new mayor, Harold Washington, was black. Kellman said Washington could help the young upstart with his career. Being a rebel without a cause, a political campaign in Chicago sounded appealing to Obama. So he moved to Chicago.

In his book, Obama chose to change the name of the boss he had when he first came to Chicago for, I believe, ominous reasons. Kellman, not Marty Kaufman, was the chief of the Developing Communities Project and was the one who hired Obama as director and lead organizer.

Kellman was trained or schooled by Saul Alinsky in community antagonizing/organizing. Alinsky is the author of *Rules for Radicals* and has some very strong socialistic views.

Kellman's description of Alinsky is quoted from David Maraniss's book, *Barack Obama, The Story*. It states, "He was not unwilling to take risks, but was just this strange combination of someone who would have to weigh everything to death and then take a dramatic risk at the end.

He was reluctant to do confrontation, to push the other side because it might blow up—and it might. But one thing Alinsky did understand was that within reason, once something blows up, to a certain degree it doesn't hurt, it helps."

I can see the implementation of this strategy, blowing something up to "help" the situation in the Obama-nation. Now, with the influence from Alinsky, Obama again has the opportunity to have connection to or association with Bill Ayers. Coincidently, Bill Ayers' father, Thomas Ayers, had founded the Chicago United and the Alliance for Better Chicago Schools.

I found in part III of *The Synarchy*, by Barbara Aho, and an article, "The Obama Files," by David Horowitz, instead of in Obama's book, that the elder Ayers, Thomas, the father of William (Bill) Ayers, a known terrorist, was probably the one that brought Obama on board because he was the Developing Communities Project organizer at the time. I can certainly see why Obama would want to hide this information.

Chapter 8

I have always been amazed by the double standards of those who live by an abstract or optional set of rules that can change due to mood, reaction, or pride instead of those that are concrete and everlasting. They rearrange or change their justifications and write and rewrite the rules they live by, continually. They misplace their faith in the capacity of the human cranium. All that can, and usually does, fail.

While Obama was familiarizing himself with his new Chicago digs, he stopped by a barbershop for a haircut. There he listened to the black men talking about their new black mayor, about how unfair the white politicians were, and that just voting the straight Democratic ticket rewarded them. They also excused the mayor's tax evasion and justified it as something that white politicians do, too.

I can understand that these men wanted to be proud of a black man achieving a position of power and authority, but it should never be just because he is black. Why do some black individuals believe black men or women should be held to a different set of standards of white men and women or any other people with different skin color, for that matter? I believe it comes from an ethnic pride based on their view that a black person actually managed to achieve a position such as this in a white world. That is all that matters to them. Integrity, ethics, values, and good character are all artificial ideas so, needless to say, are substandard, flawed, and not required. But does that not show a lack of faith in their own race?

The angst that Obama believes to be true for black Americans is that they will always be subject to a lifetime of insults, failed ambitions, and abandonment just because they are black living in a white world. He also expressed his feelings of shame for his white heritage. He fails to consider the premise that all mankind, not just white people, are fallen. He has failed to grasp the bigger picture.

Obama reveals his slant on Christians in a statement he made while visiting a factory.

"Blacks, whites, Hispanics, all working the same jobs, all living the same kind of lives, but not having a thing to do with each other outside of work and calling them the brothers and sisters in Christ," Obama said (para. 7, p. 149).

If this is true, all this statement says to me is that I would not want to work in Chicago.

Obama seems to be pushing for a revolution under the disguise of working-class solidarity or social justice. And the foundation for his revolution seems to be vengeance or Marxism. Marxism favors government ownership of factories, manufacturing, and producing goods and services—being the job provider for the whole country under the rule of the mob or a classless society where everyone has the same income and there are no opportunities for advancement because everyone has to be in the same class. This is income equality Marxist style.

Continuing on with his book, his days were filled with interviews of people absorbed by self-interest. He was looking for an issue to exploit. Obama was perfect for this job. He was able to utilize his hard-headedness and his lack of sentiment. It was all politics and no religion.

After listening to the disparaged populous of Chicago, Obama decided the black mayor was something they all had in common and that he might be able to have some "collective redemption" (para. 2, p. 158) through the mayor, so he refocused his idea of organizing on how he could use him and his office. The idea of manipulating people and probing their psyches to gain their trust was not an issue for him. He relied on it. One thing he learned was that "in politics, like religion, power lay in certainty and that one man's certainty always threatened another's" (para. 3, p. 163).

Chapter 9

His cynicism toward white people is still predominantly a leading factor in this chapter of his book. He addresses the issue of the Altgeld Gardens public housing project, which houses poor black people extremely close to a sewage treatment plant.

The story behind this development is a sad one, so it presented the perfect target.

The development was built in 1945 with 1,498 units on more than 190 acres to satisfy the housing needs for African American veterans returning from World War II. It originally was owned by the federal government and is the oldest public housing development in the country. In 1956, it was granted to the Chicago Housing Authority and is currently surrounded by substandard and hazardous real estate.

Indeed something needed to be done about the existing squalor, but Obama's predisposition is that corruption is somehow unique to white people when it comes to the management of the poor black man. Obviously white people are not immune to corruption and indifference. Just look at our history and the past neglect we have committed. But all mankind, no matter what their heritage, is subject to malfeasance. The mismanagement and neglect of The Gardens is an example of neglect for the poor not racism.

His focus was always on looking for ways to treat the condition of poverty as a black issue and not a community issue. The latter probably would have brought more success.

The disenchantment and lack of faith in his fellow black people resounded when Obama came to the conclusion that there was a permanent disconnect between white people and black people and that treating everyone equal does not work. He believes black people need help to overcome poverty more than whites do, and it is this that explained Altgeld Gardens (para. 2, p. 170).

At a community organizing meeting, the group came close to identifying the true problem that was being seen in Altgeld while reminiscing about life there in yesteryear. Apparently a few of the participants had fond memories and were puzzled over the lack of public decorum that was now being observed. What puzzles me is their inability to see that the behavior on display by the youths at Altgeld reflected the condition of their hearts and minds (para. 1, p. 178).

Obama tells of an older black man who was the owner of small private business. This man had decided it was too hard to compete against big companies. He also felt that black people, considering their adverse history and opportunities denied to their ancestors, should not have to break their backs just to survive. He referenced Koreans who have their family members working really hard just to survive. The old man then said that this is what he teaches his kids (para. 1, p. 182).

It seems the old man believes that freedom should be easy for black people just because they are black. Why? Because his ancestors were mistreated by the ancestors of white people. Freedom is not easy for anyone. It is hard to get and is hard to keep and, in my opinion, is worth having and fighting for. The things this man is complaining about are the things I am grateful to have. It is all about choices—and perspective.

Obama, I believe, associates small-business owners with the impoverished and unemployed—only in a different way. He sees their long hours and sometimes back-breaking efforts as pointless and seems to be blind to the satisfaction and sense of accomplishment it can bring. He does not see the necessity of small business in the grand plan of making life better and easier for black people because of the black community's inability toward coherence and networking and the lack of trust for each other. This explains his disregard for the small-business plight happening today. It does not fall in the perimeters of what he considers important for black people. This explains the overtones of indifference toward entrepreneurship and self-employment (para. 1, 2, p. 183).

After poking around trying to sniff out something upon which to focus, Obama found an issue that might fit the bill. It was one that they could use to rally the troops and establish their presence, force, and power. It was one that would make the statement to the residents that they were doing something to solve the poverty issue in the projects (para. 4, p. 185).

Chapter 10

The associations Obama seeks out are often wounded individuals, an assortment of special-interest, community-organizing people with trust issues. They are never focused on solutions extending past the immediate issue and bringing permanent resolutions because they fail to see the whole picture. They are all about biography and opinion formed from some traumatic or haunting experience that overshadowed their logic, objectivity, and common sense resulting from unresolved emotional injury—what he refers to as "sacred stories" (para. 2, p. 190). He insinuated that black people cannot love themselves without begrudging white people because the only stories he hears about courage, sacrifice, and overcoming great odds were centered around experiences indulging resentment toward white people (para. 2, p. 193).

> Then Jesus used stories to teach them many things. He said: "A farmer went out to plant his seed. While he was planting, some seed fell by the road, and the birds came and ate it all up. Some seed fell on rocky ground, where there wasn't much dirt. That seed grew very fast, because the ground was not deep. But when the sun rose, the plants dried up, because they did not have deep roots. Some other seed fell among thorny weeds, which grew and choked the good plants. Some other seed fell on good ground where it grew and produced a crop. Some plants made a hundred times more, some made sixty times more, and some made thirty times more. You people who can hear me, listen."[11]
>
> The followers came to Jesus and asked, "Why do you use stories to teach the people?" Jesus answered, "You have been chosen to know the secrets about the kingdom of heaven, but others cannot know these secrets. Those who have understanding will be given more, and they will have all they

need. But those who do not have understanding, even what they have will be taken away from them. This is why I use stories to teach to the people: They see, but they don't really see. They hear, but they don't really hear or understand. So they show that the things Isaiah said about them are true:

You will listen and listen, but you will not understand.

You will look and look, but you will not learn.

For the minds of these people have become stubborn.

They do not hear with their ears, and they have closed their eyes.

Otherwise they might really understand what they see with their eyes and hear with their ears.

They might really understand in their minds and come back to me and be healed. (Matthew 13:3-15)

Obama thinks that black people have a self-loathing issue and that they wish they were white instead of black. That sounds more like a personal problem to me. He thinks that all black people are self-conscious about their physical characteristics and won't discuss them in front of white people. That would be like admitting their doubt about themselves or being subjected to general examination by white people, who caused so many of the issues in the first place. This is ridiculous and not true. Being self-conscious is not unique to black people. White people don't necessarily discuss their physical characteristics with others, white or black, because of our own insecurities . . . well, maybe a very close friend in a humorous way.

This delusion could easily be remedied if Obama actually allowed himself to have a close white friend. As far as thinking that such discussions would somehow be admitting to self-doubt or imperfection to white people, does he really think white people see themselves as perfect? Again, this sounds more like a personal issue. He even says that expressions such as these would not cause white people to "look at their private struggles as a mirror into their own souls" but would rather see it as evidence of just more black pathology (para. 2, p. 193). White people do not see black people as an abnormality. They are a creation of God, made in His image.

I believe Obama projects his own feelings of self-loathing onto black people as a whole when he said that all black people suffer from self-loathing, and exposing it openly in front of white people would be "to open up our psyches to general examination by those who had caused so much of the damage in the first place" (para. 2, p. 193). He also believes those who teach "black self-esteem as a cure for all our ills, whether substance abuse or teen pregnancy or black-on-black crime" (para. 3, p. 193) are wrong, and that is somehow a waste of time. He also cynically refers to a mock psychiatric question, "Or was it because deep down you imagined a godless universe?" as a path of infinite regress (para. 1, p. 194). How could anyone that professes to be a follower of Christ think that dignity, self-respect, and the willingness to do the will of God or living within God's grace are paths of infinite regress? History tells us that the nature of God, laws of nature, reality, logic, common sense, grace, wisdom, etc., all do work.

John Locke said, "The law of Nature stands as an eternal rule to all men, legislators as well as others. The rules that they make for man's actions must . . . be conformable to the law of Nature—i.e., to the will of God."[12]

Obama thinks self-worth only comes from tangible skills, such as knowing how to read and doing math. Not from good moral aptitude because it requires too much self-reckoning, self-reflection, and self-honesty to work, and Obama apparently does not believe black people should be expected to exhort these logical demands to promote good self-esteem (para. 2, p. 194).

I believe he missed the point. I believe self-worth cannot come from a "what's in it for me" or a self-centered existence. That is careerism. I believe self-worth comes from identifying one's God-given talents and responding to it in obedience to be used as an avenue to serve humanity. It also involves trust, commitment, hope, joy, assurance, acceptance, and love. Through grace, Obama, along with everyone else, would find the answer to the question, who am I?

Obama linked up with another fellow organizer, who was a former gang leader that became a Muslim. This new friend thinks that white people are poison and that they are the enemy. This friend believes black people waste too much time and energy worrying about what white people are thinking and fighting feelings of hatred toward them. He preaches that vengeance is the only means for black people to gain self-respect (para. 2, p. 197).

Obama showed a considerable amount of interest in his friend's perspective on the situation. It got political. He described how his friend believes all black people are potential nationalists. Attributes of nationalization can implement a steady attack on white people and provide a constant recitation of their brutal experience in this country with blame for their current condition falling on white people instead of themselves to extort generosity (paras. 1 and 4, p. 198); they can blame their self-loathing and bad behavior on white people because that is what white people want them to do (para. 3, p. 198); and blame them for the voice inside that says, "You don't really belong here" (para. 2, p. 199). This is a quote, "So long as nationalism remained a cathartic curse on the white race, it could win the applause of the jobless teenager listening on the radio or the businessman watching late night TV" (para. 2, p. 202).

Obama rationalizes that if nationalism could bring promise of good things for black people, "then the hurt it might cause well-meaning whites, or the inner turmoil it caused people like me, would be of little consequence" (para. 1, p. 200). His only problem with black nationalism was its effectiveness and not its sentiment (para. 2, p. 200).

According to Wikipedia, nationalism is a belief system or political ideology that involves a strong identification of a group of individuals with a nation. They identify with Africa instead of America.

My ancestry is not Native American, but I identify with America over any other. The adoption of a national identity to America by blacks is what we need to create a unified community. Constant recitation of the brutal experience of their ancestors to have an excuse for whatever current plight in which a black person finds themself, those who refuse to try to practice self-control and self-discipline, and finding blame for self-dissatisfaction is not good for anyone, no matter what his or her status or condition.

Obama confesses he thinks his friend is right as far as directing the innate hatred that black people have of white people toward white people instead of turning it inward by stating, "whether a black politics that suppressed rage towards whites generally, or one that failed to elevate race loyalty above all else, was a politics inadequate to the task" (para. 3, p. 199).

"Elevate race loyalty above all else"?

Our Declaration of Independence states,

> We hold these truths to be self-evident, that all men are created equal, that they are endowed by their Creator with certain unalienable rights, that among these are life, liberty and the pursuit of happiness. That to secure these rights, governments are instituted among men, deriving their just powers from the consent of the governed. That whenever any form of government becomes destructive of these ends, it is the right of the people to alter or to abolish it and to institute new government, laying its foundation on such principles and organizing its powers in such form as to them shall seem most likely to affect their safety and happiness. Prudence, indeed, will dictate that governments long established should not be changed for light and transient causes; and accordingly, all experience hath shown that mankind are more disposed to suffer while evils are sufferable than to right themselves by abolishing the forms to which they are accustomed.

Barack Hussein Obama considers the moral framework of this country inescapable and one that black Americans can no longer afford. He thinks it weakens the resolve of black people and causes confusion within the ranks. With more concern about effectiveness than sentiment, he states, "If nationalism could create a strong and effective insularity, deliver on its promise of self-respect, then the hurt it might cause well-meaning white people, or the inner turmoil it caused people like him, would be of little consequence" (para. 1, p. 200).

Sounding open to the idea of nationalism here in America, he saw a need for a "strong organizational support" to change nationalism from just an attitude to a "concrete program," and not just "a collection of grievances" and "without any corporeal existence" (para. 5, p. 200). He then expressed admiration to the Nation of Islam for its success to "hoist the nationalist banner" along with sympathy for it and for Minister Farrakhan's ministry for its attempt at capitalism with some toiletry items. Under the brand name of POWER, they use the propaganda strategy of encouraging black people "to keep their money within their own community" (para. 2, p. 201). He contributes that the failure of their endeavor of creating a huge retail business was due to the difficulties that are unique to all black businesses: "the barriers to entry, the lack of finance, the set up that your (white) competitors possessed after having kept you out of the game for over three hundred years" (para. 3, p. 201). He found their newspaper, *The Final Call*, an interesting read, especially with tabloid-style headlines like *"CAUCASIAN WOMAN ADMITS: WHITES ARE THE DEVIL"*(para. 2, p. 201).

Obama blamed the failure on the "white man" and not to anything they did. This kind of justification I find harmful to him more than to the white race. Without self-reflection, there can be no self-improvement. We all learn from our mistakes.

Obama exposes his disdain for competition and capitalism in a revealing assault on the decisions resulting from a free-market economy and majority rule. He detests the rules governing capitalism and the potential wealth and power that can be gained in this environment. He believes white people influence the black businessman's psyche negatively. As an active and varied fact of their everyday lives and wishes, Obama wants to expunge white man phantom dreams of success from black people's aspirations (para. 2, 3, p. 202; para. 1, p. 203).

Obama sees Ronald Reagan as using verbal trickery when Reagan expressed the dynamics involved in the relationship between black and white people as temporary and not indissoluble. Obama thinks black people cannot "afford such make believe" (para. 1, p. 204). After all, this would imply forgiveness or forgetfulness over the expanse of time. Healing. He actually says that giving hope and opportunity to the black community is a delusion if white people are involved. He thinks attempts to adopt honesty in our public businesses would cause the loosening of their grip on what he perceives as a deception or delusion leading the black collective psyche to go wherever it pleased, including despair (para. 1, p. 204).

For the first time in several chapters, Obama has a moment of clarity. He concludes that "purity of race or of culture could no more serve as the basis for the typical black American's self-esteem" than the bloodlines they inherited. This is not only true for black Americans. He goes on to say that a black person's "sense of wholeness would have to arise" from his or her individual experiences and opinions (para. 2, p. 204). This is not exactly accurate. This is just what he has done. Obama can receive a sense of wholeness and purpose from faith in God. God does not show favor based on skin color. To Him we are all members of one race—the human race.

Obama ends this chapter with a story about going to a contemporary black play about life as a black person. The woman on stage danced and recited poetry and at the end said, "I found god in myself and I loved her . . . I loved her fiercely" (para. 3, p. 206).

Lovely.

Chapter 11

In this chapter, Obama was treated with a visit from his sister from Kenya. He tells her a story about a white girl he loved while living in New York. After he became president, he was questioned about the girl's identity. He said she was not a real girl but a composite character in his book. She was an entity of several people in one. The fact that his book was not fully, admittedly true was not the significant thing to me. It is what he said about this girl that struck me as interesting. I found his decision to end the relationship because her long, historically rich, white heritage intimidated him. Considering that she was a composite white girl, my conclusion was his insecurity in his own white heritage overwhelmed his appreciation of hers or, more accurately, theirs (para. 1, p. 211).

Obama said he broke up with her by taking her to see a black play expressing anger and contempt for the white man. She could not understand why black people are still so angry. He got defensive, or should I say offensive, and they got into a confrontation. He later confessed to feeling ashamed for making her feel bad, though. My question is, have the girls that make up this composite person ever read his book and realized what he really thinks about them?

His sister gives him some insight as to the type of person his father was, his practice of infidelity, and the children his adulterous behavior produced. From the history story, I gather Obama has two older half siblings and two younger half siblings from a black woman and four younger half siblings from a white woman. The two youngest siblings that were mothered by the same black woman as the two eldest siblings were never seen by the siblings of the white woman. They were products of Obama's father's infidelity with the black mother of the eldest two while married to the white woman, with whom he was living at the time. (pps. 213, 214).

Obama realized the image he had built up in his mind of his father in his absence was not accurate. He felt liberated from the self-imposed accountability of being the son of Africa and for the predominate "blackness" of his bloodline. He seemed to welcome the contradictory intrusion on his father's image, which was the part of himself he had focused on above all other influences. If this part of his book is true, I question why his political ideological resolve, which was also an attribute of his father's philosophies, did not wane along with this newfound liberation and freedom (pps. 220-222).

An old motto of mine that I have never let go of is: never be afraid to sacrifice what we are, for what we could be.

Chapter 12

Obama starts out showing displeasure with his fellow Developing Communities Project (DCP) officers when they seemed to lose focus on their goal. This happened after they became enthralled with their beloved black mayor, who showed up at a ribbon-cutting ceremony for a new Mayor's Office for Employment and Training (MET) intake center. He also got annoyed when a colleague of his said, "You don't have to prove nothing to us, Obama. We love you, man. Jesus loves you!" (para. 9, p. 226).

Obama started to gain influence in the political arena, where, I believe, he had his sights set all along, after some success in the Chicago area. Now, however, his feelings had changed from wanting to live up to his father's expectations to feeling he had to redeem himself for all his father's mistakes (para. 4, p. 227). He feared he might be subject to his father's fate. This change did nothing toward his focus on blaming white people for any and every hardship that arose, though. His path of monogamy and having a continuous personal influence in his children's lives, to his credit, was a move in the right direction. It is this behavior alone, not necessarily his ideology, that has won him so much favor among black people.

He speaks disparagingly about suburban parishioners expressing concern about the "white flight" into the suburbs "and dropping property values" and contends that it is all based on "racism and delicacy" (para. 5, p. 227; paras. 1 and 2, p. 228). He will not consider any other reason, and there are plenty of reasons to consider. Obama seems to always focus on only the promotion of black people in positions of power. He believed having a black mayor would make Chicago city services more equitable, resulting in black professionals getting a bigger share of city business. Their ethics, moral values, and principles are irrelevant.

This feeds the narrative that white people think themselves superior and could not care less about poor black people. So why was the situation in Altgeld Gardens not getting any better even under Chicago's black mayor? He does not understand (para. 1, p. 231).

A minister from an area church offered a suggestion. He implied that part of the problem was due to teenage pregnancy and the breakdown of the family, but Obama would not consider this idea. Again, he concludes the reason for the lack of prosperity in black communities was not the fault of the black officials in power, but stemmed from the constraints he attributes to white oppression of black people "an inheritor of sad history, part of a closed system with few moving parts," and "felt a prisoner of fate" (para. 2, p. 231).

I found it interesting that he referenced a group of women as *"innocent"* that he interviewed at a nearby elementary school. These women openly talked about their blatant abuse of the welfare system through having babies by multiple fathers. Their disregard of morality and absence of shame or remorse for their lifestyle and the emotional well-being of their children was heartbreaking. Obama sees that "they had mastered the tools of survival" (para. 1, p. 234).

At a meeting with some other organizers, one of them showed up with a newspaper clipping telling about a renovation transpiring at the Housing Authority's main office. It mentioned something about one of the subcontractors exposing some asbestos, and now the substance had to be dealt with. They figured maybe there was asbestos at the housing projects location, too, and if the substance was being handled in the main office, then the organizers could force them to deal with it in the residences also. There was no mention of asbestos exposures or known cases of mesothelioma. That did not seem to be their focus. It was just a means they needed to turn into a crisis so they could be seen as solving it.

The issue surrounding the asbestos issue finally came to the forefront and resulted in a few people coming to a show-of-force gathering at a city office, were Obama said, "They build these big offices to make you feel intimidated. Just remember that this is a public authority. Folks who work here are responsible to you" (para. 4, p. 240).

The emotional high was extremely satisfying in forcing the Chicago Housing Authority (CHA) to do tests for asbestos in public housing apartment units, even though no evidence of exposure was mentioned; whether or not asbestos existed did not seem to be the issue.

The group's success and the media exposure that followed inspired Obama to achieve his goal of black empowerment even after a lack of decorum and civility caused the CHA director to abruptly leave a town hall meeting. Even negative media coverage did not hinder their resolve. The asbestos issue was fixed, and most of the residents turned back to normal routines and personal daily life issues. They lost interest in keeping up the pressure to get leaders to change more of the problems.

Residents had long had a general consensus to focus on moving out of the neighborhood as fast as they could using whatever means necessary. That goal regained its momentum. Obama thought this was a cop-out, but wrote it off as the white man's vast bureaucracy disheartening their belief that their condition could not be altered by any amount of activism. The idea to try other avenues that did not involve community organizing and black empowerment did not occur to him. Besides, that would detour him from his primary objective.

Obama had thoughts of himself sitting down with the mayor to discuss the fate of the city. That was what he aspired to, to be in charge of the whole city. Sticking with finding solutions for the Altgeld Gardens public housing project was not his main focus and didn't satisfy his political appetite. The real issues that needed to be addressed, including lobbying to have the sewage treatment plant relocated and/or having the nearby landfills inspected for toxic waste and cleaned up and/or raising awareness about the industrial waste and the living conditions were not mentioned. He had a hunger for something more, and the Gardens was just the appetizer.

Today, the Gardens have gang problems. They suffer from horrid health problems due to the polluted air, land, and nearby waterways. It is one of the densest concentrations of potentially hazardous pollution sources in North America. Obama came in poised as their savior and could have been, in my opinion, but he dropped the ball. He left them in a situation no better than when he arrived. The asbestos was dealt with in the units, but their larger problems still remain.

Chapter 13

Sometime in 1987, Obama and his new employee, a "philosopher of the blues" whom he hired due to his "appreciation of the absurd," noticed a change for the worse happening with the young black kids on the street. They were becoming violent, challenging new limits in public and at home, and showing no loyalties, morals, or self-reflection or respect. Obama had to come to the realization black and white people now shared the same image of the young, black, violent, hostile males in the projects, and the image had merit.

He makes a comment about how he never thought a child could somehow set the terms of his own development (para. 4, p. 253). He does not consider the effect that a lack of a male influence has on young boys growing up with just one parent. In some cases, they are completely on their own with a working mother and, in other cases, the mother is not an adult herself. Even in his case, his mother instilled in him a "bigger than life" image of his father that had a major influence in his life. Also, Obama had his grandfather. The behavior of the black kids on the streets is what happens when limitations, discipline, and instruction based on love and morality are absent.

Obama continues to blame the evil white man when he questions how to analyze those in poverty and where they would sit "along the spectrum of goodness . . . a wayward gene . . . or just the consequences of a malnourished world" (para. 1, p. 254). He does not consider the consequences of an immoral and self-indulgent world to be the cause of hardship.

His conclusion is "that school reform was the only possible solution for the plight of the young men I saw on the street" (para. 3, p. 256). Would not the need for stable families or unemployment be a cause of their dilemma? He went to a school and met a black high school teacher who was starting a mentorship program for young men. It sounded good until I read what he was teaching.

The man said, "The public school system is not about educating black children. Never has been. Inner-city schools are about social control. Period. They're operated as holding pens . . . miniature jails, really. It's only when black children start breaking out of their pens and bothering white people that society even pays any attention to the issue of whether these children are being educated." This man believes that the reason black children are not doing well in school is because they are being taught someone else's history and culture. He thinks the culture they are learning systematically rejects them and denies them their humanity.

This man stated that he gives his young black students "a different values orientation—something to counteract the materialism and individualism and instant gratification" (para. 1, p. 259). This could be heard as a counter to capitalism, free thinking, entrepreneurship, and supply and demand.

Everyone in America, if you are not Native American, is from somewhere else. America's culture is just as much his or theirs as it is anyone's. They are systematically rejecting the American idea, the American dream, the American culture—not the other way around. He believes, as do I, that the starting point of education is the promise of being part of something unique and grand and of mastering one's environment. I am afraid his reasons for it are considerably different from mine, though. More importantly, I believe this is what Obama believes.

An academic education does not make you a better person. It does not change what is in a person's heart and soul. My only conclusion to this man's discontent is with the rules and laws that heed to the Judeo-Christian ethic and moral values and principles. He references them, not by name, but by their substance, which he thinks is too hard for black kids to live by. He sees it as unkind, unfair, and too restrictive.

Obama, however, concludes that guns are the cause of violence by young black men because having possession of a firearm will "shut off access to any empathy they may once have felt" for other people (para. 2, p. 270). He seems to think an education could create a tender soul and a wholesome conscience.

Chapter 14

This is the last chapter of the second part of his book. It is a common theme among the people, with which Obama associates in Chicago, that all the woes of the poor are caused by some of the black people becoming successful and moving to greener pastures instead of staying in the midst of the resentful and jealous unsuccessful. They cannot—or will not—be glad for those who do well or rejoice in their prosperity. They take pride in their self-pity and scoff at those who do not dedicate their lives to serving their needs.

Obama tells about a minister he knows who talked about the slaves' rituals and traditions practiced in the early years of slavery. They developed customs that were immersed in these practices to demonstrate their suppressed anger, their uncertain survival, their quest for freedom, and their hopes and dreams. From this, Obama believes emerged the black Christian church. I believe he is making a reference to Reverend Wright's church not evangelical Christian churches—one more akin to a social or civic center and the other more akin to a house of worship.

The minister also expressed disappointment of his declining church and blamed it on the better-off members moving to the suburbs so they could have "tidier neighborhoods . . . suburban life," (para. 3, p. 273) as if there was something wrong with wanting these things. He was displeased when interests changed to wanting more security than wanting to give more service to the church and community. True charity, which is just another word for love, is helping someone become reliant on God's grace by showing, not necessarily giving, him or her, the means to provide for one's self. Any or all of these is showing charity or love. Making someone reliant on people, systems, and policies, not offering continuous resolutions, discouraging their success and virtue and their well being and competence is not love.

Being successful is not just about being happy, wealthy, or accomplishing academic achievement. The Bible teaches that underlying all of these things is the dominant motif of character. Successful people are successful because of who they are, not because of what they do or how much or who they know. The writer of Proverbs, the book of wisdom, underscores the secret of success by writing:

"Knowledge begins with respect for the Lord, but fools hate wisdom and self-control" (Proverbs 1:7).[13]

Success is rooted in character. In terms of success, the Bible is much more interested in showing us where it comes from than in describing all of its results.

In furthering his quest for organizing, Obama hears about the Reverend Jeremiah Wright Jr. This is also when he decides to further his education and take a trip to Kenya. He feels not knowing enough about the affairs of the world puts him at a disadvantage in making the kind of impact he expects. He wants to learn about: "interest rates, corporate mergers, legislative process," how businesses and banks are structured, "the way (they) . . . were put together," real estate investing, "how (they) . . . succeeded or failed," how to achieve power and wealth, "learn power's currency in all its intricacy and detail." He wants to learn how to fundamentally change our structure and foundations to make this a world more accommodating to his idea of a perfect society (para. 7, p. 276).

In a brief and disparaging statement, Obama discloses his opinion that Dr. Martin Luther King Jr.'s message of "all of God's children" to have the same rights and principals is an unstable idea. He believes black people cannot fully experience and appreciate freedom because it would involve escaping from the knowledge of the past and the power of the white man or disappear in it. Here he is substituting "the knowledge of the past and the power of the white man" for the American heritage, American history, and the American dream (para. 2, p. 277).

I happen to be proud of our heritage, both the bad and the good, because it tells a story—the American story. It is an ongoing story where good prevails over evil. It is really a shame that some black people do not appreciate and take pride in their American heritage because they played a big part in making America great. If America had not identified the sin of slavery and turned away from it, if emancipation had never happened, then how would that particular evil deed even have been vanquished? This was a victory for the souls of both white and black people and for God's grace.

If I understand Obama, he thinks black people, here in America, cannot, should not, or will not forgive white people and throw off the shackles of despair, discontent, vengeance, hatred, resentment, bitterness, and unhappiness. The only real "power of the white man" that the white man shared with them was the Heavenly Father. The same "power" that laid bare the iniquity and the wickedness of slavery. As far as disappearing in it, I am trying to every day with every prayer.

Obama, however, sees the attributes of the civil rights movement as at least making it easier for someone, like himself, to maneuver from one community *"class"* to another without drawing attention or inviting judgment from peers in either group. He believes his black peers do not expect self-sacrifice from him because just being black was "enough of a cross to bear" (para. 2, p. 278).

In his efforts of trying to bring more churches into the organization, Obama exposes his cynicism of non-Catholic Christian pastors. He took special notice of some of them having a suspicious nature and evasive behavior. I can only speculate, but maybe they saw him, the real him, his character and his personality, as suspect. His perception of them was as "sanctimonious graybeards preaching pie-in-the-sky," or "slick Holy Rollers with flashy cars and a constant eye on the collection plate," pastors as referenced in novels or speeches by Malcolm X (para. 4, p. 279).

Some pastors did impress him, though, and proved to be the best organizers. Some gave Obama their testimony of self-corruption and the redemption through the resurrection of Christ. However, his misinterpretation of their redemption was as self-resurrection, making themselves better by creating a new focus of self. He got close. They did have a new focus, but all in all, he totally missed their message. Some of these pastors did not have a very high opinion of Reverend Wright.

However, Obama does not make note of his thoughts or feelings when he was asked, "Had I heard the Good News?" and "Do you know where it is that your faith is coming from?" (paras. 2, 3, p. 280). The Good News is the plan of salvation, as in John 3:16, which he does not wish to understand, and he guesses that his faith is in himself, but does not believe that could be enough (para. 2, p. 279).

Obama's first encounter with Reverend Wright was, in his estimation, a positive one. He thought the reverend had a talent for connecting the dots concerning the black American experience. He is also impressed with the reverend's knowledge of Islam, black nationalism, the history of religion, Hebrew, Greek, Tillich (literature like *Dynamics of Faith*—describes faith as an act of personality and not in the belief of dependence on God, and examines how faith participates in the dynamics of the personality), and Niebuhr (who is a Christian ethicist concerned about the way human beings relate to God, to each other, to their communities, and to the world) (para. 2, p. 282).

This is anti-Christian literature and black liberation theology doctrines. Reverend Wright received a PhD from the University of Chicago in the history of religion. This is not the same as going to a seminary. Obama makes no mention about his studies of the Bible or biblical literature and Christian studies. I can only wonder why. They either do not exist or they do not matter to Obama, or they would have been mentioned.

Reverend Wright had a big impact, and Obama became a big admirer. The reverend said all the right things that could appeal to a personality like Obama's. He appealed to Obama's attitude toward acceptance and tolerance of everything and everybody, making no distinctions as far as faith goes or putting importance on any doctrine but one: the doctrine cloaked in a true lack of tolerance for the theory of "the declining significance of race" (para. 7, p. 283).

The criticism continues of those who want to escape the violence of the city; it is expressed by this reverend, too. The knack that Obama has in finding this bias is uncanny. And this one is preaching that "life's not safe for a black man in this country . . . Never has been. Probably never will be." This one promotes his own "Black Value System" (para. 3, p. 284).

Obama's overview of what every religion hopes to offer to its converts is just "a spiritual harbor and the chance to see one's gifts appreciated and acknowledged" (para. 3, p. 285). I do not think he is referring to what the Bible teaches as *gifts*. He thinks religion is just for assurance and acceptability. Somewhere to be remembered. Somewhere to "redistribute values and circulate new ideas" and not for learning about salvation and communion with God (para. 4, p. 285). Somewhere for what Reverend Wright's church calls "the flow of culture . . . in reverse," which is where the wealthy black professionals and the poor uneducated black people have an opportunity to converse (para. 1, p. 286).

Obama confessed Reverend Wright's Trinity United Church of Christ was a "cultural community" that was "more sustainable than my own brand of organizing." Again, a civic center not a house of worship. He also confessed that he "could no longer distinguish between faith and mere folly, between faith and simple endurance." He remained skeptical of Christian faith, even seeming sincere; he questioned and does not see salvation as a necessity (para. 1, p. 287). His dismissive attitude toward salvation as a gift that cannot be earned or bought somehow got lost. He believes it is too easily won.

Obama attended a Sunday worship service at Reverend Wright's church and listened to a sermon titled "The Audacity of Hope." The reverend references a painting he once saw titled *Hope*, which exhibited a tattered and bruised harpist sitting on a mountain with all manner of evils illustrated below (paras. 6, 7, p. 292). The remark in his message exchanged all the manner of evils in the painting for "where white folk's greed runs a world in need" and then said, "That's the world . . . on which hope sits" (para. 2, p. 293). You have to ask yourself, is this how God perceives hope? Or is this just the rendition of how Reverend Wright perceives a painting of his version of hope?

Kenya

Chapter 15

This chapter begins with Obama seated next to a British citizen on the flight to Kenya discussing the plight of black South Africans and his disbelief that the Africans themselves hold any blame for it. Obama thinks that a native black South African should be getting the mining company job the young man was flying there hoping to get (para. 3, p. 299). Obama was irritated that the man was a colonialist (British), but was even more aggravated that this man would assume that Obama, as an American, would be in agreement with his views on the sad state of affairs in South Africa. The assumption that Obama shared his lack of personal motivation to solve South Africa's problems did not help.

In the attempt to apply a racial bias, Obama has constructed a well-cultivated opinion that all European things are unfamiliar. He considers it a sign of maturity to cling to this thinking but admits to an emptiness (para. 1, p. 302). Emptiness such as this cannot be filled with such things as racial obsessions. These will only leave him wanting.

The Founding Fathers were right in step with some ideas coming out of Europe. Sir William Blackstone wrote in *Commentaries on the Laws of England*, "Man, considered as a creature, must necessarily be subject to the laws of his Creator. This will of his Maker is called the law of nature. This law of nature being coeval with mankind, and dictated by God, Himself, is of course superior in obligation to any other. It is binding over all the globe in all countries, and at all times: no human laws are of any validity, if contrary to this."[14]

Obama does not seem to appreciate that humans are spiritual beings. We do not just have a spiritual life. Spirituality is not a part of life; it is life. And because we are made in God's image, we have the capacity for relationship with God, others, and ourselves. We possess a hunger for religion, for community, and for self-awareness. Spirituality creates, sustains, and guides the human quest in each of these areas. At the deepest level, it means we can know God and be known by God. It is God's nature to reveal; it is our nature to respond, allowing it to shape us in all the particulars of our lives. Obama simply denies himself this process.

This is a revelation about Barack Hussein Obama. If spirituality is rooted in our essence as human beings, then it is exemplified through dimensions of our personhood: integrity, morality, and fidelity, among others. We need to look no further than the Bible to see the Spirit and the qualities of character, which are essential for spirituality:

"But the fruit of the Spirit is love, joy, peace, longsuffering, kindness, goodness, faithfulness, gentleness, self-control. Against such there is no law" (Galatians 5:22-23 NKJV).[15]

Obama's emptiness is not necessarily a sign of failure, but it is a warning light in his soul, telling him that something is wrong and needs attention. Paul put it well when he wrote:

"This happened so we would not trust in ourselves, but in God" (2 Corinthians 1:9 NCV).[16]

His emptiness was and is his opportunity to draw close to God and to know from whence the ultimate source of spirituality comes. It is a reminder that the spiritual life is not grounded in emotion and opinion, but in faith.

Obama tells a parable about an African he met while traveling in Spain. He referred to him as "just another hungry man far away from home, one of the many children of former colonies—Algerians, West Indians, Pakistanis—now breaching the barricades of their former masters, mounting their own ragged, haphazard invasion" (para. 3, p. 303).

Or maybe he was just looking for work to support his family, like the man said. This statement tells more about Obama than the man he is talking about.

Furthering his confirmation of his ill-conceived notions about white people, Obama compares tourists in Hawaii and in Kenya. He sees the comfortable feelings of life in America as being a lie or somehow committing betrayal (para. 1, p. 311). Obama reminisced about the confidence of some white tourists in Hawaii that plainly intimidated him. He defensively laughed at the tourists in Hawaii, but in Kenya he saw them as more of "an encroachment," finding "their innocence vaguely insulting." He says the lack of self-consciousness the white people in Kenya exhibited expressed a freedom that he and his sister could never have, and thought it unfair because they were white imperialists. He saw it as their "confidence in their own parochialism, a confidence reserved for those born into imperial cultures" (para. 3, p. 312). It is as if Obama resents the spiritual joy and peace and sees Christian faith as just an imperial culture. It is insulting to him.

The Kenyan customs are quite different from customs and perceptions here in America. We can thank God's grace and our Christian heritage for that. Everyone in Kenya seems to judge everything and see everything through race, which contributes to his demonization of white people. There is an abyss in Kenya that only a monumental revolution of spiritual revelation could dismantle. Obama's spiritual blindness or emptiness is causing him to miss a golden opportunity to transform a nation of despair into an oasis of hope and prosperity. Oh so blind are those who *will not* see (para. 9, p. 313; para. 1, p. 314).

He believes Kenya's racial troubles are "just an unfortunate matter of economics" where native Kenyans hold no blame, have no shame, and see the white people from foreign lands as abusers and manipulators. He uses this belief to justify the behavior of Kimathi in Kenya, black people in Soweto, Detroit, and the Mekong Delta when they engage in street crime or revolution. Accountability is not applicable (para. 2, p. 34).

Obama's paradox is the white man's world of power that seduces the black man in every country. He thinks black people have been sold out to the power of white people and when told that "he's serving the interest of neocolonialism or some other such thing, he will reply yes, he will serve if that is what's required . . . a voice says to him (the black man), yes, changes have come, the old ways lie broken, and you must find a way as fast as you can to feed your belly and stop the white man from laughing at you. A voice says, no, you will sooner burn the earth to the ground" (paras. 2, 3, p. 315).

I have to remind myself, at times like this, of the stories about the miracles of Jesus and the holistic character they show in resolving troubled lives, physical conditions, and spiritual renewal. They are not just half-gospels of spiritual consolation and change but also of human bodies, social relationships, and situations. He came to help the poor, to set the prisoner free, and to heal the sick, as well as to save the soul and work all sorts of wonders—physical, mental, spiritual, emotional, and social.

Chapter 16

Obama came to the question of "what is a family?" (para. 6, p. 327). He devised a surrogate in the place of family, describing it as "a series of circles around (himself)" with borders that shifted but offered the illusion of control. An inner circle or band for love; a second band not as close for negotiated love to which he might or might not commit; and a third band even further out for colleagues, acquaintances, and different races (para. 1, p. 328). Due to his father's promiscuity, he is not really sure who is blood related, which proved to be a problem in settling his father's estate. So determining who belongs in the inner band is questionable (para. 9, p. 333).

Jesus exhorts us to love and honor our parents and has no patience with excuses for not doing so. Many instances of biblical conflict between God, the father, and his children have to do with idolatry. It is a form of idolatry to give human family life such elevation or greatness that we derive from that relationship the kind of relationship reserved only for God. To do so is to reverse the proper order of reality. God formed humankind in His image, not the other way around. Seeking to know God in order to know how to live, in families and in communities, is what the Bible teaches. Taking what we know of our families, especially our earthly fathers, like Obama's, and believing that knowledge is worthy of adulation instead of God is foolish.

Meeting members of his family was turning out to be a good experience, and Obama observed a kind of hospitality that he thought to be unique to Africa. "An obvious contrast to the growing isolation of American life . . . in cultural terms," Obama said adding that he thought the simple ways of life have been lost to Americans. They are "what we sacrificed for technology and mobility," and we no longer have "the insistent pleasure of other people's company" or "the joy of human warmth" (para. m1, p. 329). His misperception of America, as a whole, is more a reflection of Chicago and New York City, perhaps, not the small towns and cities in Texas, Louisiana, North Carolina, Florida, and Georgia where I have lived.

He indicates that to be wealthy in Africa involves trade-offs and compromises of family values and family responsibility because it is irresponsible to not support poorer family members. Their wealth should be available for family affairs and should support family members financially, and Obama believes they should not be prudent with their possessions. That would be unnatural and un-African (para. 2, p. 330).

He actually expressed shame for his success and feels that all black poor people are justified in their resentment of other black people's success. He believes a black family member's success puts that person in a position to make up their own rules, which justifies their actions. He views resentment and jealousy as just and correct. This possibly could have come from something his aunt told him about his father. She said his father suffered because his heart was too big, and he gave to everyone that asked for help. She told him everyone asked for help—even the ones that were "just too lazy to work for themselves" (para. 4, p. 336; para. 3, p. 337). He imprinted on his father's disposition instead of hers.

Obama associates wealth with negative things such as loneliness and unhappiness. Due to some visits he had with some of his wealthier classmates in Hawaii, he equates happiness with "disorder and the laughter disorder produced . . . of pain a boy could understand" (para. 8, p. 340; para. 1, p. 341). The "pain" to which he is referring comes from poverty and financial struggles, and he believes those struggles make for a happier existence—less guilt from one's prosperity. Does the pursuit of happiness mean the pursuit of unsuccessfulness and disorder? I think happiness is an emotion and a state of mind and can be experienced in both high and low financial circumstances. I have experienced both myself.

What escapes Obama is that happiness comes from our response to life's situations and to the way we live that life. It comes from a positive mental well-being and the satisfaction that that life grants. It is synonymous with joy, blessedness, peace, and prosperity.

Happiness should never be the ultimate goal of life but a result of a good life lived.

Chapter 17

This chapter opens with definite overtones of resentment toward nonblack rich people or colonialists in Kenya, mainly from Obama's sister. He associated nonnative Kenyan nationalities who carry arrogant attitudes to those in other countries by saying, "like the Chinese in Indonesia, the Koreans in the South Side of Chicago, outsiders who know how to trade and kept to themselves, working the margins of a racial cast system . . . a matter of history, an unfortunate fact of life" (para. 1, p. 348). His sister's general consensus of all non-Africans was that they deem themselves superior to black people.

Here is where he revealed something his aunt had told him: "If everyone is family, then no one is family" (para. 2, p. 347).

He tried to interject the idea that all Africans are all part of one tribe, the black tribe, due to some relative stereotyping (para. 3, p. 348). Obama is convinced that the innate gift he received from his African father based on the resembling image, resounded message, and instinctive nature comes from fellow Kenyans and relatives. His message was different from his sister's, but his obsession with race is evident and also that he sees all through that prism.

Every negative political notion, suspicion, and gloomy conversation he has with downhearted Kenyans emboldens his posturing. One individual complained about the corrupt government and the Kenyans' resistance to pay taxes. He accused the white big businessmen of refusing to pay their fair share for infrastructure expenses (para. 1, p. 353). That message resounds today. Obama said "attitudes aren't so different in America" (para. 2, p. 353). It is amazing how his focus is always drawn to people's resistance to give away their earnings as being the cause for decline, desolation, and injustice, instead of corruption, dishonesty, and immorality of government.

Obama's overview of Christianity became obvious to me when I read of a discussion he had with a safari guide. The guide said he thought Christianity had too many rules and is not good because it changes everything. Obama's perception of Christianity is that it is synonymous with colonialism (para. 13, p. 357). To him the two are the same. Next, he accredited a scene of hyenas and vultures eating the carcass of a dead wildebeest to "this is what Creation looked like" (para. 2, p. 356).

"In the beginning there was the Word. The Word was with God, and the Word was God. He was with God in the beginning. All things were made by Him, and nothing was made without Him. In Him there was life, and that life was the light of all people. The Light shines in the darkness, and the darkness has not overpowered it" (John 1:1-5).[17]

My view of creation is a much broader vision, less sinister and violent.

Chapter 18

Obama starts out this chapter maintaining the opposition position. He confirms this by expressing that basically any and every thing that the British Empire created had a negative impact on Africa during the colonization of different regions. He casts the six-hundred-mile railway from Mombasa to Lake Victoria as a project of immeasurable conceit (para. 2, p. 267). He sees mass transportation availability as the beginning of the end of Africa's virginity and purity. It brought more white people flocking to Africa to consolidate lands, and to cultivate and establish missions and churches (para. 2, p. 367). The uninvited colonialist's Christianity.

It seems Obama sees progress and modernization as the enemy. Would static isolation be what would sustain Africa? Is this the mind-set of an individual who grew up with American ideals and dreams? (para. 1, p. 368). In fact, he was somewhat surprised at his uncle's idea that "undaunted by his circumstances, certain that persistence would eventually pay off," even though his uncle had no higher education (para. 7, p. 381). The idea that someone could learn a trade or gain a skill without higher education and through committing time and effort and self-discipline would pay off eventually was a concept that seemed foreign to Obama. It still is. I believe Obama believes it is not what you know, but who you know that creates success. Both are wrong. It is who you are that makes you successful.

Chapter 19

Obama had a rude awakening when his step-grandmother told him of his family tree, stories that centered on his grandfather. Apparently, his grandfather was not of the opinion that all white people are evil, desiring only to oppress the black man. His grandfather had a certain respect for white people—their competence, their potential, their capabilities, or "power." Their inventions, weapons, organizational skills and practices, and the drive to constantly improve themselves intrigued him (para. 1, p. 407).

When South Africa's independence was progressing, his grandfather said, "The white man alone is like an ant; he can be easily crushed. But like an ant, the white man works together, his nation, his business— these things are more important to him than himself. He will follow his leaders and not question orders. Black men are not like this. Even the most foolish black man thinks he knows better than the wise man. That is why the black man will always lose" (para. 2, p. 417).

Obama's initial image of his grandfather was that of "an autocratic man"—Independent, "a man of the people, opposed to white rule." That image changed, however, to "Uncle Tom, Collaborator and House nigger" (para. 2, p. 406). Later in life, his grandfather changed his opinion and lost respect for many of the white man's ways and customs because of the corruption the white man brought to Africa. One of the white man's ideas lost on Obama's grandfather was Christianity. His grandfather rejected it because he could not understand mercy toward one's enemies or that Jesus could wash away a man's sins (para. 3, p. 407).

These principles are not inherent in the Islamic religion; therefore, his grandfather found Islam the religion of choice. It's the idea of making your religion conform to your ideas rather than conforming your ideas to the religion. This motto is what pushes most into Islam, and so his grandfather fell for the great lie. Converting to Islam caused a hardening of his heart and an offensiveness that did not do well with one of his wives and also the mother of Obama's father. She tried leaving him several times and eventually succeeded (para. 3, p. 412).

She did not feel the stress alone. It also had an impact on Obama's father, who she left behind with his grandfather. Obama's father felt abandoned by his mother and resented her but found no fault in his father (para. 2, p. 413). Obama's grandfather doted on Obama's father and wanted him to become highly educated while he denied education to his daughter, Obama's aunt, because she was female. Muslims do not hold females in high esteem (para. 3, p. 414).

Being brought up under the Muslim mantra, Obama's father did not think female teachers were smart enough to teach him anything he did not already know (para. 2, p. 415). At first, he rebelled against them in school. The Muslim mind-set unraveled slowly but surely, and he began to understand that what he was being taught at home did not necessarily ring true out in the world. Obama's father did well in school even though he was an uncooperative student, laying out until the ninth hour and then cramming a few days before a test. As he succeeded academically, Obama's father became arrogant, manipulative, and belligerent (para. 3, p. 415).

Stories of his father and his grandfather turned to memories of World War II and the rebellion that rose against Christian churches because

Africans saw the white man's Christianity as distorting and demeaning everything African. Obama associates Christianity with white man's oppression and with being a main source of forced labor—Colonialism (para. 3, p. 416; para. 1, p. 417).

Obama's father was accepted into a prestigious African school, but was expelled because of his frequent misconduct. That infuriated Obama's grandfather, resulting in the beating of his life (para. 3, p. 418). He then got sent off to work as a clerk where he would have to earn his own meals. He lost that job after getting into an argument with the owner. He found another job, but this one was for less pay. Obama's grandfather caught him in a lie about it, so he sent Obama's father away out of shame (para. 2, p. 419). Unconditional love is a tenet of Christianity not Islam, apparently.

Listening to his great-aunt's rendition of both his grandfather's and father's lives, Obama assumes his grandfather feels rage and self-condemnation and ridicule from his brothers and peers for pursuing life in the white man's world. This was just speculation on his part. Obama refers to it as "a mocking fate" as his grandfather "waits to die, alone" (para. 1, p. 428).

Not to be detoured, Obama idolizes his father for overcoming the trappings of what seems to be the white man's rules, "with its fissures of anger and doubt and defeat, the emotions still visible beneath the surface, hot and molten and alive, like a wicked, yawning mouth, and his mother gone, gone, away" (para. 1, p. 429). He does not see their problems stemming from the inability to adapt.

Obama thinks that faith is born out of hardship and that we get faith from other people. He does not associate faith with reliance on a higher power (para. 2, p. 429). He gets faith from others and himself; he has adopted their struggles as his birthright to carry on (para. 1, p. 430).

Faith is the word describing our acceptance of God's saving grace. On one hand it is simple: faith is saying "yes" to God's steadfast love. On the other hand, faith is complicated. It involves trust, commitment, obedience, hope, joy, assurance, acceptance, and love.

"For God so loved the world that he gave his only begotten Son, that whosoever believeth in him, shall not perish, but have everlasting life.

God sent not his Son into the world to condemn the world, but that the world through him might be saved" (John 3:16-17).[18]

The first message here points out God's love for the whole world. The second message is that our response to God's love is to believe in him. In the original language, "believe" and "faith" are two forms of the same word. To believe in Christ is the same thing as to have faith in Him. Everyone who responds to God's love by faith is given eternal life, which is salvation. Those who do not believe in Christ have the opposite destination—they are lost.

Faith is the means by which we are saved. God's grace, or the willingness to do God's will in all things, is the result of our salvation. In this relationship of trust and commitment, we accept God's word as true and God's promises as trustworthy, and we willingly allow Him to be the Lord of our lives. It is the Christian's answer to the question, "Who am I?"

Obama's identity and purpose of life could have been a positive and fulfilling experience growing up if he had been exposed to this kind of faith in God instead of in other searching and stumbling human beings. Putting faith in things that can, and often will, let you down will just lead to despair and frustration.

Obama's Epilogue

Obama's conclusion, that "the study of law can be disappointing at times, a matter of applying narrow rules and arcane procedure to an uncooperative reality; a sort of glorified accounting that serves to regulate the affairs of those who have power—and that all too often seeks to explain, to those who do not, the ultimate wisdom and justness of the condition" is so revealing.

In other words, he considers our laws and rule of law too complicated and unrealistic. But I ask, is what we have now due to his efforts, such as Obamacare, less complicated and more realistic? This might explain his disregard for the Constitution and the unimportance of things being legal or illegal. He mocks the system that regulates his power, ignoring the fact that power can corrupt and needs regulating, while promoting the system of regulating as something of value to those who cannot escape it.

He asks the questions, "How might that community be reconciled with our freedom? How far do our obligations reach . . . mere power into justice" . . . while thinking our rule of law often sacrifices conscience to expedience or greed (para. 1, p. 438). Is what we are seeing but a man that wheedles his will using a system of law for which he has no respect?

And how to reconcile with our freedom? Try acceptance, harmony, unity, understanding, forgiveness, love, honor, and respect for God, family, country, friends, and community. How far do our obligations reach? How about being responsible for ourselves, our actions, our behavior, our words, and our family, and supporting the church, for starters.

Power into justice? I understand that at one time or another, nearly everyone has uttered the complaint, "It's just not fair!" Although people may disagree over defining what's fair and unfair, the common complaint shows that human beings all share a sense that there is a difference between fair and unfair, right and wrong, justice and injustice. In order for this difference to be more than a matter of personal opinion or the whims of an ideology, justice must be weighed according to a universal and absolute standard.

The Bible and our Constitution are dependent on the universal and absolute standard of justice in God and in His Judeo-Christian ethics, moral values, and principles or laws of nature. God is the absolute standard of justice because justice comes from His nature. God defines justice for us by his actions and commands. Lawyers, judges, and juries may seek after justice, but only God can deliver it perfectly through his nature and laws because He is the source of justice. Man is flawed.

Corruption may be found in human courts as a result of our deviating from God's justice—or true justice. Some question why God permits injustice, such as widespread suffering and oppression in the world. The Bible recounts the doubts of even godly people as they wonder about God's justice. It does not offer a simple explanation of injustice, but it clearly states that God is not responsible for it.

Injustice does not come from God's hand, but from our own. Since the beginning of the world, people have turned away from the knowledge God has revealed in order to hide the evil of their own deeds. Because we willingly chose to do evil, God allows us to live out the consequences of our choices in violence, deceit, and injustice. Suffering injustice comes from that sin. It is God's way of jolting us into awareness of our sin.

But rest assured that God will not allow injustice to continue indefinitely. His justice will be openly demonstrated on the last day when He will judge everything, even what is done in secret. On that day he will reward and punish each person according to his or her faith in Christ. For those who have been made just through faith in Christ, that day will not bring punishment but forgiveness as Christ confesses them before the Father.

My Conclusion to His Book

It took a few days after reading Obama's book for it to all sink in and quiet down so I could gain perceptive and rational thought again. I experienced a sort of numbness or a paralyzing sadness and ill-feeling. I felt traumatized. I felt as if I had been on trial for a crime I had not committed. Lashing out emotionally was hard to avoid, and I am afraid I did just that for a day or so. I am not guiltless. With prayer and consulting my Bible the hurt and anger faded, and I saw Obama as misfortunate, not unfortunate but misfortunate and needing prayer.

My anger was a response to what felt like an assault. I remember Obama's boss when he first arrived in Chicago saying that anger was a necessity for the job. I believe Obama is an angry man and has lived most of his life focused on that anger.

Anger is an emotion that can run from a minor irritation to an intense rage or fury. Without the Bible as a map to point you in the correct direction, or a relationship with Jesus Christ, there is no wonder that Obama has come to this point in his life—wounded and feeling disgraced, with a misplaced faith and feeling of emptiness. He rejected the one thing that would have brought him peace and fulfillment. He so needs prayer for his eyes to be opened and to come to know God's grace.

As human beings and as Christians, we struggle with any anger we feel. The effects that our anger have on other people can be quite damaging, and the guilty feelings that we often feel after we cool down also give us pause. We often respond by labeling all anger as wrong or bad. As I turn to the Bible, I am surprised to see that God does not always condemn anger. As a matter of fact, God Himself, is frequently described as angry toward humanity.

We must distinguish a destructive anger from a righteous anger. That some anger is wrong is clear from the Bible's warnings to avoid it: "Wait and trust the Lord. Don't be upset when others get rich or when someone else's plans succeed. Don't get angry. Don't be upset; it only leads to trouble" (Psalm 37:7-8).[19]

Anger here is a response to a perceived injustice. A good person deserves something, but godless people get it instead. The psalmist tells the angry person to be patient because in the long run people who follow God will come out on top.

God wants us to adopt a selfless, gentle approach to those who assault us. As Jesus instructed in the Sermon on the Mount, "If someone slaps you on the right cheek, turn to him the other cheek also."

"If someone wants to sue you in court and take your shirt, let him have your coat also. If someone forces you to go with him one mile, go with him two miles" (Matthew 5:39-40).[20]

Indeed, selfish, unthinking anger is often an automatic response when our desires are not met, and it is ultimately directed at God. It causes us to become rebels. Of course, we can see the wisdom of God's advice, especially after we let anger take over our minds and make us act in ways we should later regret. I believe this is the type of anger Obama has.

As a mother of two boys, I often assumed the position of referee when disagreements started to accelerate into an all-out fight. Sometimes the justification of "well, he started it" would resound, usually followed closely by a "no, I didn't." My response would be, "It doesn't matter which of you started it because neither one of you did anything to stop it. The both of you are guilty of fighting." I believe two wrongs do not make a right.

However, the Bible does not teach that all anger is wrong. We should not become angry easily, but there are times when anger is the only appropriate response. The Bible recognizes that it is possible to be right in our anger. There is anger without sin. I hope the anger I feel about the actions taken by Obama and the Obama-nation to reject the laws of nature and the will of God and the attempt to establish a godless, man-made illusion of reality for this nation falls into this category.

While we are angry, we should be careful not to adopt the world's methods of dealing with anger, such as lashing out with violence and hate. We should rather remember that our weapons, be they bold or meek, loud or quiet, are the more powerful spiritual weapons of prayer, faith, wisdom, and love.

"God grant me the serenity to accept to things I cannot change, courage to change the things I can, and wisdom to know the difference" (Author Unknown).

What is most wonderful, though, is that the focus of God's anger against sin has not been directed against us. God loves us sinners but hates our sin. And we should follow suit.

Chapter 10

The Obama Brand

Obama's presidential campaign pennant

Even after reading his book, I am still unsure about who this man is due to his disclaimer about the names, places, and events that may not be accurate. If his book did give some insight into how he thinks, maybe, it can give us the reason why he is where he is, how he got there, and what his intentions are. What actually did he mean when he said he wanted to "fundamentally change" this country?

Personally speaking, some questions of my own have arisen that I would like answered. One of them is: Was his book what got him recognized by the secular statist progressives who were looking for a figurehead? One with all the credentials; unknown to the world of scrutiny, and with all the desirable leanings, connections, disconnections, vulnerabilities and, insecurities. One that could be persuaded or dissuaded to move in their prescribed direction.

What about Obama's allegiance to the United States and the Constitution? Here are some things to consider along with some examples of his motivations.

Mysterious Past

Example:

Some say Obama is a national security threat since he definitely has questionable allegiance to the United States, or more specifically, to the Constitution, not to mention his refusal to complete and release full, frank, and truthful answers as to his background. Well-known businessman Donald Trump was instrumental in forcing Obama's hand at producing a birth certificate after serving a couple of years as president already.[1] This delay in answering ongoing questions and concerns demonstrated a blatant disregard for the public safety and security for our nation.

Example:

Obama was asked at a live TV press conference on July 22, 2009, about a situation concerning a friend arrested on a disorderly conduct charge after a break-in, called in by a neighbor, became a public report. Obama—after confessing he was not there so he was not privy to all the facts—automatically sided with his friend and said that the Cambridge police officer acted "stupidly" for arresting his friend.[2]

This friend was a black Harvard professor by the name of Dr. Henry Louis Gates, Jr., who went ballistic, started acting out against the police officers responding to the call, and then claimed he was arrested because he was black. In not allowing the officer to be in charge of the situation, Gates was forced to experience humility, and Gates didn't like that lesson. The officer was doing exactly what he was supposed to do.

Obama retracted his statement but would not apologize to the officer for his earlier comments or for the behavior of this friend. What became known as the "Beer Summit" transpired, and Gates labeled the experience a "teachable moment." But I think the "teachable moment" taught everyone that there are those who expect and receive privilege and special consideration whether they deserve it or not.

You see the professor, as of the time of this publication, sat on the board of ProPublica. ProPublica was founded with a $10 million yearly grant from Herbert and Marion Sandler, the former chief executives of the Golden West Financial Corporation.[3] Golden West was one of the nation's largest mortgage lenders and savings and loans. The nonprofit ProPublica contributes to the news operations of all NBC-owned-and-operated stations. NBC affiliates will get early access to investigative reports from ProPublica, which describes itself as an "independent, non-profit newsroom that produces investigative journalism in the public interest."

The journalistic integrity of the Sandler-backed ProPublica has been repeatedly called into question. A report by The Capital Research Center concluded that ProPublica "churns out little more than left-wing hit pieces about Sarah Palin and blames the U.S. government for giving out too little foreign aid."

Slate reported that Jack Shafer raised questions about ProPublica's ability to provide independent nonpartisan journalism in light of the nature of Sandler's political donations, which include "giving hundreds of thousands of dollars to the Democratic Party campaign." The watchdog website UndueInfluence.com slammed ProPublica's claim of independence, stating the site is "as independent as a lapdog on a leash with allegiances sworn in advance to left-wing causes." NBC's deal with ProPublica is not the first time a major news outlet distributed reporting that is provided by questionable ProPublica pieces.

The Associated Press announced in July 2009 it would allow its subscribers to publish free-of-charge work by four nonprofit groups, the Center of Public Integrity (CPI), the Investigative Reporting Workshop at American University, the Center for Investigative Reporting and ProPublica. George Soros' Open Society Institute funds CPI. NBC-owned television stations in cities across the nation have now teamed up with nonprofit "journalism" groups funded by the billionaire husband-and-wife team who not only have spent millions campaigning for Obama but also topped donor lists to groups such as ACORN and MoveOn.org.

It is amazing what can be found when acquaintances pop up from Obama's well-guarded and unquestioned past associations. Considering some of those associations, it is unnerving to get a glimpse of just how deep the Obama rabbit hole goes.

Example:

"Whether we like it or not, we remain a dominant military superpower and when conflicts break out, one way or another we get pulled into them and that ends up costing us significantly in terms of both blood and treasure."[4] This was a direct quote from Obama on April 13, 2010, at a news conference at the closing of his "Nuclear Security Summit." Some do not hear what I heard in this statement. There is so much more being said here than just the words—intent, regret, agenda, and lack of pride in our country.

Sometimes, the greatest use of words is to hide our thoughts, and Obama seems to practice this often. It is almost like he speaks a language inside a language—a secretive idiom of ideology hidden within the vernacular of the English language to which only a privileged few are privy. Because of my lack of training to identify such espionage, I can only guess that I miss most of it. But I do know of One that understands it all. He hears what is being thought before it is ever uttered. He knows all that has been done, even behind closed doors, what is being done, and what will be done. He is the One from whom no one can hide his or her ambitions, thoughts, feelings, words, and actions. If I am not fooled, He isn't.

I know Obama professes to be Christian. I pray he is. Only God can judge his heart. But he surrounds himself with those who profess otherwise and do not encourage Christian values and principles in policy. Would saying he is, when he isn't, give him some sort of advantage? All we can judge is his actions, behavior, and words. According to the Bible, using discernment, believers should be able to identify a fellow believer. Obama's actions speak louder than his words, and his life speaks contradiction.

Matthew 7:15-19 (NCV):

> Be careful of false prophets. They come to you looking gentle like sheep, but they are really dangerous like wolves. You will know these people by what they do. Grapes don't come from thorn bushes, and figs don't come from thorny weeds. In the same way, every good tree produces good fruit, but a bad tree produces bad fruit. A good tree cannot produce bad fruit, and a bad tree cannot produce good fruit. Every tree that does not produce good fruit is cut down and thrown into the fire. In the same way, you will know these false prophets by what they do.[5]

Galatians 5:19-21 (NCV):

> The wrong things the sinful self does are clear: . . . hating, making trouble, being jealous, being angry, being selfish, making people angry with each other, causing divisions among people, feeling envy. I warn you now as I warned you before: Those who do these things will not inherit God's kingdom.[6]

Contentious and Quarrelsome

The apostle Paul argues in Romans 1:18-32 that everyone knows that God exists. He has clearly revealed himself to all people by what He has made, even though some will deny it. One of the differences between Christians and non-Christians is not that Christians know God and the non-Christians do not. It is that Christians thank God and non-Christians choose to ignore him. Thanksgiving is at the heart of Christian faith and worship. Gratitude toward God is also very rare among selfish persons.

Example:

Obama's speech in Osawatomie, Kansas, on December 6, 2011, was well received by the mainstream media. The *Baltimore Sun* wrote that the president has finally found "his voice," while other press said that Barack was "channeling Teddy Roosevelt."[7] What did Obama say that brought cheers from the progressive media outlets and jeers from everyone else? Among other things, he stated that our relatively free-enterprise system not only "doesn't work" but that "it has never worked." The first thing to note is the willful blindness and ingratitude evidenced by this statement. Our nation enjoys wealth unprecedented in man's history, with its supermarkets stocked with thousands of products from the world over; and with its "poor" people who have, or have access to, transportation, TVs, cell phones, education, and necessities of life, including food and health care. Obama just resents America's *means* of prosperity and the fact that it does work.

Example:

In what I think almost all Americans would call odd, Obama delivered a Thanksgiving address with a speech titled "On Thanksgiving, Grateful for the Men and Women Who Defend Our Country." In the text of his speech, he referred to Thanksgiving as a "celebration of community." He did not include any reference to God during his address. His remarks were void of any religious references altogether. Thanksgiving is a holiday traditionally steeped in giving thanks and praise to God. Obama said his family was "reflecting on how truly lucky we truly are." For many Americans, though, Thanksgiving is a time to reflect on how blessed and thankful they are. He apparently decided to do something a little different and celebrate "the community" and "the troops" instead of God.[8]

Obama obviously has a conflicted soul. He continually sends out mixed messages. He repels away from the tradition giving thanks to God, which one would think he would be compelled to do as a Christian. This causes a disconnection with both individuals and nations.

James states that conflicts come from selfish desires within us. Obama wants things. He becomes angry when he does not get them. He gets angry with those who do not want the same things and equates them as troublemakers. Obama sets out to cause others to be angry and jealous also with rhetoric of discontent in regard to race, gender, income, and moral issues.

Example:

Obama used a San Francisco fund-raiser to express disappointment and sorrow for America and our failure to meet his expectations. He said Americans have "lost our ambition, our imagination, and our willingness to do the things that built the Golden Gate Bridge."[9] He is wrong about a great many things, but this is the thing he is most completely and dangerously wrong about. We Americans have not "lost" our ambition and imagination. We suffer under plans devised by central planners who lack imagination, and they have informed us that our ambitions are reprehensible. Vast numbers of people out there are brimming with creativity and drive. What they need most is to have the government stop interfering and get its hand out of their pockets. They need to know they can keep the fruits of their labors and the rewards of entrepreneurial risk, without being accused of "greed."

Example:

Obama did it again overseas (well, it was Hawaii, but Obama apparently thought he was abroad because he said, "Here in Asia . . .").

"We've been a little bit lazy, I think, over the past couple of decades. We've kind of taken for granted . . . 'Well, people will want to come here' and we aren't out there hungry, selling America and trying to attract new business into America," he said at the Asian Economic Summit in Hawaii.[10] Was he wanting more foreign investors to invest in America? What about American investors? That is what I would prefer. Maybe the same reason that American investors invest elsewhere is the same reason foreign investors do not seek out investments here in this country. The American worker has not lost his "ambition (and) imagination," is not "lazy" or gone "a bit soft." We have just put a rover on Mars. What about fracking? Corporate taxes and excessive regulation have driven business away.

Example:

The "Obama For America" website sent out e-mails with the subject line "In honor of the GOP" that encouraged readers to give three dollars or more to Obama's reelection campaign and become eligible to win a dinner with the president and his wife. The e-mail also promised donors that OFA would taunt a Republican acquaintance on their behalf with the Democratic donation if they provided an e-mail address to which to send the taunt.[11]

Disunity with Israel

Example:

He accused Israel of taking territories of Palestine that were changed as a result of the Six-Day War in 1967 in a May 19, 2011, speech on US policy in the Middle East and North Africa. In his speech he said, "The United States believes that negotiations should result in two states, with permanent Palestinian borders with Israel, Jordan, and Egypt, and permanent Israeli borders with Palestine. We believe the borders of Israel and Palestine should be based on the 1967 lines with mutually agreed swaps, so that secure and recognized borders are established for both states. The Palestinian people must have the right to govern themselves, and reach their full potential, in a sovereign and contiguous state."[12]

Granting Palestinians that particular territory back would cut Israel into two parts. This is disturbing considering what the Bible says concerning God's chosen people and what will happen to those who do not bless them.

"I will bless those who bless you, and I will place a curse on those who harm you. And all the people of earth will be blessed through you" (Genesis 12:3).[13]

He favors Palestine over Israel. Mistreatment of Israel by America is a sure way to invite God's judgment.

Example:

The *Los Angeles Times* has a video showing Obama attending an anti-Israel event in 2003 in which he delivers a glowing testimonial for Rashid Khalidi, a pro-Palestinian professor. The video surfaced after the *Times* would not release it due to a promise made to the source. The paper only published an article about the video. The article failed to report what later research revealed: An anti-Israel group, the Arab American Action Network, led by Mona Khalidi (Rashid Khalidi's wife), sponsored the event. Her group receives large sums of money from the Woods Fund, an ultraprogressive Chicago nonprofit group. Obama served as a board member on the Woods Fund, alongside Weather Underground radical William Ayers.[14]

He sees the poor as deserving of more and feels they are being denied what is owed them by the rich, who are undeserving of what they have earned. He believes all riches comes by way of greed and exploitation of the poor. His anger is a response to a perceived injustice. It is this selfish, unthinking anger, which is often an automatic response when his desires are not met. He sees the poor as enslaved to poverty by the rich and that the rich are just lucky. This is an impossibility here in America, at least, for right now. No one is "enslaved" to a particular station in life, whether it be poverty or riches.

Example:

Why did Obama bow to the king of Saudi Arabia?[15] I saw it with my own eyes, but he said we did not see what we saw. Disregarding the lie, why did he do that? What message did it send to Israel?

Example:

French President Sarkozy was heard saying to Obama over an open mike, "I cannot bear Netanyahu; he's a liar." Obama childish retort was, "You're fed up? But I have to deal with it all day."[16] This was Obama's "reset" Middle East foreign policy—appease America's enemies in the Middle East while sticking it to America's sole ally in the region. Obama has done a very poor job of hiding his disdain for the State of Israel and her prime minister, who are on the front line of the war against the fascist enemies of the United States. The antagonism our president feels toward Israel is obvious, especially to Israel, and disgraceful.

Contentment with Debt

Example:

Deficit spending results in the devaluation of wealth. Higher prices are the result. Deficit spending is theft by dilution. The only way governments can fund anything is by printing money (deficit spending) or taking it from people who produce it (disproportionate taxation). Printing money is called "fiat money" because it is created out of nothing. This is a god-like act, except, governments are not gods.[17]

There are further consequences. Being in debt puts us in the position of slaves: the rich rule over the poor, and the borrower becomes the lender's slave. Who bought our debt? China did, so we are now slaves to China.

Approximately at his three-and-a-half-year mark of his presidency, Obama and the Obama-nation sent our national debt soaring to over $17 trillion. It took two hundred years to accumulate not even half that amount.

"Foreigners will lend money to you, but you will not be able to lend to them. They will be like the head, and you will be like the tail" (Deuteronomy 28:44).[18]

Printing money when there is no commodity to back it up (e.g., gold or silver) dilutes the value of dollars that are in circulation and that are exchanged for goods and services. This is called inflation, and the result is higher prices because each new dollar dilutes the value of those dollars already in circulation in the same way that water dilutes wine and a less valuable metal cheapens silver. This is designed American economic decline.

"Jerusalem, you have become like the scum left when silver is purified; you are like wine mixed with water. Your rulers are rebels and friends of thieves. They all accept money for doing wrong, and they are paid to cheat people" (Isaiah 1:22-23).[19]

These tactics or little dirty tricks have been used for centuries. Granted, the Obama-nation did not start it, but they have opened the floodgates. We may get away with it temporarily. It will rear its ugly head eventually. God indicted Israel because of these very actions, and the economic policies, both then and now, end up hurting the most vulnerable.

Those on fixed incomes, like my own mother, are the ones that are hurt by the creation of fiat money. I can't help but think of the many other elderly people that cannot move in with a family member to care for them and need care or do not have a family member who can afford to pay for their care or cannot afford it themselves. Those in the most need of health care are the ones that have turned to the state for security, and yet it was the state that created the mess in the first place, not insurance companies or the medical industry. Government control through regulation of the health-care system makes it more expensive to do business by its inflationary nature. Government control means less care and more taxes and higher prices.

"The Lord All-Powerful says, 'Then I will come to you and judge you. I will be quick to testify against those who take part in evil magic, adultery, and lying under oath, those who cheat workers of their pay and who cheat widows and orphans, those who are unfair to foreigners, and those who do not respect me'" (Malachi 3:5).[20]

The Jewish people long ago had a custom of "temporary slavery" for those not repaying their loans. The debtor would sell himself into slavery only long enough to repay the debt. He would be released when the debt was paid. Jesus spoke against this kind of slavery and any other kind. No one should be a slave to another. This is also a statement about being in debt because it can make you a slave to the one holding the note. We should avoid debt. If Obama is concerned about slavery or making America a slave nation to another, why has he indebted us into oblivion?

Biblical Unfamiliarity and Disrespect

Example:

Obama used "God rhetoric" in vain, claiming, "God wants to see us help ourselves by putting people back to work" during a jobs speech at Key Bridge in Washington, DC. White House spokesman Jay Carney said

Obama was trying to make the point that "we have it within our capacity to do the things to help the American people. I believe the phrase he was aiming for was, 'The Lord helps those who help themselves.'"[21] We have all heard it. Unfortunately, Carney did not do his research. That phrase is not found in the Bible. I believe it is true. But if God helps those who help themselves, it seems to me that the responsibility resides with the individual and not the state. The well-known phrase does not say, "The Lord helps those whom the state helps." God wants us to follow His rules to get people back to work, and the only jobs that the government can create are government jobs, and in my humble opinion, the government needs to *stop* creating those jobs.

"You yourselves know that you should live as we live. We were not lazy when we were with you. And when we ate another person's food, we always paid for it. We worked very hard night and day so we would not be an expense to any of you. We had the right to ask you to help us, but we worked to take care of ourselves so we would be an example for you to follow. When we were with you, we gave you this rule: 'Anyone who refuses to work should not eat'" (2 Thessalonians 3:7-10).[22]

If Obama and the Obama-nation want to use "God rhetoric" and evoke scripture to justify their agendas and support raising of taxes and deficit spending, they might need to actually read it first.

Example:

At the September 15, 2010, Congressional Hispanic Caucus meeting, Obama quoted from the Declaration of Independence during two speeches. In talking about what bound together people from so many cultures and made them Americans, he said, "We hold these truths to be self-evident, that all men are created equal, endowed (leaving out *by their Creator*) with certain unalienable rights, life and liberty and the pursuit of happiness."[23] I am guessing he assumed this particular audience would be oblivious to what it really says. He also misquoted the Gettysburg Address by dropping *under God* and rearranging the verbiage from the original text.

Example:

I watched a June 28, 2006, video of Obama. This numbing exhibit of pure distain for Christianity and the Word of God was very revealing.

He specifically refers to the books of Leviticus, Deuteronomy, and the Sermon on the Mount as examples of how ridiculous he considers biblical values to be.[24]

"'Now see what has happened,' says the Lord. 'Another nation has taken away my people for nothing. This nation who rules them makes fun of me,' say the Lord. 'All day long they speak against me. This has happened so my people will know who I am, and so, on that future day, they will know that I am the one speaking to them. It will really be me'" (Isaiah 52:5-6).[25]

His disregard of God's authority shows in his defiance of God's word in glorifying and celebrating homosexuality. He insulted the sanctity of marriage and was dismissive to those whom God has sent to act on his behalf in the speech he made at the National Prayer Breakfast in 2011—the one he did not cancel.

Jesus said,

> If the world hates you, remember that it hated me first. If you belonged to the world, it would love you as it loves its own. But I have chosen you out of the world, so you don't belong to it. That is why the world hates you. Remember what I told you: A servant is not greater than his master. If people did wrong to me, they will do wrong to you, too. And if they obeyed my teaching, they will obey yours, too. They will do all this to you on account of me, because they do not know the One who sent me. (John 14:21)[26]

Social Justice Schemes

Example:

It is easy to see why Obama sees and considers things as unjust and unfair because to him they are issues of personal opinion. In order for these issues to be weighed according to a universal and absolute standard, you would have to understand that the standard of justice is God himself. God is the absolute standard of justice because justice comes from His nature.

"Evil people do not understand justice, but those who follow the Lord understand it completely" (Proverbs 28:5).[27]

In my opinion, Obama sees the world through racial and cultural divisions. He draws boundaries between ethnic groups, rich and poor, men and women, adults and children, healthy and sick, those of higher learning from those of basic, common knowledge, and religious from secular associations. He sees the world in absolute groups of status or station. He sees only class, and when found on the unfavorable side of such boundaries, as having little hope for change. The poor cannot climb a ladder to success, the chronically ill usually do not get better, social outcasts stay on the fringes of everyday life, and the rich never lose their wealth and never are willing to give to the needy. None of those philosophies are true and are all devoid of hope. Because of his view, government is the only way to achieve justice.

Example:

Imagine that you had the chance to sit down with the president of the United States and you could ask him any question. What would you ask? Why Obamacare, cap and trade, trillions in debt? Why not work with Congress, energy independence, and small government? What do you think he would say?

ABC affiliate WVEC's David Alan was able to ask some interesting questions. "How have we become a country where so many members of the middle class go to bed at night wondering if they're going to be able to keep their homes and put food on the table and send their kids to college?"[28]

Alan asked the president other questions. "Do you take any personal responsibility for your administration creating that condition?"

"We didn't create the condition. We haven't solved it fully yet because it was three decades in the making," Obama replied. "I mean, if you look at the trend lines, essentially what's happened is that because of automation, because of globalization, you had a lot of manufacturing move out of the United States. Businesses got more efficient; they needed fewer workers, they had more leverage over workers, and all this added up to a tougher time for middle class families."

So, if one is to understand Obama correctly, Ronald Regan, George H. W. Bush, Bill Clinton, and George W. Bush created the current economic crisis facing middle-class America? It has been exacerbated by "automation?" "Globalization?" Does he think the majority of Americans work, or should work, in factories? He does not assume any fault for anything? Even though Alan's question was loaded and was designed to prompt an admission of failure from Obama, it is very difficult to view his response as anything but being evasive and flat-out dishonest.

The president continued, explaining his plans to "grow the middle-class" and then arguing in favor of his economic policies.

"The good news is that we still have the best universities in the world, the most innovative businesses in the world, the best workers in the world, (and) the freest market system in the world," he said.

This statement is only true from a secular progressive point of view. Did not Obama blame automated innovation for shrinking the middle class? Second, Boeing might disagree with his assessment that the United States has the "freest market system in the world."

"We've seen our exports go up, we've now seen twenty-one months of job growth (in the private sector?), so we've got all the tools to refocus and make sure that we're growing our middle class again," he said. "But we're going to have to do some smart things to do it: improve (propaganda and indoctrination) our education system, invest (raise taxes) in infrastructure, invest (raise more taxes) in basic science and technology, and make sure the rules of the road are fair (increase regulations) and that everybody (the wealthy) is doing their fair share (paying higher tax rates)." (Items in parentheses are from the author and not in the original speech.)

"The fact is, new jobs are being added at a far lower rate than a decade ago. And it's that tepid job growth that explains America's unacceptable high unemployment rate," writes Mike Brownfield of the Heritage Foundation.[29] Indeed, the US Bureau of Labor Statistics would show that Obama's "twenty-one months of job growth" has not worked out too well for many Americans.

The National Aeronautics and Space Administration (NASA) must be thrilled to hear Obama's pledge to reinvest United States resources in science and technology. Recently, they have been a little "under-utilized." Then there is Obama's oft-repeated call for the wealthy to pay their "fair share." Even though "fair share" has been questioned, dissected, and disputed, no one but the Obama-nation wants to hear it being repeated any more.

Example:

Remember when Obama announced, during his consideration of a replacement to retiring Justice David Souter on the United States Supreme Court, that he wanted a court justice who will "use empathy and compassion" on the bench.[30] Are they not supposed to interpret the law according to our Constitution? So what exactly was he saying he wanted this person to do?

Obama appointed Sonia Sotomayor to the US Supreme Court. This person believes that the court is a vehicle for making policy instead of interpreting the legality of policies developed by elected officials in our legislative branch. She considers empathy and compassion as tools in making those policies instead of the absolute, non-abstract, non-emotional, non-opinionated, Constitutional law. I see this as dangerous. She exposed her view on the matter with her own mouth while serving as one of the judges in the Second Court of Appeals. For some reason, the question about judicial activism was omitted from her questionnaire.

Example:

While Obama made speeches that he wanted more American-made products, his National Relations Board was engaged in what could be seen as bureaucratic and government intimidation. They used legal threats against a great American company, Boeing, who was seeking to make planes here in America but was looking to do it in the nonunionized state of South Carolina to lower the cost of manufacturing.[31] The cost of manufacturing has to be competitive in order to survive in a global market, right? What Boeing was seeking to do was not wrong or unfair.

"Lord, judge the people. Lord, defend me because I am right, because I have done no wrong, God Most High. God, you do what is right. You know our thoughts and feelings. Stop those wicked actions done by evil people, and help those who do what is right" (Psalm 7:8-9 [*A shiggaion of David*]).[32]

Integrity is made up of several ingredients—honesty, truthfulness, and wholeness. To be whole and undivided we must stay away from evil and pursue the things of God with all our heart; to respect and honor innocence over evil thoughts and selflessness. No one can serve two masters.

Integrity is an all-encompassing concept most often having to do with the matter of personal character or relationships. It is by no accident that the word "integral" is a derivative of the word "integrity," because at its very core the word has to do with the condition of something or someone being undivided, and thereby suggests a simplicity and completeness. Do you see personal integration and completeness in Barack Hussein Obama? What about the Obama-nation? Or do you see complications, unreliability, detachment, and division? Truthfulness is at the core of integrity.

"Doing right brings freedom to honest people but those who are not trustworthy will be caught by their own desires" (Proverbs 11:6).[33]

Example:

Obama, while addressing the University of Michigan, told students not to call socialism, "socialism," and he referred to conservatives as "right-wing nuts."[34] He praised the socialistic schemes of past presidents and said calling his agenda socialism prevented learning and compromise. Compromising our principles is what got us where we are today. Socialism is a political movement for establishing a social organization or government based on the principles of production and distribution of all goods and services under the control of that social organization or government. I call it a scheme. The Obama-nation calls this social justice.

"Many will follow their evil ways and say evil things about the way of truth. Those false teachers only want your money, so they will use you by telling you lies. Their judgment spoken against them long ago is still coming, and their ruin is certain" (2 Peter 2:2-3).[35]

Obama has the misperception that success and prosperity mean power, wealth, status, and self-fulfillment. These are perhaps things that accompany success and prosperity, but they are not the same thing. He has shown contempt for our nation's power by apologizing to other nations for what he sees as abuses in our past, our wealth and our wealthy, our status, or what he sees as unjust economic class based on individual achievement—all while seeking out their company and adulation. This idea is in opposition to the foundations and standards this country stands on and what has always been seen as the American dream.

"Live as free people, but do not use your freedom as an excuse to do evil. Live as servants of God" (1 Peter 2:16).[36]

Antiprocreation Championship

Obama will go down in history as the abortion president.[37] Reading this was quite eye-opening for me given the tragedy of abortion. I believe that Obama was an easy mark for the population-control enthusiasts that think too many people are on the earth and will hurt the earth. This is the same crowd that pushes the global warming propaganda being the results of human influence. Like Satan, they just want fewer humans in existence. The weight of this fact gets awkward when the blinders are blown off of people when confronted with the consequences of their own actions when put on stage for world view.

There are unintended consequences to what people believe and implement into law. For example, Chinese men are realizing the disastrous effects of their country's one-child policy. If a family can only have one child, most Chinese families opt for males. As a result, there aren't enough women for men to marry. Low birth initiatives and aggressive pro-abortion policies have created a birth dearth in many European countries and Russia.

This is happening in the United States as well. This is especially true among progressives. So let's apply the unintended consequences of progressive abortion policies to progressivism as a movement. The Bible presents this concept:

"Don't give fools a foolish answer, or you will be just like them. But answer fools as they should be answered, or they will think they are really wise" (Proverbs 26:4-5).[38]

While pro-abortion progressives are doing what they perceive as the environmentally friendly and politically correct thing by not having children and supporting abortion for others, conservatives with their large families will dominate the culture in a generation or two. The push for abortion by Obama and his Obama-nation may satisfy progressive sensibilities, but in the end, it will result in their demise.

Example:

Attitudes and the acceptance of homosexuality are good examples of what happens when the presence of God is missing, and our country's leader sets out to undermine traditional American family values.[39] The vacuum is filled with evil things. Homosexuality is hedonism. It is a hurtful moral issue and not a social issue. It is mentioned directly only three times and referenced dozens of times in the Old Testament, but in both the Old and New Testaments, it was assumed that everyone would recognize that homosexual practices are not allowed by God.

"You must not have sexual relations with a man as you would a woman. That is a hateful sin" (Leviticus 18:22).[40]

This view of it was taken for granted throughout the Bible. In reading biblical text that rejects sexual relations between men or between women, it is not surprising that desires of this kind and the sexual activities that accompany them are seen as signs of something gone wrong in God's creation. Homosexuality is a result of people rebelling against God's intentions for human beings just like the sins committed by others in other ways. Just like the rest of us, homosexuals are people among whom God is at work so that we all might be members of God's family.

Example:

The Obama-nation announced it intends to make the United States the global sex cop. They plan to intervene in the operations of other nations where homosexuality is not championed as well, as they like to create special arrangements for homosexuals and those with other lifestyle choices to gain special admittance to the United States. Among the arrangements is a specific call for the United States government to "enhance" its effort to provide services to "LGBT refugees and asylum seekers." The White House statement is called the Presidential

Memorandum—International Initiatives to Advance the Human Rights of Lesbian, Gay, Bisexual, and Transgender Persons.[41]

In the document's introduction, Obama explains that he has already instructed agencies "engaged abroad" to start "taking action to promote the fundamental human rights of LGBT persons everywhere." That would happen through United States government agencies that would "strengthen existing efforts to effectively combat the criminalization by foreign governments of LGBT status or conduct and to expand efforts to combat discrimination, homophobia, and intolerance on the basis of LGBT status or conduct." Sex cops.

Further, special access to the United States needs to be provided to any "LGBT" person, he explained.

"In order to improve protection for LGBT refugees and asylum seekers at all stages of displacement, the Departments of State and Homeland Security shall enhance their ongoing efforts to ensure that LGBT refugees and asylum seekers have equal access to protection and assistance," he wrote. He explained that federal workers must be trained to help LGBT members in their desires. He wants them to be treated as if they are a race of their own.

These enhancements include that those agencies helping with foreign aid should step up their involvement with LGBT interests, and a special "standing group" should be organized to make sure the United States is responding as Obama wants. Also, the State Department and other agencies "should strengthen the work they have begun and initiate additional efforts in these multilateral organizations to counter discrimination on the basis of LGBT status and broaden the number of countries willing to support and defend LGBT issues" and other outreaches.

The Obama-nation is not trying to make us a post-Christian nation; it is trying to make us, or make us be seen as, anti-Christian. They are directly at war with Judeo-Christian ethics, moral values and principles. They are turning human history on its head all the while claiming they are on the right side of history. Obama and his Obama-nation literally are "redefining sin." These are their new versions of human rights that they want us to lecture to other countries and force them to follow? Human rights are rooted in the Bible, but they are twisting the definition of it.

If homosexual behavior qualifies as acceptable, then it is not hard to conceive that soon we will be forced to accept all immoralities, such as polygamy, adultery, incest, bestiality, and pedophilia, as normal, with each requiring protection and rights.

Matt Barber of Liberty Counsel told World News Daily (WND), "How dare we, the United States, export our decline in morality to other nations. This president has brought shame upon our nation by using extortion. I use a strong word there, extortion, in an attempt to compel other nations to adopt every demand of the radical homosexual lobby." He noted the urgency of Obama's concern about homosexuals under fire around the world, yet notes that it is Christian men, women, and children that are "slaughtered" daily under anti-Christian regimes.

Randy Thomasson of SaveCalifornia.com has been involved in his state's fights over the indoctrination of sexual alternatives in public schools as well as the fight over the voter-approved constitutional amendment that defines marriage as being only between one man and one woman. He said the promotion by Obama and Clinton of homosexuality simply is not rooted in facts.

"Homosexuality has never shown evidence that it is inherited or has a genetic or biological origin. The 'gay gene' doesn't exist. Race and ethnicity are inherited, but homosexuality is not inherited," he said.

"Barack and Hillary need to take a science course on human sexuality and genetics and learn what they think is right is scientifically wrong," he said.

He said the classification of homosexuality as a "right" is a "fatal error" that threatens children, accurate science, good health, real marriage, religious freedom, free speech, and property rights. He's assembled information about homosexuality and releases it through his NotBornThisWay website. He contends homosexuality is not genetic, nor is it healthy. His site also includes offers of assistance for those struggling to leave homosexuality.

It was Rep. Michele Bachmann, R-Minn., who said the Senate's vote to repeal the military's sodomy and bestiality ban was "absolutely abhorrent."

She made the comments on Glenn Beck's web television program. Les Kinsolving, WND's White House correspondent, asked press secretary Jay Carney, "The Family Research Council and CNS News both reported a 93-to-7 United States Senate vote to approve a defense authorization bill that, quote, 'includes a provision which not only repeals the military law on sodomy, but also repeals the military ban on sex with animals, or bestiality.' Does the commander-in-chief approve or disapprove of bestiality in our armed forces?" Carney had no comment.

So here we are at the next attack on American family traditions and sensibilities: gay marriage and the recognition of the institution of marriage between two people of the same sex. Again, this is a moral issue not a social issue. What is marriage? It is the ordained by God union or institution between a man and a woman, as husband and wife, for people to best live as God created them. Together as male and female, their union reflects God's image by becoming whole again as one body, and they are able to fulfill God's instruction to go unto the earth and multiply. Antiprocreation or global population control is a doctrine in direct opposition to the will of God.

Example:

A legal appointment became necessary due to Obama's instruction to Attorney General Eric Holder to no longer defend the Defense of Marriage Act (DOMA), which affirms marriage as the union of one man and one woman for purposes of federal law.[42] Obama and his Justice Department would have us believe that traditional marriage laws are unconstitutional. A petition was introduced to state opposition to the Justice Department, and Obama made a political decision to reverse the policy of defending the DOMA, a federal statute passed overwhelmingly by Congress and signed into law by President Bill Clinton.

The duty of the Justice Department is to enforce and defend laws passed by Congress and signed by the president. They are not editors. Marriage is a fundamental human institution and is ordained by God, and its practice predates the law and the Constitution. At its heart, it is a historical human and moral reality for society, not a legal one. Laws relating to marriage merely recognize and regulate an institution that already existed.

It is no wonder that the secular progressives, (a.k.a. the "separation of church and state" statists, or the Obama-nation,) reject and refuse to acknowledge the foundations and duties of natural law abiding individuals in this nation in order to parade this prideful disgrace and blasphemy as something that we should all respect and embrace with open arms. The hatefulness lies with them in their bed of rebellion, not with Christians or God. Even Moses labeled homosexuality a hateful sin.

Same-sex marriage is just an insult to this injury. Do you really think that God will sanctify sin just because they don't accept that He sees this as sin? Or do you think the rebellion of God's instruction is something He would want our nation to ordain through the institute of marriage? Is this God's grace or will? Barack Hussein Obama should be ashamed for allowing this movement to gain so much momentum on his watch. After all, he claims to be Christian.

Romans 8:5-8 (NCV) says,

> Those who live following their sinful selves think only about things that their sinful selves want. But those who live following the Spirit are thinking about the things the Spirit wants them to do. If people's thinking is controlled by the sinful self, there is death. But if their thinking is controlled by the Spirit, there is life and peace. When people's thinking is controlled by the sinful self, they are against God, because they refuse to obey God's law and really are not able to obey God's law. Those people who are ruled by their sinful selves cannot please God.[43]

Because of Obama's family lineage being wrought with abandonment and betrayal, would this give insight into his quest to remove chance procreation? Due to his estranged deposits of kin being broadcast over different continents by the irresponsibility and carelessness of another, has Obama found a way to indulge sexual impulse without the possibility of offspring?

God's authority allows disobedience for a time but not forever. God sends confrontational messengers to confront political, spiritual, and moral evil. The Bible offers safeguards against blind acceptance of authority. You see, the Bible teaches us that God and His laws have to be obeyed above all human authority when that authority has set itself against the known will of God. A good exercise of authority is to be humble and to use one's authority to serve and build up. A negative example is to use it for status, control, and power. Proper use of authority is not for gaining or flaunting wealth or prestige, or for showing off one's power over the people.

Has No Shame

Example:

Inspector General Jerry Walpin was fired by Obama for investigating his friend Kevin Johnson, who was found guilty of fraud and misappropriation of funds after his nonprofit youth organization, ST. HOPE, received grants from Americorp tarp money.[44] Americorp's parent organization is Corporation for National and Community Service. Americorp is also the same company that bailed out ACORN. Why did Obama fire Walpin? Was there something about the bailout that Obama did not want to be found that linked him with ACORN?

Firing an Inspector general wasn't something Obama should have been able to do without notifying Congress thirty days in advance and providing a reason, which he did not do. Why didn't we hear more about this? There are implications and cover-ups all over this one.

Good leadership is best defined by how a leader treats people and not so much by how well they use people toward other ends. Care and compassion are the hallmarks of good leadership, at least in God's eyes. It is self sacrificial, like a good shepherd that is willing to give up all of his glory and prestige to care for and save his sheep. Good leaders are humble and have learned godly ways. Through good leadership, compassion and patience should be used to show care and build up others. God teaches that the most effective leaders lead by example using compassion, patience, and loving care. This is their strength. Because of their influence, leaders must be reputable and behave in such a way as to deserve the respect of others.

Example:

At a Los Angeles fundraiser, because the Obama-nation only wanted us to see Obama bash the rich, only approved Obama-nation press corps covered the various rallies and speeches, where he claimed average people can't get a break, and the wealthy aren't paying their fair share of taxes. Predictably, the Obama-nation does not want us to see Obama schmoozing the rich so that he can pocket some of their money for his campaign. Nothing could be more antagonistic and counteractive than a Los Angeles fundraiser, brimming with movie stars, athletes, and cinema moguls who embody the very prestige and abundance Obama states he detests. So not surprisingly, conservative news photographers were barred from both of his LA fundraisers. The best the public could get were bare-bones written descriptions of the events that gave only a hint of the lavishness surrounding the president.

He believes wealth comes from greed, and he sees the greed of rich people as a tool to manipulate them. That might be an avenue for his justification to associate with them. Greed can bring wealth, but most of the wealthy got rich from being successful and not from being greedy. Prosperity does not come from greed. Greed is wealth through ill-gotten gains. Obama does not make the distinction.

Greed is something we all find in bad form. That is actually consistent with one of the most-often-talked-about evils in the Bible. Unfortunately, Obama's misperception of greed is that it is the sole reason for the success of the wealthy. That might be true for some rich people. I'll take the chance and say they probably will not be able to stay rich because of the nature of greed itself. Wealth from success and good financial decisions is not greed. True greed is risking one's wealth, convictions, and character to gain more wealth.

Greed is an inner desire and feeling that can tempt anyone. It is not only the rich who can be greedy. All of us have, at one time or another, taken more than we should have. Wanting more money, food, property, or possessions is not wrong or greedy; it is the *excessive* wanting of these things that is wrong. The result of the sin of greed is wanting things so much that we do injury, harm, or wrong to others, such as cheating others or accepting pay for doing wrong. Obama has redefined the true meaning of greed to accommodate his ideology of social justice.

Greed is idolatry. Idolatry is when anything becomes more valuable than our relationship with God; the issue is whether money and possessions are more important than God. There is nothing wrong with having possessions as long as they do not possess us. It is not money or the ability to gather or possess great wealth that is evil; it is the *love* of money that is the root of all evil.

John Wesley, an eighteenth-century revivalist preacher, probably said it best: "Earn as much as you can, save as much as you can, give as much as you can!"[45]

"Riches and honor come from you. You rule everything. You have the power and strength to make anyone great and strong" (1 Chronicles 29:12).[46]

Example:

To equivocate is to use equivocal words or give equal voice to a word or words in order to mislead, according to *Webster's New Dictionary*. Some words can have two distinct meanings, or they can be used to misdirect what it is that is being said because we sometimes assume, or rely on, one meaning over another and are accustomed to giving the benefit of the doubt.

Obama equivocated on the issue of rich people not paying their fair share of taxes by arguing that billionaire Warren Buffett pays less taxes than his secretary, Debbie Bosanke.[47] This was an equivocation because Buffett and his secretary are not subject to the same tax rate. Some would call this a lie, but I will not equivocate over the details at this juncture. The president's uses of "tax rate" made it sound like there is only one for all income types. Rates are based on how people are paid, as in this example: capital gains tax rate versus salary tax rate.

In reality, Buffett and his secretary are subject to the *same* tax rate if both of them receive income from capital gains or money invested after paying taxes on it once already. If Buffett's secretary invests in stocks that pay a dividend or capital gain, then she would pay the same rate as her boss—15 percent. Salary tax rates are higher than capital tax rates for a good reason. It has already been taxed as income. The money that was invested was taxed already at the salary tax rate when it was earned. Buffet's secretary is still paying the salary rate just as her boss would be if he were receiving income from a salary. In fact, if Buffett were paid a salary, at his income level, he would pay a higher rate than his secretary because the tax rate on salaries is progressive; the more you make, the higher percentage you pay.

Example:

Obama told an audience in Nevada that he would be regularly announcing "executive actions" the Obama-nation will be taking to "heal the economy" without the "dysfunctional" Congress.[48]

"I'm here to say to all of you and to say to the people of Nevada and the people of Las Vegas, we can't wait for an increasingly dysfunctional Congress to do its job. Where they won't act, I will," he said. "I've told my administration to keep looking every single day for actions we can take without Congress—steps that can save consumers money, make government more efficient and responsive, and help heal the economy. And we're going to be announcing these executive actions on a regular basis," he said.

Obama then explained the home mortgage refinancing plan the Obama-nation would announce.

"Where we don't have to wait for Congress, we're just going to go ahead and act on our own, and we're going to keep on putting pressure on Congress to do the right thing for families all across the country," he said. "And I am confident that the American people want to see action," he said. "We know what to do. Question is whether we're going to have the political will to do it." These statements revealed the strategy that would set the stage for Obama to implement the "fundamental change" he was broadcasting at the inception of his campaign, among other things he had in mind. Being a lecturer of Constitutional law, I suppose he missed the concept that the legislative process was set up to be slow in order to make time for the process of thought and analysis. Laws are not meant to be passed quickly based on irrational emotion.

Example:

Obama really showed a lack of courage and strength when he failed to condemn the treatment of the Iranian protestors by the Iranian regime that had the support of Supreme Leader Ayatollah Khoneini.[49] That gave Mahmoud Ahmadinejad support and encouragement for the "open door" policy that Obama wanted with him, which he did not want to undermine.

It is clear that individuals and groups throughout global history often aim to gain power, security, or status by excluding or mistreating those who are ethnically and culturally different. What is also clear is God's contrasting perspective: He cares and has a redemptive purpose for all the peoples of the world—no exceptions, no exemptions, and no special considerations. All need to be saved from sin. This was expected of all Jews and Gentiles, no matter where one was from, who one was, or who their ancestors were.

There is no distinction or excuse accepted due to your skin color or culture. Morality challenges people who believe that they are exclusively entitled to receive favor from God or from government. The Judeo-Christian ethics, moral values, and principles are the tools that cut through the lines of prejudice and racism, from which comes the idea of "all men are created equal."

Example:

He and his Justice Department sided with a foreign government (Mexico) and sued the state of Arizona in order to force the continuation of illegal immigration.[50]

Example:

Obama overruled both immigration statutes and court orders to suspend deportation of illegal immigrants, which is a violation of the law.[51]

Example:

About the first of April, 2011, Dalia Mogahed, a member of Obama's Advisory Council on Faith-based and Neighborhood Partnerships stated during an interview to the satellite channel MEHWA: "Washington has no worries concerning the Muslim Brotherhood in Egypt."[52] Since she is Muslim herself, she is practicing the art of taqiyya (obligatory act to lie to deceive non-Muslims so as to advance the religion of Islam as ordered by the Quran). She further elaborated that Obama respects the Muslim Brotherhood due to its organizational skills.

Mogahed's remarks came a month after Obama's director of National Intelligence, James Clapper, claimed during a rare public hearing of the House Intelligence Committee that the Muslim Brotherhood was a "largely secular" organization with no "overarching agenda," a viewpoint that was thankfully criticized on the national stage for its complete absence of truth.

These are just a few examples of the ambitions and motivations, from my viewpoint, that may present a glimpse into the mind of our country's leader and what drives Barack Hussein Obama. Is he driven by love of country or anger? Does he consider our Constitution and our principles the solution or does he consider them to be the problem? Does he want the same things that Americans have fought and died to achieve and protect? Has he shown us his ideas of the right to life through his push to protect the killing of the unborn? Has he shown us his ideas of the right to liberty? Is his dream for America the same as the American dream? How about the right to pursue happiness or property, assuming our money is our property, too?

Has he shown loyalty to the Constitution in upholding and protecting its prescribed process of law? Has he shown his appreciation for the power that America has built, or does he consider us to be a Colonialist regime that should stop sharing our philosophies or brand of freedom? Has he embraced the idea that we are "one nation under God," or does he want to diminish the majority of white Christians that we have in this country with his open borders policy? Has he strengthened the bonds of the family? Has he strengthened the ties and bonds with Israel and the Jewish people, who are at the center of God's world? Do you really believe that what you believe is really real?

As a youngster, I lived in an America that protected children's innocence. In those carefree days we would never have contemplated the act of sodomy as somehow proper, much less qualify as a monogamous marriage. In my youth, which now seems like a distant memory, Christian virtue was actually applauded. You were taught to look up to people who believed in the difference between right and wrong and acted accordingly.

There has been a paradigm switch where what is wrong is now considered right and what is right is now considered wrong. I am a stranger in my own homeland. Yet, I will never give up hope. I am awake now. Hope, to me, is a "will-happen" thing and not a "might-happen" thing. It is a promise. So, before the America that I love becomes even more foreign, the brakes must be applied to the run-away secular progressivism that is destroying America from the inside out. It will be a beautiful thing.

Are you willing to take a stand for what you believe is really real? Do you really want to go where this country is headed? Hopefully, the answers to most of these questions will come to you by the end of this book. Stay tuned.

Chapter 11

Whetting Worldly Appetites

Obama's global appeal

The Norwegian Nobel Peace Prize Committee decided to award the prize to President Barack Hussein Obama in 2009 for his extraordinary efforts to strengthen international diplomacy and cooperation between peoples. The committee attached special importance to Obama's vision and work for a world without nuclear weapons.[1]

I believe that Obama sees the United States as a bad actor on the global stage of world peace. He sees stability as being equality and everyone being on the same level of economy, military might, and international acceptance. I believe that Obama's focus is the global community and not America. I am not a scholar or an academic, and what seems so clear and obvious to me is something the intellectuals miss today. They still are looking at his dream of America through their own eyes and not through his. All of the actions of this man are to wane American capabilities through crippling legislation within the country or international interaction while waxing any and all entities that he sees as having been a victimized by the United States in one way or another. He is trying to weaken the strong and strengthen the weak.

Even the Nobel committee could see that Obama as president created a new declining climate in international politics like no other United States president had done prior. Multilateral diplomacy, or compromise, gained a central position, with emphasis on the role that the United Nations and other international institutions could play. They consider dialogue and negotiations as the preferred instruments for resolving even the most difficult international conflicts. This is acceptance, not resolution.

The vision of a world free from American nuclear arms, instead of the "peace through strength" strategy that the United States has always stood on, was stimulating, and the plans for disarmament and arms control bargaining, including domestically, within our own borders, gained momentum. Thanks to Obama's initiative, the United States is now playing a more "constructive role" in meeting the great climatic challenges some world leaders want to control. They believe democracy and their idea of human rights can finally be implemented worldwide.

They celebrate the opportunity that has only very rarely presented itself for a person such as Obama to capture the world's attention and give them the attention their vision needs for the future. His diplomacy is founded in the concept that those who are to lead the world must do so on the basis of values and attitudes that are shared by the majority of the world's leaders—not by the Judeo-Christian moral values and principles, or laws of nature, representative of the United States.

For 108 or so years, the committee has sought to stimulate precisely that international policy and those attitudes that Obama was fulfilling as the world's leading spokesman. The committee endorsed Obama's appeal: "Now is the time for all of us to take our share of responsibility for a global response to global challenges."

The choice of Obama to be the recipient of the 2009 Nobel Peace Prize, less than nine months into his eventful presidency, was an unexpected honor that caused both praise and puzzlement around the globe. Normally the prize has been presented, even controversially, for accomplishment. However, the Nobel committee awarded this prize to Obama in what seemed to be an appeal to encourage future endeavors and for a more consensual American leadership.

Back at home, it was not received well. Some were less impressed and contended that he had won it more for his star power and oratorical skills than for his actual achievements. Even some in the Obama-nation privately questioned whether he deserved it. Considering the ambitions of the ones giving the award, I personally believed he did.

The Nobel committee's jubilant embrace of Obama was due to its rejection of Obama's predecessor, George W. Bush, who stayed the course when it came to representing the United States' foreign policy. The committee stressed it made its decision based on Obama's actual efforts toward nuclear disarmament as well as American engagement with the world. Officials want the world to rely more on diplomacy and dialogue when intervening into the affairs of its members, but previously America had always put American interests at the forefront of their involvement, and America's interests were often in opposition to their agenda.

"The question we have to ask is who has done the most in the previous year to enhance peace in the world," the Nobel committee chairman, Thorbjorn Jagland, said in Oslo after the announcement. "And who has done more than Barack Obama?"

Still, Obama, who was described as "very surprised" when he received the news, said he was not quite convinced he deserved such an honor, adding that the award "deeply humbled" him. "To be honest," he said, "I do not feel that I deserve to be in the company of so many of the transformative figures who have been honored by this prize, men and women who've inspired me and inspired the entire world through their courageous pursuit of peace."

He said, though, that he would "accept this award as a call to action, a call for all nations to confront the challenges of the twenty-first century." Please consider that less prominent figures have also won the award, and, in his case, flattery can bring cooperation. However, the reaction inside the Obama-nation was one of restraint. Perhaps Obama-nation members were reflecting the awkwardness of winning a major prize amid a worldwide debate about whether it was deserved.

Republicans in Washington reacted in disbelief. In an official statement, Michael Steele, chairman of the Republican National Committee at the time, said, "The real question Americans are asking is, 'What has President Obama actually accomplished?'" Good question.

But there was much praise as well, even if much of the praise came from Europe. President Nicolas Sarkozy of France said the award marked "America's return to the hearts of the world's peoples," while Chancellor Angela Merkel of Germany said it was an "incentive to the president and to us all" to do more for peace.

"In a short time he has been able to set a new tone throughout the world and to create a readiness for dialogue," she said.

Both of these leaders are socialists.

For a world, and especially for the United Nations, which felt at times that the Bush administration saw them as insignificant, with good reason, the prize seemed wrapped in excitement at Obama's more-than-willingness to listen and wheel and deal to promote their positions on climate change and American disarmament.

The next year's laureate, former President Martti Ahtisaari of Finland, saw the award as an endorsement of Obama's goal of achieving Middle East peace.

"Of course, this puts pressure on Obama," he said. "The world expects that he will also achieve something."

The prize was announced as Washington officials, including the president, were asleep, and caught the White House off guard.

The other sitting American presidents to be given the award were Theodore Roosevelt, who I consider a socialist, in 1906 for negotiating an end to a war between Russia and Japan; Woodrow Wilson, an outspoken progressive, in 1919, for the Treaty of Versailles; and Jimmy Carter, who won in 2002 for his efforts over decades to spread peace and development. Carter called the award to Obama "a bold statement of international support for his vision and commitment." Even socialists and progressives can want world peace, thankfully.

> Socialism, according to Wilson, is a proposition (program) that every community (the whole country), by means of whatever forms of organization may be most effective for the purpose (by any means necessary), see to it for itself(will enforce) that each one of its members finds the employment

(put to work) for which he is best suited (where the government decides it wants you) and is rewarded according to his diligence and merit (only allow as it sees fit), all proper surroundings of moral influence (accommodations for private practice of faith) being secured to him by the public authority (allowed by government).'State socialism' is willing to act through state authority (domestic policing power) as it is at present organized. It proposes (designs) that all idea (hope) of a limitation of public authority (limited federal power) by individual rights (our freedoms and liberties) be put out of view (taken away), and that the State may not cross at will (federal laws would trump state laws, which is contrary to the Constitution); that omnipotence of legislation (all powerful federal government) is the first postulate (automatic assumption) of all just political theory (the federal government is the only source for theoretical social justice).[2] (All additional text in parentheses was added by the author.)

Former Vice President Al Gore won the Nobel Peace Prize in 2007, sharing the prize with the Intergovernmental Panel on Climate Change, for his work on climate change. This helped to promote the massive global charade of negative human effects on climate to create a revenue stream with the potential to rake in billions. Gore called Obama's award "well deserved."

Obama had been praised for generating considerable good will overseas, and he has made a series of speeches with arching ambition. He vowed to pursue a world without nuclear weapons; to reach out to the Muslim world; and sought to restart peace talks between Israel and the Palestinians, at the expense of offending some of his Jewish supporters.

Due to the major economic crisis and other domestic issues here in his own country, many of his foreign policy efforts have not been able to take off as quickly as he had hoped. Even Ahmed Youssef, a Hamas spokesman, congratulated Obama but said the prize was based only on good intentions. Muhammad al-Sharif, a politically independent Gazan, was skeptical: "Has Israel stopped building the settlements?" he asked. "Has Obama achieved a Palestinian state yet?"

To celebrate the ascendancy of Barack Obama, the famous Bruce Springsteen wrote a song in 2008 in praise of the then-presidential candidate. In "Working on a Dream," Springsteen sang, "Out here the nights are long, the days are lonely. I think of you and I'm working on a dream."[3]

Who can forget the song sung by the children at the B. Bernice Young Elementary School in Burlington Township, New Jersey, "Barack Hussein Obama mmm mmm mmm," originally posted in June 2009 on YouTube? It seems the teacher, Charisse Carney-Nunes, a senior vice president of The Jamestown Project, is also an award-winning author of a children's book, *I Am Barack Obama*. She is a graduate of Harvard Law School and was Obama's schoolmate.

The Obama school song video she taped shows her book featured on an easel next to the children hailing dear leader. She promotes her book as a tool to spread her unique message to schoolchildren across the country. It is a message that she states "allows children to see themselves through the inspirational story of President Obama growing up as an ordinary child asking, 'Who will change the world?'"

The first song starts with "Mmm, mmm, mm! Barack Hussein Obama" which have overtones of the song "Jesus Loves the Little Children" by referencing all the different nationalities and then saying that they are all equal in his (Obama) sight.[4]

The second song is more of a hail to the king rendition. It starts out with "Hello, Mr. President we honor you today!" and continues on with praise and a few hip, hip hoorays. [5]

Indoctrination of America's schoolchildren with propaganda about any president is disturbing at best, particularly when that one is still in office. Teaching the children about the candidates is one thing, but these songs are not teaching them about the candidates. This is indoctrination about Obama's "fundamental change" toward secular socialism as social justice.

These are just a few examples of the world's idol worship. At least that part of the world that advocates or is open to the concept of socialism or worse as acceptable. An article written by Fox News blogger Todd Starnes on September 4, 2012, just after the Democratic National

Convention began, exposed another abomination of the Obama-nation. Street vendors all across downtown Charlotte, North Carolina, were selling posters and artwork depicting President Obama as Jesus Christ. One poster in particular quoted, "Barack is of Hebrew origin and its meaning is 'flash of lightning,'" stating it was referencing a passage in the Old Testament book of Judges.[6] The problem is that there is no such reference in Judges, and the Hebrew name Barack means "blessed." There are, however, several references to lightning associated with the weather in the Old Testament—just not in Judges. The references in the Old Testament using the term "flash of lightning" are in the books of Ezekiel and Daniel.

"The living creatures ran back and forth like bolts of lightning" (Ezekiel 1:14).[7]

This is referencing angels or cherubim, who were shaped like humans with four faces facing in four different directions, with four wings. I do not see the resemblance.

"His body was like shiny yellow quartz. His face was bright like lightning, and his eyes were like fire. His arms and legs were shiny like polished bronze, and his voice sounded like the roar of a crowd" (Daniel 10:6).[8]

This is, again, referring to an angel. I am guessing, but this one sounds like an archangel because he references another archangel, Michael, that came to his assistance. I still would not read too much into this because Satan was an angel also.

The New Testament references to lightning that are not associated with weather that I found are in Matthew and Luke.

"When the Son of Man comes, he will be seen by everyone, like lightning flashing from east to the west" (Matthew 24:27).[9]

The next scripture is very fitting in discussion of national and world leaders. Jesus warned about false prophets, saying, there he is; he is in this place or in that place but not to believe him. Now this sounds more true to form.

Jesus said, "I saw Satan fall like lightning from heaven" (Luke 10:18).[10]

Those seeking to lift up Obama during the DNC insinuated that Hussein is a biblical word meaning "good and handsome." The problem is Hussein may mean good and handsome—but in Arabic. I believe they are confusing the Bible with the Quran, which distinctly are two entirely different documents.

The poster further read, "So you see, Barack was destined to be a good and handsome man that would rise like a flash of lightning to win victory in a battle against overwhelming odds."

This would be comical if it weren't so desperate.

This poster, along with an Obama calendar with religious images of him accompanied by biblical scripture and references, was being sold outside DNC security zones, so DNC officials claim they did not sanction these items.

That may be true, but some photos obtained by Fox News showed a similar theme being depicted in a stage design resembling a giant stained-glass window. I am assuming someone with good sense made the decision to change it.

These comparisons between Obama and Jesus Christ were not completely overlooked. One pastor of the First Baptist Church in Dallas, Texas, Robert Jeffress, said, "If Barack Obama is the promised Messiah, I think there are going to be many Christians who are profoundly disappointed. One only has to look at Obama's record to understand that he is absolutely, positively not the promised One." Amen, brother.

2 Peter 2:1-3 (NCV) says,

> There used to be false prophets among God's people, just as you will have some false teachers in your group. They will secretly teach things that are wrong—teachings that will cause people to be lost. They will even refuse to accept the Master, Jesus, who bought their freedom. So they will bring quick ruin on themselves. Many will follow their evil ways and say evil things about the way of truth. Those false teachers only want your money, so they will use you by telling you lies. Their judgment spoken against them long ago is still coming, and their ruin is certain.[11]

PART 3

Islamic Shariah Mirage in America

Chapter 12

Islamic Modus Operandi

Muslim Vesture

"The angel added, 'You are now pregnant, and you will have a son. You will name him Ishmael, because the Lord has heard your cries. Ishmael will be like a wild donkey. He will be against everyone, and everyone will be against him. He will attack all his brothers'" (Genesis 16:11-12).[1]

Has America reached the saturation point by the anti-God or anti-Christ ideology? At first, this may sound like an absurd question deserving of a knee-jerk answer, but consider the evidence.

President Dwight D. Eisenhower said this in his address at the Centennial Commencement of Pennsylvania State University on June 11, 1955: "If we are to have partners for peace, then we must first be partners in sympathetic recognition that all mankind possesses in common like aspirations and hungers, like ideals and appetites, like purposes and frailties, a like demand for economic advancement. The divisions between us are artificial and transient. Our common humanity is God-made and enduring."[2]

Besides reading news articles and watching and listening to correspondence in the news media concerning the Middle East, I started reading books and going to lectures on the subject. My husband and I also took a course called *"Christianity's Collision Course with Islam and the Far Left: Understanding the Koran."*

The United States Muslim Engagement Project or Initiative, proposed by the Leadership Group on US-Muslim Engagement in 2009, is a strategy for the United States to improve relations with key Muslim countries and communities. The strategy's goal is to resolve conflicts in the fields of foreign and defense policy, politics, business, religion, education, public opinion, psychology, and philanthropy.[3] This explains the awkward and off-center policy changes, political speech changes, and the diversion from Western culture and ideology. This is to develop and work to implement a widely supportable program supposedly to make the United States and the world safer by eliminating the primary causes of tension between the United States and the Muslim world: the application of Sharia law.

Project supporters are The William and Flora Hewlett Foundation, Rockefeller Brothers Fund, Carnegie Corporation of New York, American Petroleum Institute, the Audre and Bernard Rapoport Foundation, the W. K. Kellogg Foundation, Mr. George Russell, and other individual and institutional donors.

Shariah law is the Islamic sacred law. It is the all-encompassing Islamic religious, social, political, and military authority. Its purpose is to promote Islam as the only legitimate political religious system and to become the dominant authority worldwide. It comes from two sources: the Quran (the Islamic bible) and the Hadith (the collection of stories about Mohammed's life and behavior from various authors).

The strategic obstacle—or enemy—of this focus is Christian extremism. The central message of this strategy is that the US government, business, faith, education, and media leaders must work with Muslim counterparts to build a coalition that will turn the tide against Christian extremism. I believe the consensus is that Christians, evangelical Christians, in particular, fall into that category. We are now the extremists, instead of the terrorists being labeled as such. They are to be perceived as freedom fighters. Muslim extremists are just engaged in personal Jihad, which needs to be seen as just personal enlightenment or improvement.

Their strategy calls on US governmental and private leaders, and their Muslim counterparts, to work together to advance four goals: resolving conflicts through diplomacy, improving governance in Muslim countries, promoting broad-based economic development in Muslim countries and regions, and building mutual respect and understanding.

Here is the caveat, though. Success of this strategy would only be possible if counterparts in Muslim majority countries and communities also have to take part in moving this initiative along, such as: reducing extremism (anti-Christianity movement), resolving political and sectarian conflicts (demonize Muslim bias), holding governments accountable (Muslim oversight), creating more vibrant economies (Shariah-compliant), correcting misconceptions (hiding the truth), and engaging in dialogue to build mutual respect and understanding (propaganda). (Items in parenthesis are my assessment.)

These commitments from Muslim counterparts will ensure the adoption of Shariah law, or at least, compliance.

Implementing this plan is supposed to reshape and remedy US relations with Muslim leaders and peoples and create the foundation of mutual confidence and respect and a more peaceful world.

With Leadership Group on US-Muslim Engagement's mind-set being followed to the letter by the Obama-nation, it has opened Pandora's box, which is the opportunity for the Muslim Brotherhood's General Strategic Goals for North America to take root.[4] This strategy is not a vehicle to assimilate into or blend in with American culture, but of the assimilation of American culture into Islam Shariah law. The Muslim Brotherhood and its agenda will be talked about in chapter 13: "The American Muslim Brotherhood and CAIR."

Wanting to accommodate Muslim culture and tradition is a noble thought for most Americans. I would not object, myself, if the welcoming of their social and political ideology and the fundamentals of Islam would not be inviting the demise of our own cultural traditions. Modifying, manipulating, or mutating my belief in God the Father, Jesus the Son of God, and the Holy Spirit to accommodate someone else's religion would be an impossibility. I also will forever regard the Bible as being the Word of God. Our Christian culture would have to be altered or restricted because it is in direct conflict with what Islam finds acceptable or tolerable. The naiveté and gullibility being exhibited by this country's leadership is astonishing, to say the last, but it explains how and why the transformation of America is happening. Tolerance, according to *Webster's New World Dictionary,* is to allow or to permit, to recognize and to respect others' beliefs and practices without sharing them, to bear or put up with someone or something not necessarily liked.[5] We cannot tolerate someone unless we disagree with him or her.

Tolerance is reserved for those we think are wrong. This essential element of tolerance—disagreement—has to be changed in the modern Muslim or Shariah-compliant world. The concept of tolerance must be distorted to mean, if you think someone is wrong, you are intolerant.

This presents a curious problem. One must first think another is wrong in order to exercise tolerance toward him or her, yet doing so brings the accusation of intolerance. It is a clever catch-22. According to this approach, true tolerance is impossible.

Christianity does, however, teach tolerance. The true tolerance. To be egalitarian, or regarding persons as equal in humanity, but be elitist regarding ideas. These are the two principles for true tolerance: civility and respect. Tolerance applies to how we treat people we disagree with, not how we treat ideas we think false. Tolerance requires that every person is treated courteously, no matter what his or her view, not that all views have equal worth, merit, or truth.

The view that one person's ideas are not better or truer than another's is simply absurd and contradictory. To argue that some views are false, immoral, or just plain silly does not violate any meaningful definition or standard of tolerance.

This essential element of classical tolerance and/or elitism regarding ideas or behavior has been completely lost in the modern distortion of the concept. Now if you think someone is wrong, you are called intolerant, no matter how you treat them. Christians are supposed to, in a gracious and artful way, speak the truth and then trust God to transform minds.

"We destroy people's arguments and every proud thing that raises itself against the knowledge of God. We capture every thought and make it give up and obey Christ" (2 Corinthians 10:5).[6]

That brings us to the concept and practice of jihad, which means "struggle" in Arabic; to "strive with might and main in the cause of Allah." (jihad fi sabil Allah) refers to jihad warfare—fighting to broaden Islamic territory, called the House of Islam (dar al-Islam), at the assimilation of or sacrifice of the non-Muslim world, called the House of War (dar al-harb). A Quranic declaration that those who "strive in the way of Allah . . . have hope of Allah's mercy" is a call to jihad and a promise of reward for those who answer that call.[7] "Strive" is jahadu, the verb form of the noun jihad, and in Islamic theology "jihad for the sake of Allah" or "jihad in the way of Allah" always refers to jihad warfare; it has been used in other connotations to refer to internal or spiritual struggle but is not the original context for its meaning—Islamic offensive warfare, or Holy War.

Fighting to broaden Islamic territory at the expense of the non-Muslim world is Islamic offensive warfare. Is there any part of that you do not understand? Read the above paragraph again. Couple this with extreme patience and assertiveness and perhaps you can start to see the whole picture.

This does not sound tolerant of other ideas or religious beliefs to me.

Another practice of Islam is taqiyya. Taqiyya can be spelled several ways but is a form of Islamic religious deceit, or a legal play-acting whereby a Muslim can deny his faith or commit otherwise illegal or blasphemous acts toward Allah or his prophet while he is at risk of significant persecution.[8] It is also the act of double dealing in the attempt to advance Islam. It is lying to save your own hide or to hide your intentions, of course, all to honor Allah.

Kitman is an Islam practice of lying by omission. It is just as acceptable and is well used to deflect those who have a minimum knowledge of the Quran. They will quote only a portion of a verse, or sura, to change the meaning to make it applicable for any given situation.[9]

Another form of artful deceit is to defy or deny the Muslim faith to gain the trust of one's enemy, or a non-Muslim, or maybe a large group of people—such as a whole country. This form of lying is called Muruna.

It is completely acceptable in Islam just as long as the country has a majority or is predominately non-Muslim. A person could claim to be a Christian, for example, and if it is done in the pursuit to advance Islam, that is just fine.

This practice was emphasized in Shi'a Islam, whereby participants may conceal their religion when they are under threat of persecution. Taqiyya was developed to protect Shi'ites, who were usually in the minority and under pressure. In the Shi'a view, taqiyya is lawful in situations where there is overwhelming danger of loss of life or property even if there is not a clear and present danger stemming from their religious identity. In the Sunni view, denying your faith under duress is "only at most permitted and not under all circumstances obligatory."

Obligatory—or obliging. It is their duty to lie. They are not merely compelled to do it if it suits them. It is revered as an art form and a skill that should be perfected. I cannot stress the peril that lies ahead due to this practice.

God is called the "God of truth" (Psalm 31:5). He cannot lie. Truthfulness is what relates all three persons of the Holy Trinity together. "God of truth," Jesus is "full of grace and truth" (John 1:14, 17; 14:6), and the Holy Spirit is the "Spirit of truth" (John 14:17; 15:26; 16:13). And it does not stop with the person. Truth is the teachings God brings (John 17:17; Psalm 33:4; 119:142, 151, 160). Truth is open, uncovered, and authentic, opposed to what is false or phony. I do not believe lying, in any form, would be approved of by the God of Christianity.

The Bible places a tremendous amount of importance on freedom, or liberty, in the life of His people, too. The expression of freedom is often very different from the expression of the world around us. In the world, we may think of freedom as personal liberty or the ability to do whatever we choose without interference from others no matter the consequences. This is free will.

In Islam, free will is considered heresy and is forbidden in the Quran. The Arabic word for "free will" is Al-mashi'a: the ability to choose for yourself or exercise self-governance.[10] This is an absolute contradiction to the Bible and the principles of our Constitution. The Bible encourages us to make decisions. There is a reason that advocates for Islam are so opposed to this.

"Keep on working to complete your salvation with fear and trembling (our decision), because God is working in you to help you want to do and be able to do what pleases him (God's will)" (Philippians 2:12-13).[11]

Using our free will and making decisions is how God directs our steps from our will to conforming to His will. As a person grows in knowledge of God's will and His laws, a person's way of thinking can actually become like God's way of thinking. This doesn't happen overnight, of course, and there is no magic potion to achieve it, but it can and does happen. We do not become God; we come to know God's mind.

The Arabic word glossary near the back of this book has several Arabic words that you would be wise to familiarize yourself with and understand. Islam, Muslim, Shariah accommodation is a direct contradiction of the American mind-set and way of life. Their reality, ideas of right and wrong, what they consider sin, and what is acceptable are opposite of the Judeo-Christian ethics, moral values, and principles upon which this country was founded. It can be tolerated by us, using the true meaning of tolerance, in this country, but we need to understand the nature of its practice. However, tolerance of their constructs that are alien in the American Christian nature is not what they are pursuing or telling us.

Christianity will have to be mutated—or at least watered-down—to a faith that portrays God as a divine therapist whose chief goal is to boost people's self-esteem in order for the mingling of these two cultures to take place. This opens the door to adopt the ideology of Islam and the acceptance or compliance of Shariah law and the exchange of God for Allah. The two are not the same.

This is explained in Kenda Creasy Dean's book *Almost Christian*. The book addresses the faith, or lack of it, in teens from all walks of life. The National Study of Youth and Religion found that three out of four American teenagers claim to be Christian; fewer than half practice their faith; only half deem it important, and most cannot talk coherently about their beliefs. The study's researchers found that many teenagers thought God simply wanted them to feel good and do good. This was called "moralistic therapeutic deism."[12]

More teens may be drifting away from true Christianity, but their desire to help others has not diminished, according to Barbara A. Lewis, author of *The Teen Guide to Global Action*. She admits more and more teens are embracing an obscure belief in God, yet there has been an explosion in youth service since 1995 that Lewis attributes to more schools emphasizing community service.[13] Teens may be less religious, but that does not equate automatically to being less compassionate and not wanting to make the world a better place. This gives me hope.

Elizabeth Corrie, Emory University professor, is the director of the Youth Theological Initiative at Emory University in Georgia. YTI operates like a theological boot camp for teens and sees no shortage of teenagers who want to be inspired. She, along with Lewis, agrees with Dean's book *Almost Christian*.

Dean's solution to the problem is for churches and parents to get "radical" or inspired. She says parents who perform one act of radical faith in front of their children convey more than a multitude of sermons and mission trips. A parent's radical act of faith could involve something as simple as spending a summer in Bolivia working on an agricultural renewal project or turning down a more lucrative job offer in order to stay at a struggling church or to write a book.

Dean stresses that an act of faith has to accompany the declaration that the act is exactly that, *an act of faith*.

Point out that what you are doing is because of your faith. It will not register that faith is supposed to make you live differently unless you help your kids connect the dots. Otherwise, you are just being good or being useful.

Christianity in America is paramount to the future and survival of our union, our liberties and freedoms, our independence, and the ability to be self-governed. These concepts are foreign to Islam, however. If we remove God and the worship of God, then the government will become what we will put our faith in, and we will worship it. Anything that takes your faith away from God and sets your faith upon itself is not a good thing.

Islam is the ultimate tyrannical or unreasonable combination of religion and government. And, again, do not be deceived into believing that Allah and the God of the Bible are the same. They most definitely are not. They are in direct conflict.

One of the books I read was *For God or for Tyranny*, by ex-terrorist Walid and his son Theodore Shoebat, which exposes this very well. It addresses the demands of global unity, the progressive denouncement of God, and their idea that biblical teachings are old and that we need to advance and modernize ourselves away from God and adopt a new moral code. I highly recommend this book for an in-depth look into the Islamic culture.

Another book I read was *God's War on Terror*, also by Walid Shoebat, which gives a true eye-opening revelation based on biblical prophecy about the techniques, strategies, and aspirations to dissolve all other religions and absorb the world into a global caliphate or Islamic-dominated region or world empire. He also explains the mark of the beast, which I found extremely sobering. I highly recommend this book also. Another one is *The Complete Infidel's Guide to the Koran*, by Robert Spencer, just to get you started.

Shoebat expressed in the preface of his book that well-educated Muslims and our own elected leaders have, for years, known about the crimes and atrocities committed by Islamic fundamentalists. He believes those who are not aware do not want to know out of fear of what they are tolerating—that truth and justice differentiates between criminals and their victims. He writes, "The people of the civilized world now have to prove by deed where they stand; mere words will not be believed by a world that witnesses the crimes against God's people and my Christian brethren."[14]

But standing up for what we believe in may not be acceptable to the powers that be. Lt. Col. Matt Dooley knows the consequence of this action. In an article by Bob Unruh with WND on October 3, 2012, defense lawyers for Dooley accused the Pentagon of selling out to political correctness. "In order to appease Muslims and the White House, Gen. Dempsey and the Department of Defense rushed to punish Lt. Col. Matt Dooley," said Richard Thompson, chief counsel for the Thomas More Law Center.[15]

Dooley taught a course at the Joint Forces Staff College called Perspectives on Islam and Islamic Radicalism. He was a decorated war hero and had been awarded the Bronze Star, the Meritorious Service Medal with two Oak Leaf Clusters, the Joint Service Commendation

Medal, the Army Commendation Medal with three Oak Leaf Clusters, and a dozen other honors.

Muslim groups, including some with known links to terrorism, demanded that the material they viewed as offensive to Islam be "purged" from his coursework and that Dooley be "effectively disciplined." An Officer Evaluation Report containing high marks about his teaching was withdrawn, and he was administratively removed from his teaching assignment. These groups included the Council on American-Islamic Relations, the American-Arab Anti-Discrimination Committee, Islamic Circle of North American, and Islamic Relief USA.

Thompson charged that Dooley's commanders "violated not only our nation's core principles of free speech and academic freedom guaranteed by our Constitution, but also, a number of the military's own regulations dealing with academic freedom and non-attribution policies of the National Defense University."

General Martin Dempsey, chairman of the Joint Chiefs of Staff, publicly blasted Dooley and in a Pentagon news conference on May 10 with Defense Secretary Leon Panetta, Dempsey characterized Dooley's teaching as "totally objectionable" and "against our values." This was staying consistent with the US-Muslim Engagement Project initiative. Honoring this strategy took precedence over honoring a subordinate army officer who heroically served our nation and was subsequently prohibited from publicly defending himself.

"The final bastion of America's defense against Islamic jihad and Shariah, the Pentagon, fell to the enemy," was a charge by Claire M. Lopez, a former CIA agent and strategic policy and intelligence expert. She confirmed Dempsey's earlier order that all Department of Defense course content "be scrubbed to ensure no lingering remnant of disrespect to Islam."

The law firm contended that Dooley was betrayed by his military chain of command, which refused to stand behind their own academic freedom and nonattribution regulations and left Lieutenant Colonel Dooley and his association holding the bag, so to speak, with what had been previously acceptable educational material.

If the Islamic sympathizers in our military and in our government are oblivious to the real dangers of the premise of fundamental Islam, then what about the rest of us left to make uneducated determinations in the civilian population?

Islam analyst and Jihad Watch publisher Robert Spencer gave a great analogy in the difference in perspective of reality. He used the persecution of Coptic Christians in Egypt as an example stating, "This is a classic example of the Islamic inversion of reality. In the Muslim view, Islamic law—Shariah—is synonymous with justice and fairness, even though from our perspective it oppresses women and non-Muslims," Spencer said. "Thus when the Copts are persecuted in accord with its (Sharia law dictates, that is, from the Muslim perspective) not persecution, but justice."[16]

An independent group of national security professionals deeply critical of the Obama-nation called on National Security Adviser John Brennan to resign for what the group says was a coordinated effort to prevent "identifying, understanding and countering" threats posed by Shariah law.

The Center for Security Policy chief, Frank Gaffney, a former Reagan administration official, said in a news conference that Brennan failed in his "duty to know his enemy" when he allowed a sheik with "known ties" to Hamas through his work at the Holy Land Foundation, a known Muslim charity group whose program is aimed at helping the Muslim community. Gaffney led a group called "Team B II," which released a report earlier called "Shariah: The Threat to America."[17]

Team B II was motivated by the CIA's Team B exercise in 1976 that rooted out weaknesses in US response focused on Soviet threats. They then presented the findings to Republican members of Congress. The group, which says it sees parallels between today's efforts to engage radical Muslim groups and the 1970s efforts to engage the Soviets, says Brennan is allowing a "grave threat" to grow against the United States, its Constitution, government, and freedoms.

Chapter 13

The American Muslim Brotherhood and CAIR

Islamic Conference flag

Have you been feeling that the rug has been pulled out from under you? Not unlike waking up in a vehicle that is rolling down an embankment, not knowing where you are; being stuck in the backseat; there is no one in the driver's seat; it is nighttime, and it's raining. Or thinking that everything feels unfamiliar, abnormal, or uncomfortable or that the directions to make things work properly are wrong, and the things that used to work just fine have been replaced with something not as good. Things do not make sense anymore, and the wording is just odd. There is a reason for all that.

"Then Jesus said to the people, 'When you see clouds coming up in the west, you say, "It's going to rain," and it happens. When you feel the wind begin to blow from the south, you say, "It will be a hot day," and it happens. Hypocrites! You know how to understand the appearance of the earth and sky. Why don't you understand what is happening now?'" (Luke 12:54-56).[1]

Retired Army Lt. Gen. William "Jerry" Boykin, at a synagogue in Stoughton, Massachusetts, gave an address in July, 2012, that warned that Islamic Shariah law and the Muslim Brotherhood have had a presence in the United States since the 1960s.[2]

"The new Egyptian president, Mohamed Morsi, said he joined the Muslim Brotherhood in 1978 while he was in the United States of America. People who say that the Muslim Brotherhood is not in America are not dealing in reality," Boykin said.

Boykin told the crowd of the Muslim Brotherhood's master plan for establishing Shariah law in America, a plan where the Muslims who do not actively push will pay a price for being indifferent. It's a plan that Mark Steyn, an author and Canadian-born political commentator, indicated is the same plan being implemented in Europe, where they are just a generation away from being overcome completely in compliance with Sharia law.

The Muslim Brotherhood will need to control the dialogue to ensure people don't talk about Shariah or its objectives for the country. It will need to control the training manuals and documents concerning counterterrorism and how we engage and how we assess the enemy. I guess I did not get the memo.

These have already been done. FBI Director Robert Mueller allowed the Muslim Brotherhood to expunge more than one thousand documents for the training manuals to comply.

Boykin indicated that our school systems have already been infiltrated, and the first organization in the United States was the Muslim Student Association. He said that some of our churches have been infiltrated also and that a professor at Luther College had proclaimed that he believed Jesus was Muslim. Boykin noted that it is a lie to say that Allah and God are the same. I might add that the Muslim Jesus and the Christian Son of God are not the same person, either.

Elena Kagan, the justice of the US Supreme Court, an appointee of President Barack Hussein Obama, was an active supporter of Shariah law. During her years as dean at Harvard Law School, from 2003 to 2009, she ran and greatly expanded the Islamic Legal Studies Program. This program promoted Shariah law to be integrated into our national and state constitutions.[3]

The Center for Security Policy Chief Frank Gaffney, a former Reagan administration official that was mentioned in the previous chapter, has released a video series warning that the effort to overthrow American systems is well under way through the "civilization jihad" of the Muslim Brotherhood.[4] The ten-part course, The Muslim Brotherhood in America: The Enemy Within, has been posted on the web.

This effort is being done with the support of key US government leaders, including President Barack Hussein Obama, and six individuals such as the directors of National Intelligence, State Department, Justice Department, the Pentagon, Department of Homeland Security and NASA. Just some of the Obama-nation.

The video series unveiled a long-term process of subversion and deceit through which the Muslim Brotherhood and Islamic fundamentalists, sometimes called extremists, have infiltrated the American government and promoted their plan to implement Shariah law. This is one of the reasons the attack that killed dozens of Texas soldiers at Fort Hood military base was described as "workplace violence," even though the self-described soldier of Allah, Nidal Hasan, was shouting Islamic jihad slogans.

Another example is blaming the death of an American ambassador, along with several other Americans, in Benghazi on an anti-Islamic video trailer that no one knew anything about.

The series outlines the Muslim practice of taqiyya, which I addressed in chapter 11. The series explains the use of civilization jihad, which is a form of warfare employing manipulative financial techniques, law fare, infiltration of our civil institutions and government, and insidious information dominance. The course even shows that churches and the conservative movement are being infiltrated.

The effort to destroy American society to establish Shariah law includes keeping "infidels" ignorant, prohibiting "blasphemy," demanding concessions, using educational tools, interfaith dialogue, Shariah-compliant finance, inserting Shariah into United States courts and placing Muslim Brotherhood partners in influential positions. Why else would Obama be quoting from the Quran and the Bible in several of his National Prayer Breakfast addresses claiming they have the same pursuits?

The Muslim lobby group, Council on American-Islamic Relations, or CAIR, known for labeling opponents of Islam as "Islamophobes," accompanies our president in the melding process of the two faiths in their goal to make Islam the dominant faith and Shariah law the law of the land.

CAIR was formed by the Muslim Brotherhood and often teams up with advocates of "social justice" in the Obama-nation against what it also calls "Islamophobia." Former federal prosecutor Andrew C. McCarty, who led the prosecution of the "Blind Sheik" Omar Abdel Rahman and eleven others in the 1993 World Trade Center bombing, confirmed that the term "Islamophobia" was a strategic creation by the Muslim Brotherhood to artfully attach the stigma of "hate speech" to any criticism of Islamic supremacism.[5]

A phobia is a fear of something, not a disagreement. They want to be feared, so this term is quite appropriate in their minds. Fear registers, but disagreement does not because they do not believe we are capable of free will. And as far as hate speech goes, I do not hate Muslims. I hate the fact that they are so lost. A person and what he believes are two different things. Information can change what a person believes.

CAIR's mode of operation and main function is to establish Shariah law by protecting "any cause that increases Islamic influence and protesting any effort either to reduce Islamic influence or to subject Islamic-supremacist doctrine to scrutiny," according to McCarthy.

CAIR sued a coauthor, David Graubatz, for exposing CAIR's link to radical jihad and its origin as a front group for the Palestinian terrorist group Hamas and the Muslim Brotherhood in his book *"Muslim Mafia: Inside the Secret Underworld That's Conspiring to Islamize America."*

CAIR members claim to be moderates and American patriots while proclaiming they are in America not to assimilate, but to help assert Islam's rule over the country, which they later denied. One quote—that they claim was a misquote—was by CAIR's founder, Ahmad, who was "insinuating" that Islam is not in America to be equal to any other faith, but to become dominant and that the Quran should be the highest authority in America, and the only accepted religion on earth. The reporter stands by her story and says she just paraphrased a rather wordy quote.

An example of special or superior treatment is seen at the airport regarding the "enhanced pat down" policy that went into effect for the Transportation Safety Administration (TSA). CAIR issued a travel warning to Muslim airline passengers and told them to request special consideration for religious reasons due to the policy being against Shariah law. Muslim men can have their pat-downs done in private, and Muslim women who wear a hijab should tell the TSA officer that they may be searched only around the head and neck area and be given the option to pat down their own scarf, head, and neck, and allow the officers to perform a chemical swipe of their hands.[6]

So, as a result, the ones undergoing the "enhanced pat down or full body screening" are non-Muslim Americans.

In a rather peculiar attempt to teach students at Campbell Middle School about the pros and cons of school uniforms, the lesson featured a letter from a woman who said she is "proud and happy" to be Muslim and to completely cover herself in public. She talked about her husband, who could take another wife rather than divorce her if their marriage got rocky, and she would still be cared for. She gave a brief insight to the Muslim everyday lifestyle by adding that women do not drive cars, and they wear abuyah. She described the abuyah and says she likes wearing it since it is very comfortable, and she is protected from blowing sand. She also added that she had seen pictures of women in the West and found their dress to be horribly immodest. She then opined that women in the West do not have the protection of the Shariah as they do. She then states that she felt very fortunate that they had the Shariah.[7]

Comparing Islamic rules of dress to school uniforms? One parent complained that his daughter's homework assignment promoted Shariah law. The principal and the superintendent agreed with the parent that comparing the two was a stretch, but they would not agree with the premise that the statements put Islam in a positive light. They only found the statements on polygamy particularly objectionable.

Another part of the assignment listed requirements for women's clothing according to Islam, including that it cannot resemble the clothing of non-believing women and must protect women from the lustful gaze of men. It stated that Islam liberated women over fourteen hundred years ago, and it is better to dress according to Allah. Sharon Coletti, the founder of InspirEd Educators and the creator of the material, denied they were teaching children about Islam. The teacher has since adjusted the material for the lesson. Dale Gaddis, a district area superintendent, acknowledged that it could have been taught in a better way but did not entirely discount the material. These people are examples of willful blindness.

CAIR worked to stop author and former Muslim Nonie Darwish from addressing students at Virginia's George Mason University School of Law. CAIR wanted the school to "disinvite" Darwish on the grounds that CAIR believed her to be "a notorious Islamophobe who has stated that Islam is a 'poison to a society' that is 'based on lies' and must be 'annihilated.'"[8] CAIR stated that such hate-filled views should not be funded by student organizations or endorsed by professors. They contend Darwish's statements are reminiscent of those used to target Jews in Nazi Germany. Only one problem: Darwish's statements are warnings about an oppressive ideology and not the blaming of a race of people for the woes of a nation as proclaimed by the Nazis.

Darwish sees Muslims as largely victims of Shariah law and stated that CAIR is falsely equating the criticism of a religion with hatred for a people because "the problem for CAIR is that they cannot debate us about glaring truth, so they claim we hate Muslims, trying to deflect the attention of the American people from the true worldwide problem of Islamism, jihad, Shariah and tyranny."

All criticisms of Islam, jihad, and Shariah, CAIR spins into an attack on the Muslim people, confusing the American people between criticisms of an ideology and racial condemnation against a whole group of people. I pray the American people can identify and act accordingly to this kind of sinister spin. I believe Americans can love the sinner and hate the sin. If we cannot do that, we are all in trouble.

As for being labeled an Islamophobe, that may have validity for some. There is reason to fear a religious law in the world that condemns those to death who leave that religion. I do not think it is an unreasonable phobia to speak against such a tyrannical law.

The Learning Channel, which receives federal funding, once presented a program called *All-American Muslim* to take viewers "inside the rarely seen world of American Muslims."[9] The producers went to Dearborn,

Michigan, the United States city with the highest concentration of Muslims.

Islam analyst Pamela Geller says the perspective of Islamic cultural traditions—not the reasons and purposes of them and not the ideology—is what is so dangerous. The program is designed to counter "Islamophobia" by showing Muslims not as terrorist monsters, but as ordinary people living ordinary lives, balancing tradition and modern life, dealing with their families, their jobs, and a host of other issues.

This is nothing more than video jihad. The major problem with the program is that it does not show the reality of "pure Islam." The truth about the goals of fundamental Islam is hidden from many Americans through programs like this. Islamic fundamentalism wants to take over the world, remember. If they have to use force, they'll do that. But otherwise, they'll do it by what Robert Spencer, *Jihad Watch* publisher and executive director, called "stealth jihad."

This is so misleading. The Muslims were portrayed in the show as being free to choose their own path. This is the beauty of living in a free society such as America and not from being Muslim. The danger is in the deception or the hiding of the intended meaning with confusing, willfully ambiguous, and hard to interpret statements they call truth, which results in the intellectual disarming of the American people.

Jamal A. Khashoggi is head of the joint media venture between Saudi Prince Alwaleed bin Talal and New York Mayor Michael Bloomberg's Bloomberg News. This has raised concerns about the intrusion on the United States media by Islamists focused on establishing Shariah law, including Shariah finance, in the West.[10]

Consider a statement made by the former New York mayor's new business partner: "I met Osama (Bin Laden) in Jeddah (Saudi Arabia), and ever since, I developed a close relationship with him."

In an Arab press interview, Khashoggi revealed he grew up in Saudi Arabia with Bin Laden, and they were in the Muslim Brotherhood together. Their motto was "Jihad is our way, death the cause of Allah our highest ambition." As close friends do, they shared a dream of a pan-Islamic nation.

Khashoggi calls himself a "neo-Islamist," who define themselves as a new generation of Muslim leaders defined by their seeming openness to the idea of modernization and interaction with the West. However, they remain faithful to the central tenets of Shariah law.

He previously worked as Saudi Arabia's intelligence minister, so he follows the Wahhabism form of Islam. It is a Sunni religious movement among fundamental Muslims with an aspiration to return to the primordial fundamental Islamic sources of the Quran, the Hadith, and scholarly consensus Ijma. It is the dominant form of Islam in Saudi Arabia.

Khashoggi, along with billionaire Prince Bin Talal, launched a pro-Islamic twenty-four-hour television news network with Bloomberg's news service. It provides five hours of financial and economic news programs on the new "Alarab" channel, which the prince says will be "right of Al-Jazeera." If you don't understand what that means, they are more fundamentalist.

This is the same prince who, just after 9/11, presented a $10 million gift to then-New York Mayor Rudy Giuliani with one slight tether attached. He wanted America to acknowledge that its pro-Israeli policies brought on the attacks. Giuliani rejected the relief check. I will always regard the former mayor of New York with high honors because of this. This is in direct contrast to the mayor who appears to have no problem about doing business with the Saudi royal, even though Bloomberg is Jewish. Bloomberg is on board with the prince about other issues, such as the Ground Zero mosque. His associations may explain a few other decisions he has made that seem . . . off center.

"Some people cannot be brought back again to a changed life. They were once in God's light, and enjoyed heaven's gift, and shared in the Holy Spirit. They found out how good God's word is, and they received the powers of his new world. But they fell away from Christ. It is impossible to bring them back to a changed life again, because they are nailing the Son of God to a cross again and are shaming him in front of others" (Hebrews 6:4-6).[11]

Bin Talal's Saudi-based Kingdom Foundation has sunk more than $300,000 into American Society of Muslim Advancement. This is the United States nonprofit group promoting the Ground Zero mosque and

Bin Talal's foundation, which is run by Saudi hijabi Muna Abu Sulayman. Sulayman is portrayed on ASMA's website as one of its "Muslim Leaders of Tomorrow." Sulayman, who spends much of her time in the United States, happens to be the daughter of Dr. Abdul Hamid Abu Sulayman, a figure in the Global Muslim Brotherhood, according to the Global Muslim Brotherhood Daily Report.

The Global Muslim Brotherhood is an Egyptian-based brotherhood and is the parent of Hamas and al-Qaida and the source of most of the jihadi ideology and terror throughout the world today. This group has been cited for a plan to "destroy" America "from within" and is using its agents and front groups in the United States to carry out that strategy, the Daily Report confirmed.

Bin Talal is also one of News Corp.'s biggest shareholders. News Corp. owns Fox Network media.

According to the author and researcher Walid Shoebat, Huma Abedin, Hillary Clinton's deputy chief of staff and wife to disgraced former New York representative Anthony Weiner, who reportedly advised the secretary of state on Middle East policy, was head of the Social Committee of the Muslim Student Association (MSA). This front group was found to have ties to the Muslim Brotherhood in a 1991 document introduced into evidence during the terror-financing trial of the Texas-based Holy Land Foundation.[12]

The internal Brotherhood memo said its members "must understand that their work in America is a kind of grand jihad in eliminating and destroying the Western civilization from within and 'sabotaging' its miserable house by their hands and by the hands of the believers so that it is eliminated and Allah's religion is made victorious over all other religions."

These documents keep repeating certain phrases, such as "from within" and "its miserable house by their hands and by the hands of the believers." I have read this multiple times from different venues. The wording is the same. The MSA has nearly six hundred chapters in the United States and Canada and has gained legitimacy as a benevolent collegiate faith club. The Muslim Brotherhood leaders established it in 1963 to recruit young people into the movement.

Former MSA leaders directly tied to international violent jihad include al-Qaida cleric Anwar al-Awlaki, convicted American student Ramy Zamzam, Somali al-Shabaab leader Omar Hammami, and al-Qaida fundraiser Abdurahman Alamoudi, a former national MSA president who is now serving a twenty-three-year prison sentence.

Abedin was born in America but was raised in Saudi Arabia. An attempt to have her investigated by the inspector general at the Departments of Homeland Security, Justice, and State was led by Rep. Michele Bachmann, R-MN. citing Abedin as an example of possible Muslim Brotherhood infiltration.

So would the Muslim grand jihad be responsible for the declaration by the Democratic National Convention (DNC) at the end of August 2012 that they would open with a focus on Islam. The Bureau of Indigenous Muslim Affairs (BIMA) reported they were expecting twenty thousand Muslims to attend the convention. This is a national Muslim American nonprofit organization, which claimed to be a nonpolitical group helping coordinate two days of the event.

Question: if they are a nonpolitical organization, why were they there?

"Jum'ah at the DNC" began August 29 with Friday afternoon jummah prayer followed by other events to lead up to the Islamic Regal Banquet. The following day, is when the all-day Islamic Cultural and Fun Fest would commence, which included topics of Islamophobia, anti-Shariah, Middle Eastern crisis, Patriot Act, National Defense Authorization Act, and more.[13] I am sure it was about as much fun as a tax audit. But I could be wrong.

This group may have been responsible for doing the same thing at the United States Capitol in 2009, claiming twenty thousand Muslims would attend and only two thousand to three thousand showed up. The DNC originally called this an "official function," listing these fundamentalists as typical of the DNC community, but later removed mention of this organization's events and speeches after criticism surfaced of this group being too radical and not representing supposedly typical mainstream American Muslims. This is a slippery slope for the Democratic Committee.

The prayer was supposed to be against the Patriot Act, the NYPD, and Islamophobia and was not about democracy. It was about melding their Muslim Brotherhood and fundamentalist sympathetic groups into the very fabric of our political system and desensitizing the American people. Moderate American Muslims need to speak up and marginalize these fundamentalists, or they will find themselves subjects of the tyrannical Shariah laws from which they came here to get away.

The BIMA is tied to Jibril Hough and Imam Siraj Wahhaj, both of whom have said and done radical things in their pasts. The DNC failed on a major scale to perform their due diligence, or they just simply did not care. Jibril Hough, with which is a name many in Charlotte, North Carolina, are familiar. He is the leader of a Sunni mosque, a spokesman for the Islamic Center of Charlotte, and was an outspoken antagonist to Rep. Sue Myrick. Myrick, being a member of the House Intelligence Committee, called for a plan to fight against jihadist activity in America. Hough called the plan a fear campaign and the new McCarthyism or Myrickism.[14]

The language used by Hough sounded like it came straight out of the Muslim Brotherhood handbook. He said Muslims in a non-Muslim country must abide by the laws of that state and cannot be at war with it. He further said this system of laws is not his or the Muslims he represents, but they will follow it—for now.

He commented that he supported laws that would mandate Muslim behaviors for American-Muslims but not non-Muslims. He supports separate legal paths for each faith instead of one law. The problem with this is that these two legal systems do not work well together.

Imam Siraj Wahhaj is an equally charming fellow. He is the imam for the mosque in Brooklyn, New York, the leader of the Muslim Alliance in North American, a member of CAIR, and an unindicted co-conspirator in the 1993 World Trade Center bombing.

Wahhaj was also a character witness for Omar Abdel Rahman, or the Blind Sheik, who was responsible for the 9/11 terror attack. The imam described him as a "respected scholar," and "a strong preacher of Islam."

Wahhaj has memberships in several Muslim Brotherhood front organizations and has been quite vocal about his hatred for America. He believes the only reason he has gotten involved in politics is to use it as a weapon in the cause of Islam.

BIMA stated they had a smaller event planned for the Republican National Convention; however, convention staff members were not aware of it. I watched the Democratic National Convention, and I cannot recall coverage of what I would consider a controversial and newsworthy kick-off to the renomination convention for Barack Hussein Obama.

The only controversial thing that I saw and heard was when the question was asked on whether to include the word "God" in the Pledge of Allegiance. It had to be asked three times due the vote being too close to call. The boos and nos to not include the word "God" were shocking and numbing. They did not only deny God once or twice, but thrice. Do you see the irony and significance here?

"They knew God, but they did not give glory to God or thank him. Their thinking became useless. Their foolish minds were filled with darkness" (Romans 1:21).[15]

I believe the influence Muslim Brotherhood has in the White House had something to do with the situation in Libya where our United States ambassador in Benghazi, J. Christopher Stevens, Foreign Service Information Management Officer Sean Smith, private security employees, and former United States Navy SEALS Gen Doherty and Tyrone Woods were killed. Why has a reported $450 million in emergency cash been given to the Muslim Brotherhood-led Egyptian government?

"Do not let anyone fool you in any way. That day of the Lord will not come until the turning away from God happens and the Man of Evil, who is on his way to hell, appears. He will be against and put himself above anything called God or anything that people worship" (2 Thessalonians 2:3-4).[16]

Chapter 14

Islam in American Courts

Gavel and the Constitution

The Bible references crime in several different ways and words but speaks to it as violations of an established law with few, if any, distinctions of whether the violations were breaking civil, criminal, or religious law because all laws were established for God's people by God himself. God is the source of all law, even those that are made by corrupt, tyrannical, pagan governments, and God is the source of their authority. In the case of the United States, this is especially depressing because God lets us vote into office actually what we deserve.

"All of you must yield to the government rulers. No one rules unless God has given him the power to rule, and no one rules now without that power from God" (Romans 13:1).[1]

God gave us His law as a gift to teach us how we might obey Him and as a means to fully enjoy His blessings. His law does not form a condition for entering into God's family but the rules for those who are in God's family to follow. This law is our reality as believers in God and for those who do not follow Him but seek harmony, unity, and respect for mankind.

Civil government sets the boundaries for human behavior and uses law to control it. It is intended to "establish justice, insure domestic tranquility, provide for the common defense, promote the general welfare, and secure the blessings of liberty to ourselves and our posterity" as stated at the beginning of the Constitution. Government, however, has no place venturing or expanding its power beyond this into religious or moral areas or using foreign sources of law that are contrary to the law that we established for ourselves.

But when government does this to the point of suppressing and persecuting Christians and the law of our land, Christians may be forced to disobey civil government and law in order to maintain our allegiance to the kingdom of God.

Report by the Center for Security Policy Study:
"Shariah Law and American State Courts:
An Assessment of State Appellate Court Cases"
Washington, DC, May 17, 2011

You see, while the American people were sleeping, something else very disturbing has been taking place. It crept in subtly and quietly. Shariah law is being utilized in our US court system. These were the findings according to an extensive report by the Center for Security Policy Study called "Shariah Law and American State Courts: An Assessment of State Appellate Court Cases," which tracked dozens of cases in which the Shariah law has been applied.[2] This may seem of no concern to some, but Shariah law is in direct conflict with our Judeo-Christian ethics, moral values, and principles, and the American way of life.

Center spokesman David Reaboi said the Islamic law is being used mostly in cases where Muslim foreigners are the parties involved. "Shariah enters US courts through the practice of comity to foreign law," Reaboi explained. "This happens, for example, when a judge decides to allow the use of say, Pakistani or Saudi family law (Shariah) in a dispute between Pakistanis or Saudis." On the surface, this may appear a sympathetic or "fair" thing to do.

How is it that the laws now are supposed to accommodate the behaviors and leanings of special interest groups instead of setting the standard for the behavior for the people as a whole? Everyone should abide by the same standards and rules. That would be like having to accept different compensation for the same product based on what someone wants to pay rather than what you want to charge.

Judges are not taking into account that these cases are not in a foreign country; they are here in America and should abide by the laws of *our* land. While in Rome, do what the Romans do theorem. This should not be discretionary. Constitutional law and Shariah law are like trying to mix oil and water. They are of two completely different compounds that will not incorporate together.

Reaboi said the study only scratches the surface of Shariah's presence in this nation.

"For every case in this sample drawn from published appellate legal cases, there are innumerable cases at the trial level that remain unnoticed except by the participants," the study said. "Thus, this report is only a sample of possible cases—a 'tip of the iceberg'—of legal cases involving Shariah in local, state, and federal courts."

Among the cases was of a wife in New Jersey that needed a restraining order against her husband because of spousal abuse. "S.D. (wife) and M.J.R. (husband) were both Muslims and citizens of Morocco and both resided in New Jersey. After only three months of marriage, husband began physically abusing wife. The physical abuse administered by husband injured wife's entire body including her breasts and pubic area," the report said.

"Additionally, husband forced himself on wife and had non-consensual sex with her on multiple occasions. Husband stated to wife that Islam allowed him to have sex with her at any time he wished. Wife asked the trial court to grant a restraining order against husband shortly after he verbally divorced her in front of their imam," the report said. My conclusion was that the wife was looking to our Constitutional law for protection and mercy of the court to which she was entitled in order to negate Islamic law or Shariah law that her husband wanted to follow.

"The trial court refused to issue a final restraining order against husband finding that, although husband had harassed and assaulted wife, husband believed it was his religious right to have non-consensual sex with his wife and that belief precluded any criminal intent on the part of husband," according to the report.

"The New Jersey appellate court reversed the trial court and ordered that the trial court enter a final restraining order against husband. The New Jersey appellate court stated that the trial court erroneously allowed the husband's religious beliefs to excuse him from New Jersey's criminal code and that husband knowingly engaged in non-consensual sex with wife," the report said.

American Center for Law and Justice Shariah expert Shaheryar Gill said in the prominent New Jersey case, "the judge actually looked at Shariah Law to decide."

The report gave details of nineteen "top cases" and a summary of fifty cases from twenty-three states that have used Shariah as the basis for their court decisions. Gill says an ACLJ book, *Shariah Law: Radical Islam's Threat to the US Constitution*, discusses the problem: "The moral aptitude of Islamic reality, from Christian standards, runs parallel to each other. They may cross on occasion, but they each lead in different directions."

"In the cases of 'S.D. v. M.J.R.' the New Jersey appellate court rightly refused to accommodate the sincerely held religious beliefs of a Muslim man who physically, verbally, and sexually abused his wife in accordance with Shariah," the ACLJ book says. The report, however, pointed out that civil law is only part of what Shariah dictates. It said that Shariah law is also a religious law, and it conflicts with our American constitutional law on a number of subjects.

The following is George Washington's farewell address:

> All obstructions to the execution of the Laws, all combinations and Associations, under whatever plausible character, with the real design to direct, control, counteract, or awe the regular deliberation and action of the Constituted authorities, are destructive of this fundamental principle and of fatal tendency. They serve to organize faction, to give it an artificial and extraordinary force; to put in the place of the delegated will of the nation the will of a party; often a small but artful and enterprising minority of the Community; and, according to the alternate triumphs of different parties, to make the public administration the Mirror of the ill-concerted and incongruous projects of faction, rather than the organ

of consistent and wholesome plans digested by common councils and modified by mutual interest.[3]

I consider fundamentalist Muslims pushing for Shariah law to be "a small but artful and enterprising minority of the community." Could George Washington see into the future?

The report also said, "Institutionalized, authoritative Shariah is comprehensive and by definition without limit in its ambitions and scope, and it also includes legally mandated, recommended, permitted, discouraged and prohibited practices that are strongly biased and discriminatory against women, homosexuals and non-Muslims."

"Shariah Law provides a legal framework for violence up to and including legalized murder against apostates (people who have left Islam), homosexuals, blasphemers and especially women accused of various crimes," the report said. Shariah law is not consistent with the principles of all men (and women) are created equal.

"Just this year in 2011, in Pakistan's Shariah legal system, both apostates and blasphemers have been imprisoned and face execution. Shariah criminal punishments are extreme, including amputations and lashings for numerous crimes," the report said.

Kamal Saleem Interview

In June, 2011, former terrorist Kamal Saleem agreed that one of the methods for carrying out jihad here in the States is through the courts.

"What they're trying to do is make cases for Islam and these cases are done purposefully. We take an imam (case), there are two of them (imams). They were fighting against each other and the fight was over a mosque," Saleem said.

"That is so devious and it is a part of the culture of Islamic invasion. These two imams are fighting over a mosque in Florida. Each imam says it belongs to him. One says I built it and I raised the funds. The other one says the Wahhabi government put me over here and they're the ones who sent the money. Both of them are right," Saleem continued.

"They went to the Supreme Court in Florida. What happened is that they said this was a Muslim matter and you need to judge us by Islamic Shariah Law or you will not understand how these things work," he said.

ACLJ Shariah expert Shaheryar Gill had this to say about other recent cases that show the tactics by which Shariah has infiltrated the court system.

"There are different types of cases in which you see that Shariah or Islamic law is applied or is required to be applied, or looked at," Gill said. "For example, indirectly, there are cases in which foreign judgments are brought into the U.S. and enforced here," he continued.

American Center for Law and Justice Case Booklet

The case of *Farah v. Farah*, heard in Virginia, in which a trial judge recognized the validity of a Muslim marriage that was conducted through a proxy in England.

"The trial judge ruled that the marriage, which was solemnized in England (though no certificate of marriage was issued by any English authority) and its ceremony completed in Pakistan, must be honored in Virginia because 'the law of the state of Pakistan sanctions marriages performed under the personal law of the parties which in this case was Muslim law,'" the ACLJ booklet reported.

The problem with this particular case is Muslims have a practice of temporary marriages that are optional for Muslim men. For this practice to be accommodated here in the United States, marriage would have to be redefined.

The booklet pointed out that the Virginia court, "correctly recognized, however, that Pakistan's recognition of Shariah 'does not control the issue of the validity of the marriage under Virginia law.' Instead, the court applied Virginia law, which only granted comity according to the principles of the location celebrating the marriage, which was England."

There is also the California case of *Malak v. Malak*, which involved a Lebanese court decision. "The court determined, however, that the Lebanese order was enforceable because even though the Lebanese court had not explicitly applied the 'best interests of the child's standard, its decision aligned with California's 'best interests of the child' standard," the ACLJ book said. An Emory University Law School publication noted that the *Malak* case was cited as precedent in other Muslim child custody cases. These cases also take judicial activism to a whole new level.

Additional Evidence

Atlas Shrugs publisher and Islam analyst Pamela Geller warned about the use of Islamic law in American court decisions as turning a dangerous corner. "It is setting a very dangerous precedent. Shariah Law and U.S. law conflict in numerous ways, including issues of freedom of speech, freedom of conscience, and equality of rights for women. Allowing Shariah to be a determining factor in U.S. courtrooms threatens those rights for all of us," Geller said.

I could not agree more. The fact is this is a sovereign country. We live by our own laws and have adopted our code of ethics that is unique to this country. Some of us may appreciate them and some of us may not, but they are ours. There seems to be a growing consensus that those of us who appreciate the structure and virtues that our Founding Fathers built upon are obstructionists or extremists deserving of scorn or accusation.

Kansas Court Legislature

A bill designed to prevent Kansas courts from making decisions based on foreign legal code cleared the state legislature after a contentious debate about whether the measure upholds American values or appeals to prejudice against Muslims.[4]

Prejudice is making a judgment before due examination. It's an emotional bias based on hatred, thinking yourself better than another based on excessive intolerance or wanting to do harm. That is not the case here. Preferring American values and law over foreign law just shows we hold our legal code in high esteem.

The Kansas Senate approved the bill on a 33-3 vote. The House approved it, 120-0, a few days earlier. I believe this is a move in the right direction. The measure needs to be considered on a federal level. This is not a move against Muslims, but against any legal system other than our own system.

The bill doesn't specifically mention Shariah law. It just says that all courts and administrative agencies can't base rulings on any foreign law or legal system that would not grant the parties the same rights guaranteed by US and state constitutions. Contradicting Shariah law in the United States should be of no consequence, ever.

The bill's supporters said it simply ensures that court decisions will continue to protect long-cherished liberties and equal treatment under the law. Senator Susan Wagle, a Wichita Republican, said a vote for the legislation is a vote to protect women.

"In this great country of ours and in the state of Kansas, women have equal rights," Wagle said during the Senate's debate. "They stone women to death in countries that have Shariah Law."

The bill passed both chambers by wide margins because even skeptical legislators believed it did not represent a specific political attack on Muslims.

"We don't have any intolerance in this bill. Nobody's stripped of their freedom of religion," said Senator Ty Masterson, an Andover Republican. "This is talking about the law—American law, American courts."

Several senators noted that the bill's supporters singled out Shariah law during discussions, as examples. I question why they would have a problem with that. Shariah law is a law of dominance, violence, and intolerance. Not just for its subjects but *by* its fundamental subjects to make it the ultimate global authority. Not all Muslims want to be subjects under Shariah law, though.

"This bill will put Kansas in a light that says we are intolerant of any other faith," said Senate Judiciary Committee Chairman Tim Owens, a Republican who voted against the bill. "I would not be able to look at myself in the mirror in the morning if I didn't stand up and say I don't want to be that kind of person, and I don't want to be in a community or a state that is that way."

This gentleman needs to educate himself on the rules and expectations of Shariah law and understand that not being open to foreign laws being used in our courts is not being intolerant of a faith. He needs to understand the only reason Islamic fundamentalists still tolerate American laws is because Islamic law has not become the dominant law in this country, yet. He needs to have a solid grasp and allegiance to the principles of our Constitutional law before he makes such a declaration. In his attempt to be fair and just, he comes across as foolish and naive.

Forty-five Kansas House members, led by Rep. Peggy Mast, a Republican, sponsored a bill aimed at Shariah law last year. The House passed it overwhelmingly, but was not the case in the Senate. This was the House's second try, which put pressure on senators.

Several senators questioned whether the legislation was necessary, arguing Kansas judges and officials already must adhere to the US and state constitutions. Senator Garrett Love, a Republican, said even if no Kansas court has yet based a decision on foreign legal codes, "That doesn't mean we shouldn't still protect Kansans from those foreign laws being used in the future—a future that really may not be that far away."

Both the Council on American-Islamic Relations and the National Conference of State Legislatures admit there are anti-Shariah proposals that have been considered in nineteen other states and are not happy about it.

"It is an effort to demonize Islam," said Ibrahim Hooper, a spokesman for the Washington-based council. "As Muslims are seen participating in a positive way in society, that really irritates some people." Hooper called it "an anti-unicorn" bill. He cannot separate the person from the religious law.

"All it does is increase hostility toward Islam and suspicion of Muslims," Hooper said. These statements by our senators, representatives, and legal officials demonstrate the blatant ignorance that can cause the destruction of our judicial system, which protects men and women, Muslim and Christian alike, from the ideology of opposing rationale of foreign laws, countries, or governments.

Other Evidence

Do we really want to open the door to situations such as the upstate New York television station owner who beheaded his wife in February 2009 using Shariah law as his justification.[5] Is the toleration of this ideology what is necessary to keep from being seen as intolerant? Tolerating murder in the name of religion should be intolerable. Murder is murder, no matter how one tries to justify it.

If you did not hear about this case, it was because it did not fit within the Obama-nation-approved media narrative that they want to chronicle with attention. There was no outrage. Only silence. Do we really want a religious legal system here in this country that condones the stoning of a Muslim woman for the "suspicion" of adultery?

The Obama-nation is pushing the Muslim agenda in both subtle and not so subtle ways. They support the Ground Zero Mosque and omit the word "Muslim" from every terrorist headline while adding the words "right-wing, Christian" to non-Muslim crimes. The Fort Hood shooter has never been labeled a Muslim terrorist, though he was, to this day.

Asking questions surrounding the open border issue should be a necessary and constitutional initiative to defend the use of American Law in American courts that protects our fundamental freedoms against all foreign legal code that would threaten them. Representations to the contrary, particularly from groups such as CAIR that are tied to the Muslim Brotherhood, an organization seeking our destruction, should be seen for what they are—fraudulent deceptions—and rejected in the most effective possible way: by ensuring that every state in the union joins Kansas, Tennessee, Louisiana, and Arizona in enacting protection similar to American Laws for American Courts. The Judeo-Christian ethics, moral principles, and values, and the standards of right and wrong are based on perfection. So are God's laws of nature, natural law, or God's nature.

"He is like a rock; what He does is perfect, and He is always fair. He is a faithful God who does no wrong, who is right and fair" (Deuteronomy 32:4).[6]

Many attempts have been made to undermine our rule of law and our rights afforded to us by the Constitution, including our freedom of speech. I believe a great example of this was when it came under attack by the Obama-nation when they tried to blame a fourteen-minute movie trailer for the attacks on two of our Middle Eastern embassies. It did not work out the way they were anticipating. Americans are not that easily fooled. I believe it was the launch for an antifreedom of speech campaign that went horribly wrong—with *wrong* being the key word here.

The Bible tells us that the universal and absolute standard of justice is God Himself. He is the absolute standard of justice because justice comes from His nature, among other things. God defines justice for us by His actions and commands, not by what we faltered humans consider justice to be. This is the basis for the principles and standards reflected in our Declaration of Independence and enforced through our Constitution.

Though lawyers, judges, and juries seek after justice, only God can deliver it perfectly since He is its source.

"The teachings of the Lord are perfect; they give new strength. The rules of the Lord can be trusted; they make plain people wise. The orders of the Lord are right; they make people happy. The commands of the Lord are pure; they light up the way" (Psalm 19:7-8).[7]

Chapter 15

American Financial Shariah Compliance

Federal Reserve Bank

At the start of the Obama-nation, they announced the appointment of thirteen White House Fellows to spend a year as full-time, paid assistants to senior White House staff, the vice president, Cabinet secretaries, and senior administration officials. This student program was introduced in 1964 by LBJ to give promising American leaders "firsthand, high-level experience with the workings of the government, and to increase their sense of participation in national affairs."[1]

The first on the list is Samar Ali, a Muslim, an attorney, a specialist in cross-border transactions, Shariah-compliant transactions or Shariah-Compliance Finance (SCF), mergers and acquisitions, project finance, and international business matters. She was instrumental in bringing about and implementation of SCF and banking practices here in the United States, which is a system of banking consistent with the principles of Shariah or Islamic law.

As an associate for the law firm Hogan Lovells, Ali advised a Middle Eastern university on how to set up a Foreign Aid Conventional and Shariah Compliant Student Loan Program and advised individuals as well, according to Hogan Lovells. We need to question if this has anything to do with the Obama-nation's interest in providing student loans here in America.

This particular law firm claims it advises on many newly derived transaction types such as a "mudaraba sukuk" or Islamic finance instrument (sukuk), which acquires revenue from an arrangement based on a Shariah-compliant contractual investment between an investor and a managing trustee in which profits are shared (mudaraba). The financial instruments are issued by a "special purpose vehicle." This vehicle regulates the return in proportion to the investment.

Shortly after or more toward the tail end of the United States banking meld, March 2, 2009, the Indonesian president, H. Susilo Bambang Yudhoyono, told the World Islamic Economic Forum in Jakarta, "Islamic banking should now be able to take a leadership position in the banking world."

His next statement is what caught my eye. "Islamic banks have been much less affected by the financial meltdown than the conventional banks (US banks) for the obvious reason that Shariah banks do not indulge in investing in toxic assets and in leveraged funds. They are geared to supporting the real economy." Adding, "Islamic bankers should therefore do some missionary work in the Western world to promote the concept of Shariah banking, for which many in the West are more than ready now."

Could the financial and economic meltdown have been orchestrated to push us into the position to adopt SCF?

Was the Dodd-Frank financial "reform" bill that was paraded as the remedy to the weaknesses in the United States financial system and that is supposed to ensure transparency and accountability but gave the government unlimited empowerment, which is unreviewable and often secret, a bureaucratic Shariah-compliant financial instrument (sukuk)?

It created administrative associations that have broad and essentially unlimited power to seize banks and other financial entities it deems unsound under the guise of "too big to fail." At the same time, the new Consumer Financial Protection Bureau and Financial Stability Oversight Council created their own law.

This is somewhat of a Trojan horse. The Obama-nation is embracing this medieval doctrine of Shariah law that regulates every aspect of life and can change the basic American life and laws concerning what is required, like almsgiving to Allah, and what regulations will be changed, omitted, and/or added. Was Samar Ali brought in to learn, or was she there to teach, design, and implement SCF?

Jesus said, "Everything that is hidden will be shown, and everything that is secret will be made known. What you have said in the dark will be heard in the light, and what you have whispered in an inner room will be shouted from the housetops" (Luke 12:2-3).[2]

Some no-information or low-information legal voters might think that making the United States banking system change to accommodate and be compatible with the Arab world would be good business practices and would increase the global marketplace. But SCF is steeped heavily in the doctrine of Islam, or Shariah law, and is the vehicle by which to implement a very different concept of conducting commerce.

Consider how Muslims perceive the increase in capital by means of appreciation or interest on assets or investments. This is seen as ill-gotten gains and is prohibited by the Quran. A sin. They have the same ill feelings about collecting interest on loans or charging over 33 percent for something you make than what you had to spend to make it. This explains why the Obama-nation has contemplated confiscating some of our retirement assets to reduce the national debt, or reduce the value of the dollar, which will yield the same result—the disappearance of retirement funds.

The retirement system in place currently is a rather safe environment considering the diversification in plan options. About four in five full-time employees enjoy a retirement plan through their employer.

The "Guaranteed Retirement Account" (GRA) system, authored by Teresa Ghilarducci, would allow government to seize private 401(k) accounts, setting up an additional 5 percent mandatory payroll tax to dole out a "fair" pension to everyone using that confiscated money over and above regular contributions, whether one contributed to it or not. All of this is proposed under the pretense of "fairness"—retirement Income equality. Progressive statists use this term frequently when disparaging wealth, but there is nothing about it that is fair. This kind of thinking is reminiscent of the Social Security system that ended up being a slush fund for government whims and is now going bankrupt. This is a ponzi scheme geared to give politicians more revenue to pay for their out-of-control ambitions and buy votes, which taxpayers fund.[3]

We "Westerners" consider earned interest on investments justified income. Advocates of SCF do not. They believe that you do not deserve income from ways that you did not provide a service or product to achieve. The Arabic word for interest is riba. There are actually two types of riba, or what they see as ill-gotten gains in trade or business exploitation:

1. The exchange of commodities in unequal quantities or value is forbidden by the Quran. They believe that selling, buying, trading, or exchanging something at unequal value is a sin.
2. *Maisir* is the Arabia word for gambling—getting more back than you gave. They see the act of insuring something or purchasing insurance as "wagering on the outcome" and as being wrong. They consider this as taking advantage of them.

I hope you are thinking, "Wow, this sure explains a lot." Keep in mind, this is when Shariah is the absolute rule being used, and no other system of doing business is being applied. This is also why most of the Middle Eastern countries are economically poor.

This could explain the troubling obsession that Prince Bin Talal had with mainstreaming SCF in the West to make the banks reject the cornerstone of Western finance: credit and interest rates. SCF has also required banks to give a share of their profits to Islamic charities, which often funnel money to terrorist organizations. This is called *Zakat*. It is a required charity tax, which only Muslims have to pay to support poor Muslims. But through the use of SCF, it is a means to "purify" funds generated from non-Muslim sources. It is money-laundering in reverse.[4]

There are only eight approved forms of charity to which faithful Muslims are expected to tithe at least 2.5 percent of their income, and four of them can be interpreted as supportive of violent jihad. This may explain the silence from the many tolerant, peaceable Muslims who are not necessarily advocates for Shariah law themselves. Their jihad is more of a personal, pietistic "path to Allah." But speaking out could not only bring persecution to themselves but to some of their peaceable Muslim neighbors who are tithing to charities with known, or unknown, ties to terrorism.

Bin Talal has set up a Shariah law and finance section at Harvard University. He and former New York Mayor Bloomberg, his business partner, have opened a regional hub in Dubai, where it has developed an Islamic finance portal. This business venture provides a pro-SCF information product.

The Arab Bankers Association of North America is a group that supports Shariah finance in America. They sponsored a dinner attended by Rupert Murdock, the majority shareholder in News Corp., the parent Company of Fox News. Prince Alwaleed Bin Talal is next in line with a 7 percent investment. The prince is an admirer of the Fox News business model and expressed his desires to apply it to Eastern media profiles.

The prince has boasted of his influence over Fox News content. He said he called Murdock and had the wording of the Muslim riots in France changed from "Muslim riots," to wording that disassociated Islam from the violence. He also had a hand in the unbooking of the authors of the best-selling *Muslim Mafia: Inside the Secret Underworld that's Conspiring to Islamize America.*

Those of us that will not remain silent about our opposition to the Islamization of America will find opposition to us even at Fox News, although it is the news channel I still prefer above the rest. It is possible that my book, due to the exposures I have introduced, will not be seen as popular. But the information in this book is not for self-glorification. It is a wakeup call from out of the wild blue yonder, from an unassuming, grassroots, homespun, self-informed spectator. I expect more ridicule from this book than glory, which I accept with open arms.

Do not be deceived into thinking that there are any safe havens in the media world free from Islamic influence. Just personally knowing what is in the Bible will keep us from being deceived by those using misquotes and misdirection of biblical lessons and their meaning. This way we will come to understand what is under Shariah influence and what is not.

"Those who are careful about what they say protect their lives, but whoever speaks without thinking will be ruined" (Proverbs 13:3).[5]

In the case against Timothy Geithner and others over the nation's multibillion dollar bailout of AIG insurance filed by taxpayer Kevin J. Murray, it was exposed that some of the TARP money used to bail out AIG was used by AIG to bail out multiple Shariah-complaint insurance products. Robert Muise and David Yerushalmi of the American Freedom Law Center handled the case.[6]

The government takeover, under the umbrella of a bailout, of AIG began in September 2008, just prior to the Obama-nation transition of the government, and it violated the Establishment Clause of the First Amendment, "Congress shall make no law respecting an establishment of religion or prohibiting the free exercise thereof," and Shariah law serves as Islamic "religious" law. It was discovered in district court that AIG provided two of its SCF subsidiaries with at least $153 million. This amount was determined by the judges to be insignificant; however, I believe further inquiry should have been made.

The Obama-nation was in control of AIG while refusing to regulate the expenditures of federal tax funds by passing a federal budget, or lower spending, or the deficit. It was avoiding the responsibility of holding itself or AIG accountable for their acquired revenues according to Constitutional law.

I found involvement and the takeover of AIG by the Obama-nation very disturbing also, considering that AIG is the world leader in promoting Shariah-compliant insurance products, and Muslims are not allowed to purchase insurance as Westerners know it. Maybe that is why we have Obamacare, now, to eliminate insurance companies. Doing away with insurance companies, calling it a tax, and controlling the entire medical industry, including doctors . . . behold, America is now Shariah-compliant and the Obama-nation has the means to implement the *Jizya* or *Jazia* tax.

The *Jizya* is a non-Muslim poll tax. This tax, according to the Quran, must be collected from Jews, Christians, and other non-Muslims, as a sign of their subjugation or conquest under Islamic rule. This is the penalty for not converting to Islam. The "People of the Book" (people being Jews and Christians and the book being the Bible) are to be seen as lowering themselves to Muslims. They are supposed to collect it in a way as to belittle or humiliate us, too. In other words, not be under disguise or be hidden as something other than what it is.[7]

Muslims call Jews and Christians—besides infidels—*dhimmis* or *dhimmah*, who are made to submit to the rule of Shariah law. We are allowed to still practice our religion but not on an equal basis as Muslims, and it is their duty to make us feel subdued. In other words, practice your non-Muslim religion at home and maybe at church but nowhere else, but Muslims are free to do as they please anytime and anywhere. This is happening right now in the land of the free.

The *dhimmis* are supposed to assume a posture of lowering ourselves during the collection of the *jizya* to achieve atonement for rejecting Allah and to keep from being killed. Muslims are not allowed to honor or show gratitude or appreciation as the receiver of the *jizya*, either. *Mozarab* is the Arabic word for Christian *dhimmis* in particular.

Al-qudra is the Arabic word for "effective power" and is believed by Allah to be heresy. Wikipedia says this is the power delivered from an engine to a drive mechanism either directly or through a power transmission. Output of this power may be termed net, total, or rated. Interesting.

Is Allah angered by the "effective power" that is given from God (an engine) to a drive mechanism (Christian believers) through a power transmission (the Holy Spirit)? It could be considered a transmission of divine power through the Holy Spirit and the use of this power by the believer that is seen as the "output of this power" or be seen simply as spreading the Good News and trusting in God's will. Again, interesting concept?

I am speculating, of course. Only God and Allah really know. I do know that God is power, has power, gives power, and can take power away, and the power that has been given to all believers is the power of victory over sin.

Moving on, the United States Treasury Department created and staffed a position called the Islamic Finance Scholar-in-Residence. They published presentations by senior Treasury Department officials praising SCF and stated explicitly that the United States government "place significant importance on promoting Islamic finance" and has "recently deepened our engagement in Islamic finance in a number of ways," including a "call for harmonization of Shariah standards at the national and international levels."[8]

SCF is a soft form of jihad; some see it as "financial jihad." Soft means proselytizing and using other peaceable forms of subversion to infiltrate, and then eventually assimilate, Shariah into non-Muslim societies.

It was discovered that AIG subsidiaries obtained consultation from Shariah Supervisory Committees, which are "authorities in Shariah law and oversee the implementation of SCF products by reviewing AIG's operations, supervising the development of SCF products, and evaluating the compliance of these products with Shariah law," the court said.

The United States Treasury Department held a half-day conference called "Islamic Finance 101" for government policy makers to promote Shariah law and SCF both. Throughout the discussion at the conference, they made the argument that SCF is not about the promotion of the religion of Islam but the study of it.

If this were true, then why is SCF described by AIG as an activity strictly guided by Shariah law, which is based on the Quran and the teachings of their prophet? Could it be that AIG is fully engaged in religious indoctrination?

I believe this is so systemic that perhaps the only way it can be disrupted and forced out is with a complete and total collapse of our economic practices so we can start over minus SCF. Maybe even on a global scale. That could be the only way they would lose interest in our economy— by reducing their and our ability to exercise international commerce in any industry. That would stop their focus on us, and they would have to focus on their own domestic issues, and so would we. Considering what is happening with the bubbles being created with our dollar values and national debt, economic collapse may be exactly what God has planned in our near future. In other words, hit the reset button and have America turn their heads and hearts back toward Him. We are making a mess of *His* world.

"The Lord will help you defeat the enemies that come to fight you. They will attack you from one direction, but they will run from you in seven directions" (Deuteronomy 28:7).[9]

PART 4

Diminishing the American Populus

Chapter 16

The Truth about Homosexuality

Same-sex union symbols

It has been some time now since I worked outside the house apart from doing little, short, odd jobs for the church, neighbors, and friends, but I do not miss working in the public domain. I did enjoy it at times, but it seemed that my principles and values, which I considered at one time very accommodating, were being challenged more and more.

For instance, there's the increasing uncomfortable demand of submission toward homosexuality. Why can't we agree to disagree on the matter? Is it possible for the code of the homosexual activist movement which states that some people are born with predisposed tendencies that cannot and should not be resisted and the conviction of traditional thinking that homosexuality is a bad behavioral choice, coexist? After all, homosexuality has been practiced since Old Testament times. It has always been viewed as objectionable and unacceptable. Objectionable and unacceptable to whom? That would be God. Do they realize why Sodom and Gomorrah were destroyed, and who did it?

"Your love must be real. Hate what is evil, and hold on to what is good. Love each other like brothers and sisters. Give each other more honor than you want for yourselves" (Romans 12:9-10).[1]

Maybe they do. It was not Jews or Christians who destroyed those cities. We had nothing to do with it. That, however, does not seem to make a difference. That is why the homosexual—or gay movement—agenda is to seek, conquer, control, and destroy traditional thinking and practices. God-loving and God-fearing people who see the Bible and the Constitution of the United States as concrete, with absolute laws, who are their enemy. They reject the knowledge that these documents have stood the test of time and that the principles which they both provide us cannot and will not be changed in spite of man's changing worldviews. Neither are living documents.

"Out of the mind come evil thoughts, murder, adultery, sexual sins, stealing, lying, and speaking evil of others. These things make people unclean" (Matthew 15:19-20).[2]

I can understand the desire to be loved and happy. I also understand the heartbreak of rejection or manipulation. I have experienced all of these at some point in my life. Before I married, I was vulnerable and gullible both, just like everyone else. Some situations even lead to heartbreak and humiliation. I was guilty of making mistakes and seeking self-gratification, but, thankfully, I also, felt the need and importance of commitment. Deep down, I knew I was going at it in the wrong way. I believe everyone can feel that. I believe that some folks just *will* not see themselves as doing something wrong. They justify what they do, no matter what it is, just because they are the one doing it.

To me, marriage was freedom from all of that. I also came to believe that marriage is not just making a commitment to each other; it is making a commitment to the institution of marriage and all it stands for in the sight of God. God has a purpose for mankind to fulfill, and marriage is the institution He created to set part of that purpose in motion. It is the union that is important and not just the relationship to each other.

I have been married for more than thirty-five years, and I can give testimony to this. Relationships wax and wane. I highly recommend a good sense of humor to get through it. It has come in handy on numerous occasions. My husband and sons are my comic relief. It works out nicely because they like to make me laugh, and I like to laugh.

Most people believe that marriage is about happiness and about the relationship between the two of them only. It isn't. It is about the union and not about any one individual's feelings and his or her happiness. Things like instant self-gratification, pride, lack of forgiveness, and the expectation that someone is responsible for our happiness lead to many divorces. People incorrectly think is it about them and how *they* feel.

Happiness comes from within us. Happiness is synonymous with joy, blessedness, and peace of mind. It is an emotional response *and* a state of being. Believe it or not, we can have control over our desires and being prone to acts of passion or provocation. Our emotions should be mixed with consideration. They do not and should not control us. Our society has adopted this false idea that our emotions are what guide us . . . that somehow thinking is overrated. Self control is really the only kind of control we have. I believe we can manage time, situations, and even people, but we cannot control them.

I believe our happiness does not come from vices or indulgences such as gluttony, sex, drunkenness, or any other sins of the flesh. But practicing self-control inside a marriage, being responsible for your actions, and living in harmony are important, but it is not the only thing. It is the union that is the most important. That is why God hates divorce. It tears apart that which He joined together to be one body.

"God made husbands and wives to become one body and one spirit for his purpose—so they would have children who are true to God" (Malachi 2:15).[3]

Studies show that children of divorced parents can, and do, turn out stable, but divorce does present a handicap. One thing that helps the most is for the father to remain financially supportive and active in his children's lives. What happens without daddy around can be much different.

In a 1979 study, the National Longitudinal Survey of Youth found fatherless children to be twice as likely to drop out of school, and girls who grew up without their fathers were 2.5 times more likely to become pregnant as teenagers.

Another publication, in 1997, called *Life Without Father.* by Rutgers University sociology professor David Popenoe, concluded that boys raised without fathers were more likely to have problems with drugs, alcohol, behavior, and social interactions. Other studies found that disruptions in family structures were predictors of children's gang involvement.

These findings do not sit well with the progressive agenda being promoted by the Obama-nation. They see these nonbiased, nonreligious, scientific results as "right-wing" and say that they give a blame-the-victim message. They do not see that the problem lies within the confines of not teaching self control and responsibility and children not understanding the need to be kind and helpful. They fail to see that this formula will increase the odds of success in their lives and will plow the field for their children to achieve success, too.

Self control is the one thing we should all be trying to perfect along with our emotional state of mind. Reactions to people and things around us play a big part in that. The control of *self* is really the only thing we can control, and it seems it is the one thing we try to control the least. We choose to give in, accept, or accommodate our insecurities and weaknesses instead of trying to move away from them. We can choose to be happy or unhappy, too. Disappointments can lead to despair, if we allow them to, but they can also lead to a critical juncture of growth and virtue for all involved. Understanding that God is in control of everything else and focusing on that end is choosing peace.

I understand why some folks, such as homosexuals, try to justify their choices. They do not want to believe that their weaknesses, vulnerabilities or gullibilities are being seen as undesirable. Even believers and followers of God's laws have weaknesses and fall prey to temptations. We just know they are wrong to indulge them, and even then, sometimes we still do. We also know to ask for forgiveness and that we have to repent by turning away from weaknesses and temptations in order to receive forgiveness, grace, and peace.

Sometimes it works immediately, and we are no longer tempted by a particular weakness. Sometimes it does not, and we fall again. We ask for forgiveness, again, and turn away, again, and keep doing that until we do not have to anymore. It is really simple and rewarding. God's speed depends on our focus and conviction for doing the right thing, of course. Being a believer in Christ does not automatically make someone perfect. We just can see the benefit in the willingness to try to attain holiness. It is a process. A long process. It is all about the journey and not necessarily the destination.

It is hard for me to imagine how the gay community feels about God and living in His grace. Could it be that they feel that their will is stronger, fairer, and more righteous than God's? Do they not realize that they are really declaring war on God instead of those of us who are just the followers and observers of God's will?

Apparently, coexistence is intolerable. The intolerance isn't from those who try to obey God's laws but instead from the homosexual movement. Followers of God and of Christ have had to tolerate homosexuality since, as before mentioned, Old Testament times.

Is homosexuality a predisposed tendency based on a biological condition or a physiological condition or both? Depending on the agenda of the science, one could probably find a multitude of statistics to support the justification for this lifestyle . . . devoid of biblical study, of course.

The Bible is not a supporter of the old adage "If it feels good, do it." This is a term I personally heard all throughout the 1960s and into the 1970s. The Bible does not identify people who are homosexual by orientation from those who actually engage in homosexual behavior. It just points out that homosexuality is a consequence of sin at work in the world. It teaches that thinking about acting upon homosexual tendencies or temptation is different from actually engaging in the activity itself. This is where self control would prove useful. It is the human condition, which is the need of God's grace already at birth, and subsequent sinful acts, that separate us from God. Homosexual behavior, like all sexual relations outside of marriage, is immoral and God sees them all as the same—sin. Again, this is where self-control comes in—control of our emotions, our thoughts, and our actions.

The Bible does not indicate that homosexuality is an especially "bad" sin. The Apostle Paul said homosexuality is one of the sins that results from the rebellion of the human race against God. This may explain why it was referred to as "a hateful sin" in the Old Testament.

"You must not have sexual relations with a man as you would a woman. That is a hateful sin" (Leviticus 18:22).[4]

Is homosexuality a hateful sin to God only? Could it be a hateful sin to both the plan God has made for us to fulfill in the perpetuation of the human race and to the opposite sex they are rejecting? Is it not hatefulness that causes children to be the center of this whole issue? Is it not one-sided and hateful to deprive a child being raised by opposite-sex adoptive parents who can provide all aspects of the child's needs, which numerous studies have repeatedly stated is best for children? A hateful sin indeed.

Rebellion of the human race against God sounds ominous and dangerous. This is a prideful refusal to acknowledge the authority God claims. To rebel is to deny the preeminence of another in order to bolster oneself. They are putting themselves above God in an arrogant attempt to eliminate God's laws and the laws of nature so that they can become their own authority and make their own laws that are based on sin. This applies directly to the progressive movement in many ways also.

So what is to become of the unrepentant, rebellious homosexual? The Bible makes it clear that they cannot share in the promise of eternal rest in heaven. Seeing the popularity in the general population for homosexuality, it explains why only a faithful remnant will be sifted out of the many to receive God's eternal blessings.

Not being perfect myself, I understand why the idea of self-control is such a hard sell. The conflict between "if it feels good, do it" without regard to the consequences and responsibility versus a thoughtful and ethical philosophy are like two magnetic poles repelling each other. Self-control, without the foundation of scripture or godly laws is just seen as a stoic tradition. Therefore, it is something that can be, and from that perspective should be, challenged. The idea that temperance or self-control is one of the four cardinal virtues, along with faith, hope, and love, has been disregarded and, therefore, is unnecessary.

"Those who do not control themselves are like a city whose walls are broken down" (Proverbs 25:28).[5]

While working retail as an assistant manager, I saw folks from all walks of life both as fellow employees and as customers. I worked with several gay individuals, both male and female. One in particular, I believe, was conflicted about being gay. He was the brother of a minister and apparently had been exposed to what the Bible says about homosexuality.

He was a precious, searching soul and is someone I still think about and pray for to this day. I believe his becoming a homosexual was determined more by his life experiences and peers than by him. Even though he reveled in the acts of debauchery, which he would have to convey to all of us the next time he saw us, I still sensed a regret or solemness in his demeanor.

I went to work one day, and there was just the two of us working. He expressed what sounded like resentment of the expectations that his homosexual peers preferred him to display. I responded with, "There is so much more to you, and you have so much more to offer than all that." My statement was met with a blank stare.

What will happen to our country if we stop exercising practical wisdom? What happens to a country that fails to restrain, resist, and counsel the sinful spirit about the adverse nature of those acts? They are subject to the destructive whims of those forces. This applies to sexual continence, drug addiction, alcoholism, gambling, and so on.

Self control seems to be the adversary in this industrialized country in which we live, where efficiency, productivity, and profitability are dependent on appealing to the desires for comfort, pleasure, ease, or status of the people—indulgence, sensuality, or outright deceptions that are used to bait us at every turn.

It does not end there. An epic example of the homosexuality movement trying to justify their rejection of God's basic plan for His creation to survive that I came across is *The Queen James Bible*. A "queen" is the female avatar in the male duo scenario, for those who do not keep up with gay nomenclature. An unnamed group of gays, who claim King James was gay, has published it.[6] Even if King James was gay, why, with the forty-seven scholar-translators, are there so many anti-homosexual references? He obviously was not happy about it if he was. The book has an anonymous author, so he or they mistakenly think there is safety from scrutiny. Just one problem, God knows who they are.

This group of gays wanted to change the 1769 King James translation to one that reflects a pro-homosexual interpretation. This attempt to change reality would be rather funny if it were not so pitiful and desperate. They believe that this point of view can persuade people that the Bible says nothing negative about homosexuality. They attempt to justify their action by calling it "interpretive ambiguity." Being faced with the decision to either modify existing inconvenient passages by rendering confusion, or "interpretively ambiguous language," or just deleting it completely was a difficult one, they claim.

"I warn everyone who hears the words of the prophecy of this book: If anyone adds anything to these words, God will add to that person the disasters written about in this book. And if anyone takes away from the words of their book of prophecy, God will take away that one's share of the tree of life and of the holy city, which are written about in this book" (Revelation 22:18-19).[7]

The Queen James translation is simply animus. There is no verse condemning same-sex sexual relations in it. The story of Sodom and Gomorrah in Genesis, and verses in Leviticus, Romans, 1 Corinthians, Timothy, and Jude were additionally troublesome. Then there is the issue represented in the standard set forth when God created Adam and Eve. Jesus repeated what was established at that time in this passage.

"Jesus answered, 'Surely you have read in the Scriptures: When God made the world, "he made them male and female." And God said, "So a man will leave his father and mother and be united with his wife, and the two will become one body." So there are not two, but one. God has joined the two together, so no one should separate them'" (Matthew 19:4-6).[8]

This presents another issue of biology. There is no match of sexual biological equipment. This is why Paul described same-sex sex as "unnatural." This is willful disregard. I am sure the progressives who champion homosexuality consider the physical aspects to have no bearing on the sexual relationship, not considering having to pursue multipurpose uses of certain features. All efforts to relieve their guilt with the acknowledgement of their doing wrong, then asking to be forgiven and then repenting, seem pointless. But we should not give up hope. Truth has a way of imprinting on people's minds. Even when their behavior destroys indiscriminately the lives, relationships, and families as a result of their sin, they should not be left to their devises.

> Because they did these things, God left them and let them
> go their sinful way, wanting only to do evil. As a result, they
> became full of sexual sin, using their bodies wrongly with

each other. They traded the truth of God for a lie. They worshiped and served what had been created instead of the God who created those things, who should be praised forever. Amen.

Because people did those things, God left them and let them do the shameful things they wanted to do. Women stopped having natural sex and started having sex with other women. In the same way, men stopped having natural sex and began wanting each other. Men did shameful things with other men, and in their bodies they received the punishment for those wrongs.(Romans 1:24-27)[9]

I am sure those creating this new Bible had trouble with this passage.

If Paul described that same-sex sex as "unnatural," can we not conclude that same-sex sex goes against the "laws of nature" that are the principles our Declaration of Independence identified?

So, is the whole gay marriage revolution that they have declared even a legitimate debate? Ask yourself who established the institution of marriage in the first place? Then ask yourself whose authority they are challenging and why? This may explain the ruthless and frothy pursuit in which they commit themselves. Whether anyone is an active, deliberate part of this movement or just a passive, silent, objective observer, they are contributing to the destruction of the family unit, designed by God, and the American way of life. Silence renders consent. We have to stand up and speak out about what is right and what is not.

"They know God's law says that those who live like this should die. But they themselves not only continue to do these evil things, they applaud others who do them" (Romans 1:32).[10]

As of March 2012, 83 percent of this nation identified themselves as Christians. I believe this term is thrown around loosely, so the true question is, "What do you believe?" Jesus even said that some who minister in His name would not be in Heaven. He also said that the only ones who will enter the kingdom of heaven are those who are trying to do God's will.

God judges each one of us in the same way, and each one of us will be punished according to our own sin. So, I don't believe that saying, "But,

Lord, I didn't know that was wrong," will work. The next question He can ask is, "So why didn't you know?" I do not know for sure; I am guessing.

How do you think God sees those who applaud others who do these things that we know are wrong? What does this say about those who claim to be Christian who applaud them? How do you think God views the leader of a nation that was once dedicated to Him and founded on His reality and the laws of nature making the claim that the Bible was the basis for his pro-gay marriage position?

The homosexual movement attempts to change God's law to better fit their situation, to allow the indulgence of their declivity, and to justify their actions and behavior. The foundation of their movement is for freedom, fairness, and equality. Freedom from God's morality and the law of nature; fairness to be seen the way they want to be seen, to practice immoral behavior and not be judged against God's morality and the negative results of their actions, and equality to achieve the same level of stature and benefits of society reserved for the morally disciplined, obedient, or respectable population.

Jerome R. Corsie, a Harvard PhD and an author of many books, including *The Obama Nation* and *Unfit for Command,* had an article that I found extremely disturbing about Obama. The main theme of the article was addressing Obama's association with the Reverend Jeremiah Wright's Trinity Church and the reasons for his affiliation with a religious base.[11]

There were many revelations in the article, but the information I wish to address here is the point that Obama revealed in the other book he wrote, *The Audacity of Hope,* (p. 207). In that, Obama stated that he joined Trinity Church because at Trinity "faith doesn't mean you don't have doubts, or that you relinquish your hold on this world . . . that religious commitment did not require me to suspend critical thinking, disengage from the battle for economic and social justice, or otherwise retreat from the world I knew and loved."

He decided to join for *other* reasons than a revelation of God or a coming to Jesus moment. It was not due to conversion. Obama needed the black base for political reasons, and that seems to be the extent of it.

So when Obama said that he consulted with his Christian sensibility to come to a pro-gay marriage stance, just what "sensibilities" were those actually? Were they his sensibilities or God's sensibilities? If "truth" is God, and the Bible is the Word of God, then the obvious stance should have been to reject gay marriage. But, of course, Obama needed that black voting bloc of Trinity Church and the gay voters, which was more important. Even Franklin Graham, Billy Graham's son, both Christian evangelists, said, "Obama has shaken his fist at God with his stance for gay marriage."

Presbyterian USA and some Methodist and Episcopalian churches have adopted the "welcoming stance" to homosexuals, which is a good thing if it is for ministering to them only and not the acceptance or accommodation of their lifestyle.

"He (Man of Evil) will use every kind of evil to trick those who are lost. They will die, because they refused to love the truth. (If they loved the truth, they would be saved.) For this reason God sends them something powerful that leads them away from the truth so they will believe a lie. So all those will be judged guilty who did not believe the truth, but enjoyed doing evil" (2 Thessalonians 2:10-12).[12]

The truth is God. I am starting to understand the "something powerful that leads them away." God cannot look upon sin, nor can He lie. He is holy. So maybe those who refuse Him, Truth, and insist on doing what He has not and cannot tolerate in His kingdom of heaven, and also on His earth, are seeing "something" that God sent long ago that gets them to follow lies. It is all about choices.

Obama used a biblical passage out of context when he cited the Golden Rule, "Do unto others as you would have them do unto you," to better illustrate his "just" Christian sensibilities.[13] The Bible was not referring to sexual deviation or disobedience in this passage. The only audience that it would have appealed to would be an audience with little or no knowledge of the Bible. The misdirection of this sort brings only confusion or worse, delusion. Changing the biblical reference with which this passage is associated could make it mean just about anything. There is no more harmony, continuity, or good will toward others in doing this.

This passage is about kindness, courtesy, thoughtfulness, caring about everyone we meet, and tolerance, not the accommodation of sin. It is not about acceptance for same-sex relationships or marriages. Marriage is not just about love and devotion. If it were the only element to be considered for marriage, then someone could legitimately marry their mailbox just as long as they loved it. Confusion and delusion—and splinters.

My heart breaks for the pitiful souls that are allowing themselves to be coddled by this new-age theology and erroneous ideology, and it breaks at what this is doing to my country. This has to stop. The statists or progressives are pushing indulgence with a political twist as their drug of choice. So it is no surprise the two fit hand in glove.

Homosexuals already have all the rights that non-homosexuals have: hospital visitation, naming nonrelatives as heirs in their wills, cohabitation law protections, etc. So why are they causing such upheaval? They claim it is a civil rights issue. Is it? Are they a race in and of themselves? Civil rights such as the right to vote along with fair and equal treatment in public places are guaranteed by the Constitution to everyone already.

The Defense of Marriage Act (DOMA), from 1996, is a federal law that defines marriage as the legal union of one man and one woman for federal and intrastate recognition purposes. Section 1 is the title; section 2 grants each state an unlimited courtesy against being legally required to recognize a same-sex marriage recognized by another state; and section 3 defines the term "marriage" for purposes of federal law as meaning only opposite-sex unions. This section catalogs the nonrecognition of same-sex marriages for all federal purposes, including insurance benefits for government employees, Social Security survivors' benefits, immigration, bankruptcy, public employee benefits, estate taxes, and the filing of joint tax returns.[14]

So far, eight federal courts, including the First and Second Circuit Court of Appeals, have found issue with parts of section 3 as to their constitutionality. The United States Supreme Court heard an appeal in the *United States v. Windsor* case in the latter part of March 2013 and was anticipated to make decisions on it during the summer. It ended up with a five for Windsor to four against vote.

What amazes me is folks on both sides of the aisle doing an enormous amount of backpedaling. These were folks that were originally completely for DOMA. The Obama-nation is, of course, at the forefront of it all with topics such as whether the Constitution requires the government to treat same-sex the same as "normal" unions, equal protection, and what the appropriate "standard of review" is that a court should use to decide whether DOMA is constitutional.

Standard of review? How about the standard of natural law? Are we to live by the standard of "right reason" or by the standard of man's idea of right and wrong?

The question of what the court should use as its "standard of review" is more about how much attention the court should give the standard of natural law in the legislation, challenging the virtue of "right reason" and its use to create policy, which was why it passed in the first place— the same standards our Founding Fathers believed we had to keep to survive.

"So a man will leave his father and mother and be united with his wife, and the two will become one body" (Genesis 1:24).[15]

Marriage is an important and crucial institution established by God. Marriage unites two human beings in the most intimate and passionate relationship possible, "holy" matrimony. It mirrors, on a human level, the relationship we enjoy with God.

I cannot forget an issue that arose at work just after Christmas over some symbols of homosexuality that had been written on the wall that we used as a company chalkboard. A manager drew a Christmas tree, and each employee could draw an ornament on the tree with his or her initials inside it whenever that person managed to persuade a customer to open a high-interest credit card account. The employee with the most ornaments would win a prize.

Christmas had come and gone, and the board had not yet been wiped clean when someone drew two symbols representing the female gender linked together and two symbols representing the male gender linked together on the board. Another employee brought it to my attention because the person considered it offensive.

To this day, I regret not erasing the board right then. I now feel my procrastination and reluctance to act upon my principles caused more problems than I had anticipated. By the time I finally erased the board, words had been exchanged between employees, feelings were hurt, and everyone was either surprised or angry. Workplace drama was something I abhor, and I especially did not like being at the center of it. When human resources asked me why I erased the board, my reply was, "Graffiti of any kind is inappropriate at a workplace." I was not willing to say how I really felt, and I believe they did not want to hear it.

I wonder, though, would it have gotten a different reaction if the tables were turned, and an employee was drawing Christian religious symbols?

Case in point, remember the gunman, Floyd Lee Corkins, a volunteer in a "gay" community center, who targeted the Family Research Council (FRC) because of its Bible-based position on homosexuality on August 15, 2012. Washington Police Chief Cathy Lanier and FBI officials praised the guard at the Family Research Council building (FRC), Leo Johnson, for preventing more bloodshed. A surveillance tape showed the suspect shooting Johnson after talking with him. Even wounded, Johnson moved toward Corkins and wrestled the firearm away from him.[16]

The Southern Poverty Law Center (SPLC) had recently labeled the FRC as a "hate group," and FRC President Tony Perkins said the "reckless rhetoric" of the left-wing SPLC contributed to the atmosphere that caused the security guard to get injured. Perkins said the label of "hate group" marginalized individuals and organizations, letting people feel free to go and do bodily harm to innocent people who are simply working and representing folks from all across this country.

Another example of vicious gay propaganda was by activist Dan Savage at Winona State University in Minnesota during the "Fall 2012 Lyceum Series."[17] Investigative reporters at CampusReform.org, an Arlington, Virginia, based conservative youth group, and in Seattle at the National High School Journalism Convention uncovered most of these.

Savage reportedly

- accused the president and other Christians of wanting homosexuals dead;
- accused the FRC of telling parents whose kids "come out" (turn to homosexual behavior) to reject them;
- accused the FRC of telling parents of "queer" kids to do what he "damn well knows" drives those kids to suicide;

- said that every dead gay kid is a victory for the FRC;
- accused the FRC of arguing that the gay lifestyle is sick and sinful and dangerous and points to suicide, but then doing everything in its power to make sure that suicide rate does not come down;
- accused the FRC president of sitting on a pile of dead gay kids every day when he goes to work;
- accused all Christians of hatred;
- said, "Isn't it enough God's going to roast me on a spit in hell for all eternity . . . You don't believe that is going to actually happen (so) you want to persecute me now . . . just in case. Can you just trust that Jesus hates me as much as you say;"
- referred to Michele Bachmann, R-MN, as an "ignorant b***h;"
- said, "We can learn to ignore the bull**** in the Bible about gay people the same way we have learned to ignore the bull**** in the Bible about shellfish, about slavery, about dinner, about farming, about menstruation, about virginity, about masturbation. We ignore bull**** in the Bible about all sorts of things;"
- referred to the Bible as "a radically pro-slavery document;" and
- said the Word of God is 100 percent wrong on human sexuality.

The Southern Poverty Law Center is an interesting group of people. This organization uses a facade of legitimacy from having the word "law" in its title but has nothing to do with law. The main function of the organization was revealed by Mark Potok, director of "intelligence" at SPLC in his statement, "Sometimes the press will describe us as monitoring hate crimes and so on. I want to say plainly that our aim in life is to destroy these groups, to completely destroy them."

They were the ones who tried, unsuccessfully, thank God, to saturate the public school system with an entry-level program designed to promote "diversity" called "Mix It Up" day. Their goal was to force the acceptance of homosexuality into public schools at all levels. They believe the earlier the better.[18]

They were reprimanded by several school administrators after listing participating schools on their website because they falsely listed the schools as participants without authorization or permission.

A quote straight out of Saul Alinsky's book, *Rules for Radicals*, is an obvious tenet of the organization. Rule 12 states, "Pick the target, freeze it, personalize it, and polarize it. Cut off the support network and isolate the target from sympathy. Go after people and not institutions. (This is cruel but very effective. Direct, personalized criticism and ridicule works.)"[19]

"My enemies' mouths do not tell the truth; in their hearts they want to destroy others. Their throats are like open graves; they use their tongues for telling lies. God, declare them guilty! Let them fall into their own traps. Send them away because their sins are many; they have turned against you" (Psalm 5:9-10).[20]

How can we forget what happened to Chick-fil-A? I really never went to Chick-fil-A much until after the big hullabaloo. Funny thing is, the media's misquotes or at least changing the meaning, topic, and misinformation were to blame for the whole thing. Dan Cathy, president of Chick-fil-A, was interviewed by Ken Coleman on Ken's radio show. The original interview was regarding the growing problem of "fatherlessness" in our society today. It really was not about homosexuality at all. The context was changed by the media to make the infamous quote by Mr. Cathy in which he states that our culture is "inviting God's judgment" to be about homosexuality.[21]

The Obama-nation is part of the revolution that does not want to follow the laws of nature or the Constitution based on those laws. They are creating or adopting their own ideas of laws, and the part of society, the enemy, the extremists like myself who want to keep to the laws that we consider absolute and concrete, like our rights, and cannot be changed, they want to silence.

In order to keep to our Judeo-Christian ethics, moral values, and principles, we will have to become the target of intolerance and hatred. But we cannot give up our God-given right to practice our Christian traditions outside of our homes, remain silent about what we consider upright and realistic, stop defending ourselves and our family's lives, stop defending our reputation and business practices, or stop trying to limit our exposure to sinfulness and debauchery of the world into which we were born.

Change needs to come, but I do not believe it is the change prescribed by the Obama-nation. Hope is needed, but not the whimsical, fanciful type of hope that is more like a wish, but real hope. Not an uncertain expectation or desire that we see as looking forward to a desirable but remote possibility. A desperate hope is what we need. We need a hope of certainty as if our lives depended on it. One with a confident expectation. One with a promise.

"We know that in everything God works for the good of those who love Him. They are the people He called, because that was His plan. God knew them before He made the world, and He decided that they would be like His Son so that Jesus would be the firstborn of many brothers" (Romans 8:28-29).[22]

I have heard some signs of hope.

In Michigan, there is the case of Julea Ward, a counseling graduate student kicked out of Eastern Michigan University due to her religious beliefs after she asked the Counseling Department to refer a gay couple having relationship issues to a more appropriate counselor. The University wanted Ward to go to a reeducation camp, but she refused to have her religious beliefs remade, and that resulted in her being kicked out.[23] The case had to go to the 6th Circuit United States Court of Appeals, where the opinion was obviously from a higher power, so to speak.

The Circuit Court sent the case back for trial saying, "A reasonable jury could conclude that Ward's professors ejected her from the counseling program because of hostility toward her speech and faith. A university cannot compel a student to alter or violate her belief systems based on a phantom policy as the price for obtaining a degree. Tolerance is a two-way street. Otherwise, the rule mandates orthodoxy, not anti-discrimination."

Unfortunately, homosexuality is not the end of this. The gay movement has pried open Pandora's box and has gained footing with the aid of the Obama-nation to pry it open even further. I believe the next agenda they want to unleash on this nation is centered on pedophilia. Apparently, some folks are tired of feeling guilty about this, too.

The freedom of speech has always been a highlight for the Obama-nation when it is leaning toward their favor. The problem with their idea of "freedom of speech" is that they believe that everyone has to listen to their speech whether they like it and agree with it or not. We may all have the right to free speech, but we also have the right to listen—or not listen—and have the right to make that decision for our offspring, who depend on us as parents for, well, everything, including exposing them to what someone has to say.

A good example of this is the American Library Association's (ALA) highly publicized "Banned Book Week." This is when some in the library profession exploit the idea that some parents, especially Christian or conservative parents, are unfair and inept when questioning the value or appropriateness of certain material available to children. The ALA is a major source for undesirable values and disinformation tools to prevent traditional and wholesome values from getting much shelf space in libraries.[24]

The American Civil Liberties Union (ACLU), on behalf of the ALA, has gone as far as promoting tolerance and openly promoting homosexuality by trying to discourage schools from using filters to prevent children from accessing objectionable websites.

Robert Knight, a *Washington Times* columnist, spoke to an ACLU representative; when he asked her about child pornography, he said that she shrugged and acknowledged that it was illegal but, with a knowing smile, added, "for now, but it won't be for long." Knight said this while serving on a panel debating whether public funds should be used for "art." Activists no longer like to call it pedophilia. They prefer "intergenerational intimacy" or "minor attraction." This is the epitome of political correctness.

This is what we end up with when people remove or omit standards of right and wrong that have guided this nation for over two hundred years, leaving it up to the whims of corrupt and lost souls. Why else would they want to teach things such as incest, adult-child sex, child abuse, sadomasochism, and sorcery to our kids? Are these what they consider art?

What is the best way to institute a new social order that is devoid of godly influence? Why else would Obama appoint Kevin Jennings, a longtime radical homosexual activist and founder of the Gay, Lesbian, Straight Education Network, to the Office of Safe and Drug Free

Schools?[25] This organization compiled a recommended reading list of books to promote sex to, with, and of children.

Jesus used the example of "accepting" and "receiving" a child with the "accepting" and "receiving" of Him. To come to Him as a child would . . . humbly. In this matter, He was teaching His disciples to be trusting, accepting, and without pretense as a child. It also showed that Jesus saw children as special members of the community. Teaching and guiding the hearts and minds of our children by principle and example is paramount to their development. Seeing the truth but being taught lies creates a puzzling environment and anger. It can cause a lifelong struggle with spiritual confusion.

"The good people who live honest lives will be a blessing to their children" (Proverbs 20:7).[26]

The United States is now being the global sex cop, as I mentioned in chapter 10, intervening in the workings of other nations where homosexuality is discouraged and providing special provisions for homosexuals and those with alternate lifestyle choices to gain special admittance to the United States.

Peter LaBarbera, president of Americans for Truth about Homosexuality, an Illinois organization active in revealing the agenda behind the homosexual-bisexual-transgender movement, made this observation about the Obama-nation's mission statement called the Presidential Memorandum—International Initiatives to Advance the Human Rights of Lesbian, Gay, Bisexual, and Transgender Persons.[27] These are some of its tenets:

- taking action to promote the fundamental human rights of LGBT persons everywhere
- intervene in other nations where the homosexual lifestyle choice is at risk
- strengthen existing efforts to effectively combat the criminalization by foreign governments of LGBT status or conduct
- expand efforts to combat discrimination, homophobia, and intolerance on the basis of LGBT status or conduct
- provide access to the United States to LGBT refugees and asylum seekers at all stages of displacement

- enhance efforts by the Departments of State and Homeland Security to ensure that LGBT refugees and asylum seekers have equal access to protection and assistance
- train federal workers to help LGBT members in their desires
- train agency personnel in foreign aid to offer support for the alternative sexual lifestyle choices and respond as Obama expects

So, from where does the idea that homosexuality is a human right that deserves special protections against "discrimination" originate? How is protecting bad decisions from moral discernment a favorable practice? Should not all sexual behavior be discretionary and weighted by preference and selection? Why eliminate the element of morality?

There is no evidence that homosexuality is inherited or has a genetic or biological origin. There is no gay gene. Race and ethnicity are inherited, but homosexuality is not. It is a behavior. A choice. A seduction and indulgence that can become addictive.

If homosexuality were genetic, it could only be for one generation because homosexuality is anti-re-creational. They do not produce offspring. And how would it be possible to change their "orientation?" A seven-year, peer-reviewed study proved that a change in orientation can and frequently does happen. Mark A. Yarhouse, a psychologist at Wheaton College, and coauthor Stanton L. Jones published the study. The study reported that, over this time period, 23 percent converted to heterosexuality and 30 percent just changed to a stable behavioral chastity with significant disassociating themselves from a gay orientation.[28]

Why do Obama and the Obama-nation need to discredit the science of human sexuality and genetics and establish a new-age system of reality?

"God's anger is shown from heaven against all the evil and wrong things people do. By their own evil lives they hide the truth. God shows his anger because some knowledge of him has been made clear to them. There are things about him that people cannot see ... His eternal power and all the things that make him God. But since the beginning of the world those things have been easy to understand by what God has made. So people have no excuse for the bad things they do" (Romans 1:18-20).[29]

The Obama-nation even passed a "hate crimes" bill to protect select groups by increasing the penalties of any actions taken by any person which are, in any way, provoked into any action, including verbal abuse. Even things I have mentioned in this book would probably qualify. Protected groups include all paraphiles of any kind, homosexuals, formerly in that category, and minorities. Paraphilia is a condition of intense sexual arousal and gratification to atypical objects, situations, or individuals and is more common among men than women. HR 1913, called the Local Law Enforcement Hate Crimes Prevention Act of 2009, was not about stopping crime but was drafted to give "actual or perceived" sexual preference or "gender identity" the same legal status as race and was attached to a "must-pass" defense appropriations bill.[30]

Opposition from across the aisle expressed disdain over the inclusion of paraphiles. They tried to have veterans included instead, but the Obama-nation unanimously voted in paraphiles and excluded veterans.

If the debasement and weakening of America's moral fiber is not Obama's main ambition, then does he have special plans to use these poor souls for his own means? An army, perhaps? A political army that is predictable and easy to motivate and control. An army that is grateful and loyal to Obama and apathetic to our Constitution. An army that has no conscience, devoid of "right" reason and perspective. An army that thinks the kingdom of God hates them. An army that thinks evil deeds are right and righteous deeds are wrong. An army that is protected from Godly advice and wisdom, but is still protected when they are hateful and discriminatory. An army that brands evil as good and good as evil.

Not too long ago I would have laughed at this, but why else the push to have gays serving openly in the military along with females in combat positions? Servicemen and servicewomen who cling to traditional biblical and family values will become a shrinking minority over the next few years.

Legislation to restore religious freedom to military chaplains, to reverse Obama's decision, has been introduced because it created an "unconstitutional" divide that protects the rights of this special interest group and their supporters but disciplines those who choose to adhere to biblical standards of behavior. These are the same Biblical standards that are the standards that are found in the laws of nature and what I consider to be normal behavior.

The current military policies that are being implemented are causing many traditional members of the military to resign or opt out of service, especially chaplains. They have to choose between going against their religious convictions and performing same-sex marriages or removing themselves from being subjected to it.

This insanity was made, I believe, by the strategic inroad and the core basis for the homosexual crusade when the American Psychiatric Association (APA) made the decision to remove homosexuality from the list of mental defects in its Diagnostic and Statistical Manual of Mental Disorders back in 1973.[31]

I believe the declassification of homosexual behavior as an abnormal psychiatric behavioral disorder is what is fueling this movement to promote it as normal. It is the nucleus of the whole movement. Why there was not an extreme outrage heard and an assertive effort to expose the destructive nature of this decision by the moral majority, I do not know. If homosexual behavior is normal, then "if it feels good, do it" will soon be found acceptable behavior. Limitations, self control, mental health, psychological ramifications, boundaries, and morality be damned. Anything goes.

Dr. Judith Reisman, an American conservative writer and commentator, with a PhD in communications, and visiting professor of law at Liberty University, attended a symposium held by the "minor-attracted people" advocacy group B4U-ACT that was proposing that pedophilia should be removed from the APA's list, too, in order to spread accurate information on the subject.[32]

Dr. Reisman was the principal expert investigator for a US Justice Department study on child sex abuse. She pointed out that pedophilia advocates are using the same strategy that was successfully employed to make homosexuality a classroom subject for small children in the nation's public schools. Their campaign featured doctors and psychiatrists who seek to normalize and be sympathetic to sexual activity between adults and children of almost any age.

How will we combat this when even the National Education Association (NEA) has helped fund the homosexual agenda. This teacher's union is a big supporter of the Gay, Lesbian and Straight Education Network (GLSEN) and its human rights campaign. Christian teachers have become concerned that their union dues are being used to support activist groups that promote antibiblical lifestyles and have opted out of the union.

I recently read a book called *Only One Mommy* by Rena M. Lindevaldsen, Esq.[33] I wanted to grasp a better understanding of what transpires when children are involved, through adoption, into an environment based on an antiprocreation sodomitical relationship. This book did not let me down.

It is the story of Lisa Miller and her trials and tribulations of overcoming the lie of homosexuality and the depravities that are spawned from it, mainly a heartbreaking custody battle. If one needs to first have "right reason" to beget wisdom and wisdom to beget justice, then the state of Vermont is surely not the place to look for it.

Miller and her same-sex civil union partner became the parents of a little girl after Miller was artificially inseminated and became pregnant in Vermont. They divorced, and all hell broke loose, and I am not using that term in an allegorical way. I mean it literally. She had to eventually escape the United States, after undergoing agonizing court proceedings and the laws that protect shameful and nefarious behavior, to protect herself and her own biological child.

Miller's former lesbian partner sued Liberty University and Thomas Road Baptist Church in Lynchburg, Virginia, for allegedly helping Miller flee the United States, which was completely unfounded. A Mennonite pastor was convicted of helping Miller. God bless him.

If events such as that were not enough to see the error of our ways in allowing the persistence of this breach in morality, there is evidence that some Muslim clerics are saying that sodomy is acceptable behavior also, that is, if it is for jihad purposes. In a previous chapter and in the Arabic word glossary, I made note of the word *Muruna,* which is when the Muslim tenets of faith are denied or disregarded for the purpose of jihad to gain the trust of one's enemy. Unfortunately, there is another way this could be applied. It was also suggested that they would find it acceptable if it were for increasing the carrying capacity of certain hiding places in the body cavity for a bomb. All I have to say is good luck with this one, Transportation Security Administration (TSA).

I pray and ask God what it is that we need to do to achieve His forgiveness. Repentance was the answer. But who is listening?

"Then if my people who are called by my name are sorry for what they have done, if they pray and obey me and stop their evil ways, I will hear them from heaven. I will forgive their sin, and I will heal their land" (2 Chronicles 7:14).[34]

After finding out all of this, I understand why homosexuals and all others who engage in alternative sexual behavior were once considered to have a mental disorder. Indulging corruption of the soul can alter one's mind, one's physical health and, apparently, one's physical appearance. This is, perhaps, what makes it so hard for them to turn away from it.

Why else would a man trying to dress like a woman with exposed bra straps and a spaghetti-strap top be considered a perfectly normal-thinking person? Especially when this man shows up at work at a school cafeteria to serve kids lunch. That is what happened at Sierra Sands Unified School District in Ridgecrest, California.[35] Is this the kind of role model we want for our children?

Parents were stunned. After seeking legal advice, they found that a Senate bill (SB 58) was also responsible for mandating that schools promote transgender, bisexual, and homosexual historical figures. It also uses all social science curriculum, including history books and other instructional materials, to teach children as young as five years old not only to accept but also to endorse transgenderism, bisexuality, and homosexuality. The Obama-nation's labor laws protected this man, and he was free to express his sexual deviance at the school under California state law.

Another example of how our schools are being affected by this distorted view comes from the Howell Public School District in Howell, Michigan. In October, 2010, a teacher, Johnson "Jay" McDowell, told a student to remove a Confederate flag belt buckle because he was offended by it.[36] The student pointed out an obvious hypocrisy over the teacher's promotion of homosexuality that might be offensive to students.

The teacher, being the head of the school's organized labor union of instructors, asked the student what his feelings on homosexuality were, and the student said it offended him. The teacher ordered the student out of the classroom and threatened him with suspension.

Erin Mersino, of the Thomas More Law Center (TMLC), was the senior trial counsel for the student. Richard Thompson, president and chief counsel of the TMLC, stated, "The purpose of our lawsuit was to protect students' constitutional rights to free speech, defend religious liberty, and stop public schools from becoming indoctrination centers for the homosexual agenda." In a report by the American Freedom Law Center (AFLC) on this case, it was stated, "The school district has promoted the concept that religious opposition to homosexuality is equivalent to bullying, hate speech, and homophobia in order to eradicate such opposition." The federal lawsuit was filed against the teacher by the Thomas More Law Center on December 14, 2012, after the suit against the school district was dismissed. Federal District Judge Patrick J. Duggan of the Eastern District of Michigan was the presiding judge.

Many cases were cited by the court, such as the following: "students do not shed their constitutional rights to freedom of speech or expression at the schoolhouse gate."

With homosexuals now able to serve openly in the military, the gay rights movement's next move is probably to end the armed forces' ban on "transgenders." Now can you imagine the image this will present in the eye of the enemy?

The news seems to be a constant current of the bizarre when the topic of homosexuality is concerned, and Washington, DC, news is no exception. It seems our capital is quickly moving toward becoming the gay capital of the world due to Executive Order 13583, signed by Obama without fanfare, that makes it a goal to hire people who reflect his ideals of "diversity and inclusion." The Obama-nation describes it as "a commitment to equal opportunity, diversity, and inclusion."[37]

Obama's Office of Diversity and Inclusion, an office inside the Office of Personnel Management, is now setting a new standard for recruiting, hiring, and retaining current federal workers and is tapping into the global community to hunt for workers that also share Obama's ideas of diversity and inclusion.

I concur with Peter LaBarbera when he said, "Who knew when Reagan was talking about being a shining city on the hill the city would turn out to be Sodom" . . . on fire.

The Office of Personnel Management is pursuing an agenda to "institutionalize equality in the nation's largest workforce," referring to government employees, not only in Washington, but in all government or public positions nationwide. The director of the office, John Berry, has nothing but praise for Obama's strategy. He pointed out that the Obama-nation has treated this issue not as an issue, but as a priority.

People did not think it was important to have a true knowledge of God. So God left them and allowed them to have their own worthless thinking and to do things they should not do. They are filled with every kind of sin, evil, selfishness, and hatred. They are full of jealousy, murder, fighting, lying, and thinking the worst about each other. They gossip and say evil things about each other. They hate God. They are rude and conceited and brag about themselves. They invent ways of doing evil. They do not obey their parents. They are foolish, they do not keep their promises, and they show no kindness or mercy to others. They know God's law says that those who live like this should die. But they themselves not only continue to do these evil things, they applaud others who do them. (Romans 1:28-32)[38]

Chapter 17

The Antisanctity of Life Delusion

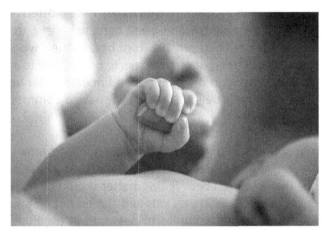

New human life

I personally have never faced the choice of terminating a pregnancy. It was not even a consideration. I can only image that a decision like that would come from an intense emotional act of fear and panic. I find it hard to conceive that it could be a cavalier and casual routine. The callousness involved is beyond my mental ability. Both my two children were welcome additions to our family unit, and I am proud of both to this day. My husband and I were married for several years before we got started on enlarging our family. Both children were planned, and, yes, I used birth control.

I believe preventing pregnancy and aborting a baby are not even close to being the same thing. As a creature that has the potential to procreate, with the proper help from a counterpart, of course, the management of the enumerated products of myself and my choice counterpart, I believe, should come with prudent regulation. To me, it is just mere common sense and self-governance. I also believe, if God's purpose was for me to have more than just two children, I would, because contraception does not always work.

This is the true choice—to regulate or not to regulate the chance of pregnancy—not the choosing to destroy a life already in progress to rectify a deed.

Some in the Christian community believe contraception is a sin. I do not agree with them. I have read the Bible on this subject with an open mind and heart, and I have not found evidence to prove it or disprove it. However, I can see the path onto which they have plotted their trek. I also believe they have a right, a God-given right, to believe, to interpret, and to practice their faith in private, in public, in their work, in their businesses, and speak freely about it to me, to others, and to each other because, if I were wrong in my belief, then I need to hear upon what principle they base their belief. After all, we have a common form of reference.

Using contraception is, in my opinion, exercising self-governance or self-regulation because my self-discipline and self-restraint have not always proved to be the greatest. I believe this matter should be no exception, since producing new life is so precious and should not be taken lightly, and considering there are volumes of passages in the Bible praising self-governance.

Contraception was quite the surprise issue of the 2012 election campaign when Rick Santorum was asked about it during the questioning in one of the many Republican debates. It was the first time he was confronted with the idea of it being an issue with anyone. He was stunned, and, quite frankly, so was I, along with everyone else on the stage, except for the interrogator, that is. We all found out later that it was thrown out there for the candidates to stumble over because the opposition wanted to bring it to the forefront in just that way. It was very clever.

There was no wonder that the Republican candidates were blindsided by this because Republicans were not participants in the construction and the passing of the Obamacare legislation requiring that employers provide health insurance for employees, including contraceptives and the drug "RU-486" that induces abortion. The FDA approved its use in pregnancies until the seventh week of pregnancy.

The question was directed to Rick Santorum, in particular, because of his open expression of his Catholic faith. This is my assumption. This was the beginning of the strategy derived by the Obama-nation that became labeled as a "war on women." In reality, it was a calculated assault on freedom of religion.

I believe only God knows the absolute, true condition of a person's heart. We make judgments, as God directs us to, based on external criteria: what one believes, how one behaves, and the way one appears. God sees beneath the surface to the heart of the matter. God sees a person's inner thoughts, emotions, will, and the sacred sphere within the core self—the soul. It is that which speaks directly with God and is subject to divine revelation, influence, and activity.

I also believe an evil force or void brought on by the rejection of God has an ability to fill the human heart, too. It does it through the allure and exploitation of our selfish nature and weaknesses and our never-ending pursuit to justify our actions. In order to convince ourselves we are not guilty of things, we project an acceptable image, and as a result, this evil force causes us great harm. This enables us to fool the masses and maybe even ourselves, but there is one who sees all, that cannot be fooled. Evil and sin walk hand in hand guiding us toward our destruction.

What better way to bring about the demise of mankind than to persuade us to destroy ourselves, our offspring, and each other. Unlike God, we elevate the life of one over another. A biblical view would call us to weigh each life as valuable before God, and to be responsive as God is to the needs of women in medically critical pregnancies and their unborn children.

Abortion has been the subject of heated debate for quite some time now. Is it murder? Does the Bible recognize the fetus as a living person? Does a woman have the right to kill her baby just because she does not want it? I believe these are moral issues, not social issues as many of the pro-choice advocates prefer to present it.

A strong implication can be drawn from several passages in the Bible that God's involvement in our lives does not begin at birth. God is shown to be "active" with the forming, constructing, and developing of our bodies in the womb and even tells us He knew us before the womb. In this sense, the development of the fetus may be seen as one stage along the way in the realization of God's design.

Even though the Bible does not address abortion directly, I believe it was not necessary because the sixth commandment, "Thou shall not murder," directly refers to any and all human beings, no matter at what stage of life.

"You made my whole being; you formed me in my mother's body. I praise you because you made me in an amazing and wonderful way. What you have done is wonderful. I know this very well. You saw my bones being formed as I took shape in my mother's body. When I was put together there, you saw my body as it was formed. All the days planned for me were written in your book before I was one day old" (Psalm 139:13-16).[1]

The condition of our heart is seen through what we believe, what we do, and how we feel about topics that arise, whether we are sincere, good, bad, or indifferent. Is it open or closed, contrite or stubborn, soft or hard?

The condition of our heart reveals itself in the argument over whether we should be able to kill newborn babies under the guise that they are "morally irrelevant" and are no different from aborting a late-term fetus.

An article published in the *Journal of Medical Ethics* addresses the question of whether a newborn baby is an actual person and would have a "moral right to life." Another question that this group of ethicists muddled over was if parents should be able to have their baby killed if it turns out to be disabled when it is born.[2]

The journal's editor, Professor Julian Savulescu, director of the Oxford Uehiro Centre for Practical Ethics, accused a few indignant individuals that responded to this article with offensive and threatening feedback as "fanatics opposed to the very values of a liberal society."

I am not an advocate for abusive and irrational rants, but someone who steps into the domain of emotion and passion should expect contention. When you drive off that cliff, you have already lost the argument. The part that drew my attention was the "values of a liberal society." From whence do these values come and who is the author?

The article was entitled "After-birth abortion: Why should the baby live?" It was written by the professor's two former associates, Alberto

Giubilini and Francesca Minerva. They argued that "the moral status of an infant is equivalent to that of a fetus in the sense that both lack those properties that justify the attribution of a right to life to an individual."

The goal of the *Journal of Medical Ethics* was not to present the truth or to promote someone's moral view, it said, but to present a reasoned argument based on widely accepted premises.

So truth is not a widely accepted premise?

The truth is murder is the unlawful, premeditated killing of another human being. The prohibition against murder may be the most widely shared moral principle across cultures and religions around the globe. I believe human life is a gift of God to be cherished and protected, and so murder is an act against God. However, even people who do not acknowledge God's existence still consider murder to be wrong.

I have a question for this group of academic ethicists: Why is the desecration of all that we Christians believe God has created, promised, and holds dear at the center of their targeted deconstruction? Who are they to self-appoint themselves as the morality lawmakers and determine which life is legitimate and which life is not?

One critic of the article, Dr. Trevor Stammers, director of medical ethics at St. Mary's University College, in reference to the term "after-birth abortion" said, "This is just verbal manipulation that is not philosophy. I might refer to abortion henceforth as antenatal (prenatal) infanticide."

On a positive note, the journal stated that it would consider publishing an article asserting that, if there were no moral difference between abortion and killing newborns, then abortion, too, should be illegal.

With the pro-abortion Obama-nation and the anti-abortion conservatives doing what they do, what is in the future for each side of this issue? If the pro-abortionists keep doing what they see as the environmentally friendly, convenient, and politically correct thing by aborting their children, supporting abortion and same-sex marriage for others, they may just be instrumental in their own demise.

I found the perfect term for this. I became familiar with the term *reductio ad absurdom* ("reduction to the absurd") whereby a proposition is disproved by following its implications logically to an absurd consequence.

In the book *The Rise of Christianity*, author Rodney Stark comments "that Christian prohibition of abortion and infanticide contributed to the success of the new religion . . . a superior birthrate also contributed to the success of the early church."[3]

"Do not be fooled: You cannot cheat God. People harvest only what they plant. If they plant to satisfy their sinful selves, their sinful selves will bring them ruin. But if they plant to please the Spirit, they will receive eternal life from the Spirit" (Galatians 6:7-8).[4]

One of the most highly promoted organizations championed by the Obama-nation is the Planned Parenthood Federation of America (PPFA). According to an annual report covering the period from July 1, 2009, to June 30, 2010, the PPFA is America's premier abortion mega-industry, which received government health services grants and reimbursements totaling $487.4 million in taxpayer funds.[5]

When compared to previous annual reports, there was a steady increase in the number of abortions performed at its clinics, ranging from 289,750 abortions in 2006 to 329,445 abortions in 2010. Funding increased from $363.2 million in 2009 to $487.4 million in 2010.

It also showed that adoption referrals to other agencies totaled 4,912 in 2007 to just 841 in 2010, a decrease of 82.8 percent. The latest annual report used, claimed that abortion services make up 3 percent of "medical services," but PPFA states it served three million people and performed 329,445 abortions, which showed that 11 percent of its customers received an abortion.

The annual fiscal year report for 2009-10 showed that PPFA's assets topped $1 billion as of June 30, 2010. This explains why Marjorie Dannenfelser, president of the Susan B. Anthony List, calls PPFA an "abortion giant." She believes, as I do, that having assets that are valued over a net $1 billion signals the time for PPFA "to end its reliance on taxpayer dollars."

The Obama-nation, however, "are unwilling to answer to the pro-life American majority that wants out of this business," Dannenfelser said, considering it was earlier reported that the organization gets 90 percent of its funding from the federal government (that would be us) or from Medicaid.

The United States Government Accountability Office (GAO) reported that Planned Parenthood Federation of America could not find some $300 million of taxpayer funds given to it by the federal government from 2002 through 2008. The report also revealed that the budget for it, back when the federal government still passed budgets, has gradually increased each year beginning in 1990 no matter who was in office. It still increased even when a pro-life president was in office.[6]

Taxation without representation. I believe that applies here. Federal taxes being sent to organizations such as this without proper explanation, disclosure, and without petition by the ignorant electorate as to actually what the money will be used for, is what I see.

David Green, the owner of Hobby Lobby, one of the nation's largest arts and crafts retailers, and a faithful Christian, has his head and his business on the chopping block because of his faith.[7] Faith is now penalized, not rewarded, like in the times that caused the origin of this country.

Green will face heavy penalties by the United States Department of Health and Human Services for the mandate that requires coverage of contraception, sterilization, and abortion-inducing drugs, with no deductibles or copay, in the employer-provided health insurance coverage. Green says his faith and conscience will not permit him to comply. This is coming from the 2010 Patient Protection and Affordable Care Act (Obamacare).

Green wrote, "Being Christians, we don't pay for drugs that might cause abortions, which means that we don't cover emergency contraception, the morning-after pill, or the week-after pill. We believe doing so might end a life after the moment of conception, something that is contrary to our most important beliefs. It goes against the biblical principles on which we have run this company since day one." Refusing to comply with the new law could cause $1.3 million *per day* in fines.

In order to impose a government-controlled health-care system such as Obamacare, the right to life will have to be established because of the dramatic and devastating effect that Obamacare will have on it in its evaluation of how it will manage its operation. I am not a fan. But for now, my focus is still on the right of life, no matter one's stage of life, how one came to be, or whether a parent or both parents want that life or not. Life is precious and should not be cheapened by the whims, ideologies, apathies, or depravities to which this world and our country have succumbed.

When I read the preamble to the Declaration of Independence and read passages such as, "and to assume among the powers of the earth the separate and equal station to which the laws of nature and of nature's God entitles them, a decent respect to the opinions of mankind requires that they should declare the causes which impel them to the separation," I think of Mr. Green's dilemma.

A "decent respect" to his opinions from his fellow "mankind" is not being fulfilled here. And the "which impel them to the separation" of what is being imposed by an overreaching governmental apparatus of which he wants no part. Whatever happened to liberty and justice for all?

Another article from the *New American* exposed the hardships being passed down to Hobby Lobby and David Green, along with some other points of interest. It points out that even though the Roman Catholic bishops and institutions have been in the forefront of the legal and public relations battle against the mandate, the Hobby Lobby dilemma is a reminder that the issue is not exclusively a Catholic controversy. Hobby Lobby's CEO is a Baptist businessman and one who is unwilling to have the federal government define the limits of his Christian faith.[8]

The Obama-nation wants to dictate to the American people which direction our moral compass should point while crying "separation of church and state." But what represents the moorings of their moral belief system? What happened to the rule of law, the laws of nature, the laws of God or the Word of God? Where does their doctrine come from, and where does it lead?

And what about the people who practice what they preach? The article continued with more intrinsic rationale of the Obama-nation. It stated that the Obama-nation sees that if a religious entity, person, or thing is not all-inclusive and keeps to itself, but interacts with the general public and other faiths, it loses its "religious" identity and its rights of expressing its faith. Basically, the Obama-nation does not want and has determined a penalty for witnessing, or what we Christians call "spreading the Good News" or openly engaging with people of other faiths. They seem to think that this should be a violation of an organized religion's principles. They are against the "reaching out" of Christianity. They want it to cease and desist.

The mandate, announced on the eve of the January 22, 1973, *Roe. v. Wade,* the pro-abortion decision, was what got the war on the value of life and liberty started, but the war on new life and liberty globally began the day Obama became president. This can be traced back to the repeal of the "Mexico City" policy that forbade funds to go to any organization in another country that performs abortions. This happened just shortly after Obama's first term as president in January, 2009.

This goes along with the idea that taxpayers should pay for "a woman's right to choose," in other words, that those of us who see abortion as the murder of innocents will have to pay for the killing for those who do not. I mean, after all, if Americans are going to support abortion in other countries, then they should support it in our own, right?

Why is choosing to kill another human a "right?" Is inconvenience or not wanting to be a parent or not wanting to be bothered with pregnancy more important? Is this not the epitome of selfishness?

In essence, the 1973 *Roe v. Wade* decision applied the Constitutional right to life as after birth only, hence making the claim that abortion does not breach a person's right to life. States, then, cannot regulate first trimester abortions; states can regulate—but not ban—second trimester abortions, but states can ban third trimester abortions, and many have.

This is a perfect example of how judicial activism or legislating from the bench creates clashes with the law of nature and right reason and a whole host of illogical laws by the individual judges using their own moral leanings to make rulings that turn into laws rather than interpreting the law as it stands, as they should. Laws that are complicated, illogical, and hard to follow and understand are all that is put forward.

Can you remember the "conscience" exemption clause that President Bush Implemented? Obama announced his plans to eliminate it just one month into his presidency. The exemption allowed pro-life nurses and doctors working in hospitals that receive federal funds to refrain from participating in abortions or other "procedures" that they considered immoral.[9]

These are just a few examples of the "war on religious liberty" that has been turned upside down to be a "war on women." The Obama-nation has shown complete opposition to Judeo-Christian ethics, moral values, and principles and is attempting to coerce people of faith to violate their moral conscience and the teachings of our foundations. There should be no question of it in anyone's mind at this juncture. The Obama-nation will go and has gone to great lengths to undermine and attack religious liberty.

This is a huge step for the disregard of conscience by desensitizing doctors to the allegiance to doing only good. It muffles the practice of self-awareness and reflection, remorse, and diverts their efforts from pointing to right reason. Human-generated conscience is fanciful, versus conscience that is based on Judeo-Christian ethics and laws of nature.

There are unintended and unexpected consequences in the deviation from the rule of law and law of nature and, also, in implementing laws in direct opposition to them. For example, the Chinese government has been engaged in a one-child policy for quite a while, and they are now starting to realize the adverse effects of their country's policy. If a family can only have one child, most Chinese families opt for males. As a result, there are not enough women for men to marry.

Since the revolution of the Obama-nation began, we have gone from birth control and abortion as a matter of conscience and personal conviction that no one could impose on anyone else, to birth control and abortion as a human right that all women deserve and must get for free, that is, paid for by other people whether they approve of it or not.

President Obama, with great pride, made a statement celebrating the *Roe v. Wade* Supreme Court decision that has resulted in 54 million abortions. To remind everyone, this court decision overturned pro-life laws offering protection for unborn children in most states across the country, which made abortions, without reason, legal and virtually unlimited.

This is the statement Obama released:

> As we mark the 39th anniversary of Roe v. Wade, we must remember that this Supreme Court decision not only protects a woman's health (viewing pregnancy as a disease, disorder, or an unnecessary consequence to suffer) and reproductive freedom (viewing this freedom as the right to kill), but also affirms a broader principle: that government should not intrude on private family matters (viewing a decision to kill a baby as private family matters and not a moral issue). I remain committed to protecting (viewing the woman as the only one with the right to life) a woman's right to choose (choosing to kill) and this fundamental constitutional right (constitutionally unsupported lie). While this is a sensitive and often divisive (fatal to the developing fetus) issue—no matter what our views (especially the view of life being sacred), we must stay united in our determination to prevent (kill) unintended pregnancies (babies or miracles of life), support pregnant woman (convince them that killing the baby is the right thing to do) and mothers (those who choose life), reduce the need for abortion, encourage healthy relationships, and promote adoption (mixed messaging). And as we remember this historic anniversary, we must also continue our efforts to ensure that our daughters have the same rights (views about abortion), freedoms (freedom to kill), and opportunities (have unwed sex without the consequence of parenthood) as our sons to fulfill their dreams.[10] (All text in parentheses added by the author of this book.)

That day was a day of mourning for some of us. For others, it was a day of celebration. A day to celebrate the loss of tens of millions of unborn children by those who value *self* over life, love, and compassion. It was a day to celebrate the damage abortion does to a woman medically and physically, emotionally, and psychologically, and to relationships with friends, family, and with God. This kind of thing has to break His heart.

It was a day to mourn due to the culture of death that abortion had brought to our nation and to our world. A culture that believes death is a solution for those who are considered too old, too ill, too inconvenient, too stressful, or too troublesome. A culture moving in the direction that sees new life as an object or nuisance, subject to manipulation or disposal.

"Jesus sat down and called the twelve apostles to him. He said, 'Whoever wants to be the most important must be last of all and servant of all.' Then Jesus took a small child and had him stand among them. Taking the child in his arms, he said, 'Whoever accepts a child like this in my name accepts me. And whoever accepts me accepts the One who sent me'" (Mark 9:35-37).

Is it possible that the lack of respect for life by some of us today is what is contributing to the corruption of the innocent minds of our children? Do we now expect the acceptance from our offspring of selfishness, broken promises and vows, and callousness toward the termination of life based on convenience? It's the mixed message of conditional love. How does a parent make his or her child respect the life of others and help the child have respect for his own life if the mother, prior to or after his or her birth, justified a non-life-threatening abortion?

Gallup released the results of a new poll in May 2010 that showed a wonderful shift, though. The poll confirmed that America is moving more toward a pro-life elevation rather than pro-choice on abortion. Could this be the new normal for the United States? In 1996, 56 percent of Americans said they were "pro-choice" while 33 percent of Americans said they were "pro-life." That was a 23 percent pro-abortion majority. Now, with 47 percent of Americans saying they are pro-life and 45 percent saying they support abortion, we have a 2 percent pro-life majority. That might not sound like much, but that means public opinion has shifted 25 percent toward the pro-life side in the last fourteen years.[11]

So why has Obama done everything in his power to advance abortion and continue the pro-abortion legacy of the Supreme Court? He even named two pro-abortion justices, Elena Kagan and Sonia Sotomayor, to the Supreme Court. So why the push to expand abortions by authorizing abortion funding in various instances and decreasing funds for abstinence education? Why is Obama creating a moral values conflict where the government is dictating the standards of what is acceptable and what is not to religious organizations and Christian businessmen? I will let you decide.

I believe Obama and his Obama-nation have declared war on Judeo-Christian family values, the family unit, children, and self-government because it is the foundation of our Western civilization, and they see this as something that needs to be fundamentally changed.

Karl Marx, the father of communism, understood that the family structure needed to be eliminated in order for his ideology to succeed, too.[12] That is especially true for a structure where parents are accountable to God and children accountable to parents.

"Honor your father and your mother so that you will live a long time in the land that the Lord your God is going to give you" (Exodus 20:12).[13]

What remains of Western civilization is being sabotaged by statists who seek to alter the thinking of our children and make a mockery of the family unit as it was originally designed. This bizarre dream of a utopian kingdom resonates well with what I discussed earlier in this book— the United Nations' "Agenda 21" movement. This agenda wants to cap the number of people the planet can have. The Agenda 21 apologists believe that humans are the enemies to the planet, and they need to establish a system of population control.

The Obama-nation policies are playing right in with the "population control" agendas focused on world dominance, all under the guise of sustainability and caring for the masses. This is the true nature of the idea of humans being the number one negative influence of the plant or the global warming agency, the advocating for homosexual antiprocreation, abortion convenience, and the efforts to eliminate the means for self-defense. These are just the few that I have addressed in this book. There are others, such as the reduction of the availability of multiple energy resources.

In addition to Obama's naming of pro-abortion justices to the Supreme Court, he appointed Kathleen Sebelius as secretary of the Department of Health and Human Services. She is the one responsible for the implementation of Obamacare and its mandate and has an extensive pro-abortion record. That record includes, while governor of Kansas,

Sebelius supported abortion rights, vetoed pro-life legislation, and was a personal friend of abortionist and murder victim George Tiller.[14]

George Richard Tiller, MD, was a physician from Wichita, Kansas. He gained national attention as the medical director of Women's Health Care Services, one of only three clinics in the nation that provided late-term abortions at the time.

Dr. Tiller had preformed about sixty thousand abortions over a thirty-five-year period. He performed more than 250 late-term abortions in 2003 alone and had an average annual income of $1 million.

"Partial-birth" abortion is one of the methods used for late-term abortions. It induces a breech delivery and collapses the fetal skull before completing the delivery. This procedure is banned in twenty-four states, but pro-choice advocates have sought to overturn state laws with a federal ruling.[15]

An example of this was that in April, 2000, the Supreme Court rejected a Nebraska law banning partial-birth abortions. Later, in June, 2000, the Supreme Court said that the Nebraska ban was unconstitutional because it had no exceptions and barred second trimester abortions, also.

I have never considered what actually goes on in an abortion clinic, and I have a fairly wide threshold for what some folks would consider gruesome or grotesque. Being the mother to two rowdy boys, I've seen my share of gaping wounds and bloody messes. But I do not think I would have the stomach for an abortion clinic.

Kermit Gosnell, a seventy-two-year-old American abortion-providing physician, performed hundreds, maybe thousands, of abortions in West Philadelphia, surrounding suburbs of Bucks and Montgomery counties, and nearby states between 1972 and 2011. He stood trial for first—and third-degree murder, illegal prescribing of drugs, conspiracy related to corruption, illegal abortions, and related medical malpractice offenses.[16]

A grand jury recommended murder charges against Gosnell and several employees, with prosecutors seeking the death penalty. One of the murder charges was for the death of a forty-one-year-old Nepal immigrant who came seeking an abortion. Three of eight murder charges were thrown out, apparently because the judge had not heard sufficient evidence from prosecutors that the three babies were viable, born alive, and then killed.

In the article I read, the journalist tells of the appalling images he saw at the trial and what a 2011 grand jury report referred to as a "house of horrors." He said what he saw was "beyond any morbid Hollywood horror."

He described the display of tiny severed feet and hands in jars in the "procedure" room; how survivor babies' spinal cords were severed with scissors, called "snipping," then having their brains removed by suction, and then having their little bodies put in a waste bin; and an exhibit depicting a large baby in the fetal position, bloody, stuffed in a bin, with Gosnell joking about it being so large.

He tells of testimony given by one employee as to how digitalis was injected into the stomachs of the pregnant women to kill the babies so they would be born dead. This employee had been working at the clinic since she was fifteen years old and was medicating and administering injections to women under Gosnell's instruction, even though she was unqualified and unlicensed as a medical technician.

This witness described how the babies born alive had heartbeats and were moving and flinching and how some made baby sounds. She also described how filthy the floors, equipment, and beds were in the downstairs area where the poor women were treated.

In the article, J. D. Mullane pointed out how court staff had set aside three rows of seats to accommodate up to forty reporters, but he was the only one sitting in the reserved media area. A few other news outlets did show up, but none of them were as dedicated to the story. They came and went, claiming their resources were thin, and trial coverage was not gavel-to-gavel.

The media's blackout of daily reporting on this trial was appalling but not surprising. A court staffer told him, "If you're pro-choice, do you really want anybody to know about this?" as he motioned to the filthy medical equipment set up in the courtroom.

Whether it be for moral reasons or for health reasons, most doctors in Pennsylvania will not perform abortions after the twentieth week of pregnancy. Abortions after twenty-four weeks are illegal. It was estimated 40 percent of the second-trimester abortions performed by Gosnell were beyond the twenty-fourth week of gestational age, according to the grand jury. Testimony revealed these procedures were "too much to count," and the ones over twenty-six weeks were "very often." By the estimates provided, Gosnell performed at least four or five illegal abortions every week.

So when does human life begin? It seems one can find data to suppose whatever end results one is seeking. The courts often focus on viability, the point at which the fetus could survive outside the womb. Naturally, this would be about six months of gestation, but modern medical advances have pushed that back substantially. So, when *does* human life begin?

Trying to avoid the truth is where complications, unintended and unexpected consequences, occur, and problems arise. There is no question in my mind that human life begins at conception. That's why having sexual relations should be held in a higher regard than just having a good time out on the town or "getting lucky." Is that not why love and commitment should be a major factor? Otherwise, it is meaningless. One of the consequences is that the more bed partners you have, the less chance you have to be happy with just one. Ignorance is bliss. What you do not know, you do not miss. Having knowledge of another will cause you to compare and can cause resentment or regret. You will remember.

> God wants you to be holy and to stay away from sexual sins. He wants each of you to learn to control your own body in a way that is holy and honorable. Don't use your body for sexual sin like the people who do not know God. Also, do not wrong or cheat another Christian in this way. The Lord will punish people who do those things as we have already told you and warned you. God called us to be holy and does not want us to live in sin. So the person who refuses to obey this teaching is disobeying God, not simply a human teaching. And God is the One who gives us His Holy Spirit. (1 Thessalonians 4:3-8)[17]

Understanding and following the truth about the sanctity of life makes decisions and perspectives so much clearer and cleaner. Truth is a moral quality, and it speaks in a revealing way. It has open, uncovered, and authentic characteristics. It makes obstacles disappear and clears the fog of misperception, confusion, and the need to force its concepts. Complications are minimized, not increased, consequences are favorable, and everyone leaves with a sense of confidence and fulfillment that they are doing the right thing.

Whether the subject is abortion, contraception, stem cell research, cloning, reproductive technologies or surrogate mothers, the jumping off place, the place of origin, the common form of reference, needs to be the same. The law of nature and nature's God need to always be at the heart of these decisions. But the sanctity of life does not end with the creative ways to start a new life or end one.

The sanctity of life is a conviction to revere human life at all stages, including, capital punishment, self-defense, military engagement, the care for the elderly, our children, widows and orphans. This is why the right to life is considered a God-given inalienable right—a God-given human right. This was common knowledge among our Founding Fathers. A right that deserves and needs to be protected. Protection of that life is not against the right for anyone else to have a right to life, but for the right to exist and not be destroyed by anyone else.

God gave instructions about capital punishment immediately after the flood where God executed capital punishment directly to the world, except for Noah and his family. From that time forward, man would serve as God's instrument in protecting life by punishing those who took the life of another.

The following passage should have special meaning for those who believe they have the authority to determine who can live and who should die on their own:

"I will demand blood for life. I will demand the life of any animal that kills a person, and I will demand the life of anyone who takes another person's life. Whoever kills a human being will be killed by a human being, because God made humans in his own image" (Genesis 9:5-6).[18]

It is God's intent to put an end to evil as quickly and completely as possible in the interest of preserving life. In the New Testament book of Romans, restrictions were made for the enforcement of the death penalty to civil authorities and were never to be used for revenge or to punish a person that killed another accidentally. The only justification to take life is to save life that is being threatened.

The shedding of blood is always painful, whether it is through violence inflicted to do harm, in using deadly force to protect or preserve life, or in healing, as in surgery. Followers of Christ see Jesus's blood as if it was the healing act of a surgeon. His blood was shed in a procedure that removed our sins and brought about our full recovery. The Bible teaches that sin is death and that blood is life, and life is in the blood. If everyone can wrap his/her head around this simple concept, the laws would get much simpler, and we would be much safer.

So, protecting our life, our family's lives, and our neighbors' lives should be a given. Deadly force should be the last resort, but its availability should always be there. I personally see my life as my right to liberty and property. This brings us to the right to bear arms and how and when it is the right time to use them.

Chapter 18

The Right of Self-Preservation

9mm handgun

I believe in good gun control: always treat a gun like it is loaded; never point a gun at something you do not intend to shoot; use both hands, and aim small, miss small. This is what my husband and I taught our sons at a fairly young age with the aid of the Boy Scouts. As far as I know, they have no self-inflected gunshot wounds nor do any of their friends or acquaintances.

All kidding aside, we wanted them to know the proper use of and be familiar with firearms in the event they would need to defend themselves or us. We never had a problem giving our sons opportunities to exercise responsibility. My husband and I found that in order to be able to trust our sons, we needed to entrust to them things that required it. Sometimes, it was information, our car, or guns, and sometimes it was the debit card and PIN number. Sometimes, It was not always well received, but we believed the principle was established because we never sensed a lack of seriousness when it came to respecting the handling of firearms.

In a country where the four biblical virtues of hope, faith, love, and self-governance still are held in high regard, the protection and preservation of life, the right to live that life, was what Americans believed in at America's inception:

- hope of future, inevitable freedom, and a chance to live with independent, individual liberties
- faith in God in which we proudly proclaimed our trust as in our national motto and on our currency
- love for our fellow man both in and out of our country
- where self-governance, and self-discipline could be expected in order for harmony and good fellowship between neighbors

I do believe these virtues are still important to most Americans. Americans have not become too soft and spineless to still stand for these virtues. I believe we are prone to try to see the better side of folks and give the benefit of doubt. We want to think that some folks who make terrible decisions can still have good intentions. Even though that is not impossible, I do not believe that is something that happens very often. At some point, we have to realize that constant bad decisions are signs of something other than good intentions.

Both sides of this debate have what sound like solid arguments. Both fear the possibility of ulterior motives and hidden agendas. One side fears the unregulated access of firearms for the general public is an unacceptable threat to society, and the other side fears being made to rely on the mercy of the unmerciful, power-hungry controllers of society, without recourse or redress, is unacceptable. Government versus the common folk. It is a lack of confidence in each other's moral compass.

Has America become so traumatized by mistrust—become incapable of responsibility to provide safety and security for ourselves and our family, so self absorbed that we want the government to provide us with things we wish not to be bothered trying to achieve for ourselves, that we fail to see the tide of control encroaching upon our house that depends on these virtues within the hearts of the people to survive?

Wenzel Strategies, a public-opinion research and media-consulting company, showed in one of a series of polls that a complacency has developed, making fertile ground for government overreach to take root right here in America. The seeds are being planted daily and the progressive harvesters can almost taste the fruits of their labors.[1]

The telephone survey was done on a nationwide scale of registered voters on January 9, 2012, and had a margin of error of plus or minus 3.22 percentage points.

The poll exposed that many in this country are perfectly content with heavily-armed domestic law enforcement. I would not have a problem with this myself if they were not so heavily unionized, and as long as the everyday Joe can be heavily armed, too. There is balance. Power is equal to a certain degree. Whether there is trust or mistrust, this is a better position for everyone.

Until recently, even I had a disbelief that our government could do anything that would make me want to revolt. My revolt was to join the Tea Party movement, not take up arms. I do not want to be the one firing the first shot, nor do I recommend it for anyone else, so relax. Thanks to God, it has not come to that.

Apparently, many still have faith in our government to do the right thing for "we the people." Are these folks on the right side or the wrong side of history? Did any of these people learn anything in world history class or in the Bible?

Here are the results of the poll:

- 73 percent said they believe the local and state police should possess military-style equipment and armaments.
- 21 percent disagree.
- 59 percent said they did not think their local or state police would ever engage in any kind of martial law because that would restrict their personal freedoms.
- 51 percent said they could not think of any circumstance or action by government that would convince them to revolt against the government.
- 18 percent said they would revolt against the government if necessary.
- 47 percent said the Second Amendment is just for hunting and self-protection.
- 8 percent believe it is for the defense against tyranny.

- 10 percent said it serves both purposes.
- 69 percent said we need to keep the Second Amendment.
- 22 percent said we should ignore or repeal it.
- 70 percent said they believe a person who wants to do harm to another person but has no gun would just find something else to use.
- 18 percent said they believe such a person would just give up.
- 48 percent said gun bans were a bad idea.
- 39 percent said gun bans were a good idea.
- 56 percent said if there were a ban on guns, then crimes would then increase because they know potential victims cannot protect themselves.
- 40 percent said they favored banning ammo or taxing it into oblivion.
- 60 percent of Democrats said they favored the ammo ban or heavily taxing it.
- 55 percent said they supported a federal government registration of all firearms.
- 38 percent opposed a registry.

Wenzel said in regard to the poll results, "This is a testament to the longstanding stability that the country has now but also shows a risk of tyranny. If government leaders know the citizenry is unwilling to revolt, and they know their law enforcement agencies are well-equipped to put down any uprising with military-style weaponry, one could argue that those leaders might be tempted to impose tyranny on the country in some form or another."

He also referenced this being the downside of more than 230 years of government stability. The idea that our government could become so bad that it would be necessary to be overthrown is understandably hard. It is an uncomfortable and unnatural thought process for Americans. After all, the last fight we had was for a more constitutional future for the country by the federal government in the Civil War. They were the good guys. This would be quite a reversal.

The question is, do we see the same courage, morals and principles being championed by our leaders in Washington today that were held by our founders that brought them to risk their lives, reputations, and fortunes?

Some Americans find it hard to be objective and realistic about the nature and appetite of government. The government of today is not the same government of yesteryear where honor and integrity were the themes of the day. Some understand that all things change in time, but the problem is they only see what they want to see and not what is really there.

On a positive note, the survey did show that most Americans understand that a firearm is a tool and an efficient one, whether it is the hands of a person with the intent of doing good or not. It showed most Americans are more focused on the person holding the gun rather than on the gun itself. It also showed that Americans are aware of the exceedingly-high violent crime rates in cities such as Chicago and Washington, DC, in spite of the strict gun-control laws in those cities. Wise observations, in my opinion.

There is hope for us, yet.

Wenzel said it best when he said, "It is clear that Americans believe in the Second Amendment, but they also want something done to prevent another Sandy Hook shooting. They want more of an emphasis on the people who create these tragedies, just as national lawmakers and leaders appear ready to forget the evil people who wield these weapons in their race to attack the individual freedoms outlined in our founding documents."

This may explain the widespread belief that the Second Amendment, which gives Americans the right to hold and bear arms, is for self-protection and hunting only and not for fighting for our own freedom and liberty against a tyrannical American government.

The emotional and frantic legislation being drafted by the Obama-nation after the Connecticut tragedy, with the pretense that the initiatives would reduce gun-related violence, made it obvious that they were pushing for an alternative agenda and not really formulating legislation to prevent senseless killings. It was predictably the same strategy, same tactic, and same pattern that the Obama-nation uses consistently. Never let a crisis go to waste.

They stood against reason, and, by the grace of God, reason won . . . so far.

Other strategies, of course, are always available. The "brainwashing" strategy is always there, but it is much slower, and the Obama-nation is an instant gratification lot, and they know their time in power is limited.

Eric Holder in 1995, while a US Attorney for the District of Columbia, admitted in a speech to the Women's National Democratic Club that they wanted to "brainwash" people into not liking guns. He actually used that word. He also said he wanted gun owners to cower in the same way that smokers "cower outside of buildings."[2]

Here is part of the speech:

> What we need to do is change the way in which people think about guns, especially young people, and make it something that's not cool, that it's not acceptable, it's not hip to carry a gun anymore, in the way in which we've changed our attitudes about cigarettes. You know, when I was growing up, people smoked all the time. Both my parents did. But over time, we changed the way that people thought about smoking, so now we have people who cower outside of buildings and kind of smoke in private and don't want to admit it. And that's what I think we need to do with guns.

This explains their calling semiautomatic rifles "assault weapons." Thought association. The media is always quick to jump on board with the new nomenclature. Some media, in an attempt to promote the Obama-nation agenda, published the names and addresses of people who legally own guns, comparing them to dirty smokers and registered sex offenders.[3]

A representative at Gun Owners of America, Mike Hammond, brought up some items in the Obama-nation gun control revolution to the forefront, such as universal background checks. He challenged them on the criteria they want to use to identify who should be prohibited from buying guns, such as veterans who sought counseling for traumatic experiences.[4]

Seeking counsel for a problem we are having a hard time dealing with should not disqualify someone from owning a firearm, especially when those challenges are from the exposures to war or combat. Seeking guidance is being responsible. We all need guidance, whether we acknowledge it or not, and whether we seek it out or not. Wisdom is something to seek out and not believing you have all the answers. If that is the case, we are all in trouble, getting counseling or not.

The universal background check in many an eye is the play-by-play, move-by-move beginnings of the national gun registry. Hammond personally drafted the Smith Amendment to stop the creation of a national gun registry. The question is whether the Obama-nation will honor it, though. They seem fairly intent on finding a way to see a gun registry implemented.

A gun registry is the vehicle necessary to implement a government confiscation of weapons, Second Amendment wording of "shall not be infringed" being of no consequence. I am pretty confident their new Constitution for America will not have the right to bear firearms. I would not want to wager a bet on it, because I think I have an unfair advantage here.

Hammond asked the FBI about the statement that Obama made about how 40 percent of gun sales have no background checks. He was told that they, the FBI, shared no such statistics and were not sure where the Obama administration had acquired it. This is a tactic used by the Obama-nation to say what will advance their agenda with little or no fact to back it up because they know it is not necessary. Low—or no-information voters will not investigate the truth. Only individuals who have never tried to purchase a firearm could or would find it believable.

Our idea of the sanctity of life and the right to protect it from whatever threatens it on an individual basis is one of the things that sets America apart from the rest of the world. Those of us who have lived under this ideology of individual sovereignty and who hold life and the right to live it and protect it as sacred, will be a hard group to convince that someone else has our best interest at heart better than we do. People that do not hold to the same ethics, principles, and standards that we do.

So, how can the phrase "being necessary to the security of a free State" be misinterpreted along with "shall not be infringed" part of the Second Amendment? This is about as understandable as it gets. The only recourse they have is to discredit the whole thing all together.

After the shooting in Aurora, Colorado, and Sandy Hook Elementary School in Connecticut, each by individuals with severe mental issues, antigun advocates want everyone to believe that America is a nation infected with violent crimes and murders. They want us to believe that we are one of the most violent, if not the most violent, nations in the world, and that guns are our nemesis.

The facts prove to be an obstacle in their race to disarm America when a crisis arises that they want to use to their imagined advantage. The FBI's Uniform Crime Reports: Crime in the United States, Table 1, shows violent crimes have dropped between 1992 and 2011 from 757.7 per 100,000 people to 386.3 per 100,000 people. That was a reduction of 49 percent.

The Obama-nation wants us to believe that assault rifles are responsible for many of the homicides that occur and that they need to be banned. In 2011, "assault rifles" accounted for less than 3.8 percent of homicides committed by firearms and less than 2.6 percent of all homicides.

What is an assault rifle, anyway? Has anyone actually made a distinction between a regular rifle and an assault rifle? Are not all firearms assault weapons? I can testify that a pencil can be used as an assault weapon—twice in my lifetime. So what actually is an assault weapon by definition? It is something which incorporates anything that can be or has been used as a weapon?

(FYI, the "A" in AR-15 does not stand for "assault." The "A" stands for Armalite, the manufacturer. AR is the abbreviation for Armalite Rifle M-15, just to clear that up.)

Distrust of our fellow neighbor and the lack of confidence in our leadership and in parents of our youth have caused a rise in fear and anxiety. Good citizenship involves much more than simply obeying or disobeying the laws; it is a reflection of the moral standards we have through our behavior toward each other and toward our leaders.

"Also do good things for the city where I sent you as captives. Pray to the Lord for the city where you are living, because if good things happen in the city, good things will happen to you also" (Jeremiah 29:7).[5]

Our individual well-being is tied to the well being of the community in which we live. I believe that God is in control of human affairs and empowers authorities to rule. However, I do not believe that folks are to blindly submit to leaders or government without expecting a high level of accountability, especially in a country such as ours. Being a republic, with elected representatives and government officials, our government is a direct reflection of the people, or so it should be. The manipulation of faction is possible, though, without proper attention and understanding to legislative reform by we the people.

And what happens when our leaders do not follow the set rules of accountability? We are to speak out, petition, pay attention, vote for godly people, and render to Caesar what is Caesar's, and give to God what is His. We need to live by the rule of law, the law of love, and the love of law. We are to practice what we preach. We need to pray for our leaders and believe that right now is always the right time to do the right thing. Welcome to the full measure of God's grace. The more we try, the more we will experience it.

The violent crime problem that we suffer from in this country is not the fault of guns; it is the fault of the culture we have morphed into. It is a culture that loves self, the world, the things of the world, and the things in the world. It is a culture that avoids self-analysis, self-control, or reflection. It is a culture where the idea of confessing fault or failure is discouraged, and the default status is to divert blame when troubles arise. It is a culture where acknowledging, accepting, and being responsible for your choices, decisions, and mistakes is seen as being foolish or weak.

If we really want to reduce violent crimes, we need to stop blaming inanimate objects for the things we do wrong and start trying to clean up our act. Culture should be about growth and the improvement of the mind and relationships with others. Unfortunately, the Obama-nation and the unrealistic politics that they hold so dear are only reinforcing the disparaging culture and keeping the people trapped in it.

There is no better example of this disparaging culture than in the inner city of most large cities in the country. The FBI's Uniform Crime Reports: Crime in the United States, table 16, in 2011, showed the national total of violent crimes was 286.3 per 100,000, with 754.5 per 100,000 in cities with populations of 250,000 or more, with the highest rates corresponding to the areas that voted for Barack Hussein Obama.[6]

The comparisons to other countries are not much better. According to the Home Office Statistical Bulletin: Crimes Detected in England and Wales 2011/12, England, with a total population of 53,013,000, had 762,515 violent crimes that year. That is 1,361.6 per 100,000, with a rate three to five times higher than ours.

It is hard to understand why people in the inner city do not see the dangerous current they are swimming in and do not understand the senseless philosophies disguised as life preservers that are being thrown at them. The result is that they eventually become victims of their own complacency, ignorance, and disarmament.

The Obama-nation continues to perpetuate these vacuums of knowledge among the poor and discouraged with enslavement through entitlements for the gratitude of their votes. The Obama-nation has no desire or intention of dealing with the real issues because solving problems would create an environment for prosperity, and they would lose the gratitude of the poor. They want control and power only for the ones in control and with the power. I pray that their prey will come to see right reason versus their empty platitudes. Disarming the American people would mean that the criminals and the government would be the only ones armed.

The attempts by the Obama-nation to restrict our gun ownership have been staggering. Obama bypasses Congressional approval on this issue with executive orders—so far, twenty-three—to further cut down the access to guns by the average American. Not one of the orders would have prevented any of the tragedies. There has to be an ulterior motive.

Why make laws, executive orders, or whatever else, based on the actions of the criminally insane or mentally ill that have nothing to do with the criminally insane or mentally ill? Does he identify the majority of American gun owners to be in one of these two categories?

After the Newtown, Connecticut, Sandy Hook Elementary shooting, Obama promised immediate action, and then sent out Vice President Joe Biden to lead an advisory panel to come up with a plan.

THE ABOMINATIONS OF THE OBAMA-NATION

The recommendations from this panel were the inspiration for the executive orders, but something unexpected happened.

A lawsuit by Freedom Watch Director Larry Klayman asked a federal court to order the Obama Gun Control Task Force to halt its meetings and the implementation of any of its recommendations based on the task force compliance with the provisions of the Federal Advisory Committee Act.[7]

Klayman's case was brought in the Middle District of Florida, stating that the White House "had a duty to the American People to provide at least 15 days notice to the public of the meetings which Biden has been chairing to recommend so-called gun control measures following the tragedy at Sandy Hook Elementary School."

He also stated, "In their zeal to use this tragedy for political purposes and to try to quickly ram increased legislative gun control measures, if not gun confiscation and/or significant infringement through executive order, down the throats of the American people—in violation of Second Amendment rights—President Obama and Vice President Biden have thumbed their nose at the law and instead been holding closed door meetings with special interest lobbyists on both sides of the issue."

Biden was reported upon by CNS News in January 2013, comparing the restrictions that the Obama-nation wanted to place on gun ownership to auto safety regulations, such as air bags, under the pretense that it was in the best interest of the people by saving lives.[8]

Infringing on my rights as a law-abiding citizen to restrict my gun ownership when criminals and mentally-ill individuals, who disregard the law, are roaming free is the height of injustice. Regulate the offenders, not the air bags. Is the Obama-nation incapable of making the distinction between offenders and defenders? Why would they fear law-abiding citizens having the means of self-defense?

The Obama-nation seems to always target freedom and liberties to solve society's woes. They see themselves as the ultimate authority on deciding what rights we will have and who will get them. They are confusing rights with privileges and responsibilities.

Saving lives was the buzz phrase Biden used to tickle the ears of the unquestioning and uninformed. Seat belts have saved lives, but if the Obama-nation was really that concerned about saving lives and removing the risk of a dangerous situation, why not ban driving altogether? Too extreme, maybe? It would save lives. About forty-five thousand people die every year in automobile accidents. Driving or riding in an automotive vehicle is a risk I personally am willing to take. The benefit far outweighs the danger. Same goes for my sidearm.

And what about abortion? Stopping abortion would save about 1.3 million lives every year. So are they really concerned about saving lives or just making it appear that way? They clamor at the prospect of removing or restricting a liberty or freedom. They see them as nuisances to be kept at a minimum. They want them seen as an obligation, danger, or inconvenience to Americans.

Restricting and regulating our God-given rights will not save lives except for the lives of those that do not respect the right to life in the first place and could care less about the rule of law. So who do they want to protect?

Self-defense is embedded deep within our waves of American grain. Taxation without representation got us up in arms against King George, which resulted in our Declaration of Independence, but it was his attempt to confiscate our guns and gunpowder that caused us to take aim and shoot.

The revolution began on April 19, 1775. Seven hundred Redcoats, under the command of Major John Pitcairn, headed out to seize the arms from the residents of Lexington and Concord. That did not turn out so well for the British. And I dare say that if it happened once, it can happen again. Americans felt strongly about their right to keep and bear firearms then, just as they do now.[9]

"But when a long rain of abuses and usurpations, pursuing invariably the same Object evinces a design to reduce them under absolute Despotism, it is their right, it is their duty, to throw off such Government, and to provide new Guards for their future security" (Declaration of Independence).

One of the Obama-nation's gun control strategies came from an eleven-page proposal by the Center for American Progress. I wrote about this group earlier in this book. It recommended a full ban on the sale of assault weapons and magazines with a capacity for more than ten bullets. It also wanted legislation to require licensing and transfer restrictions on new and currently owned "assault" rifles and for the collection of more data on new gun owners to start a nationwide database.[10]

Mike Maharrey, communications director of the Tenth Amendment Center, made this point: "The Second Amendment was not created to give the right to keep and bear arms to the people. The founders acknowledged that the people already had those rights. The Second was intended to protect them by keeping the federal government off their backs."[11]

I could not agree more. I find Mr. Maharrey's assessment of the issue right on point. The right to keep and bear arms is an unalienable right we get from God, not from the government, and not from the Constitution. This right is a necessity to secure the right to life, to protect ourselves from entities that pose imminent danger to life, limb, family, or property. Why would the government fear this right if it is not posing imminent threat to those things?

The Obama-nation's efforts to create a national gun registry, ban certain weapons, mandate universal background checks, put limits on ammunition capacities, and gain unrestricted access to medical records is not for safety. That is not their focus. It is as plain as the noses on their faces.

Why does the Obama-nation have trouble with our Constitution? I believe I have tried to address that question. God only knows what other things they are up to that I have not mentioned in this book.

Steve Stanek, a researcher for the Heartland Institute, said there "was less violent crime in the country in the 1950s, before background checks, waiting periods or age limits to buy firearms, and before licensing of gun dealers and the existence of the Bureau of Alcohol, Tobacco, Firearms and Explosives. So if easy access to guns is a major cause of violence, why was there less violence in those days?"[12]

David Applegate, a policy adviser on legal affairs for the institute, presented some positive considerations that I believe have promise:

1. Whether protection of schoolchildren is best handled at the state, local, or national level

2. Whether the answers to school violence, in general, lie in treating causes or symptoms

3. Determining the causes of such violence

4. Whether different solutions would better fit different locations verses a one-size-fits-all national policy

5. Whether enough is being done to enforce existing laws against murdering people and unlawfully using weapons

6. What the experience of the 1994-2004 assault weapons ban has been

He added that the legislative body of our government was the best suited to make these decisions and not an ad hoc commission headed up by Vice President Joe Biden.

Violence and persecution come in a variety of forms, of which only some end up as murder. Guns are not the cause of these things. The Bible speaks of the apostles being treated as "the garbage of the world" and says that people cursed, hurt, and told lies about them (Corinthians 4:11-13). It also encourages believers with "when people insult you because you follow Christ, you are blessed" (Peter 4:14). This is when it is appropriate to turn the other cheek.

Our right to bear arms is a means to defend ourselves and others, not to provide an opportunity to commit murder. I believe the Obama-nation sees the opposite. They see the gun as a means to do evil and regard the gun as evil itself. If that were true, then money, property, motorized vehicles, the Internet, even a pencil, are evil, too. An inanimate object is not evil itself. There are only evil intentions. Guns are tools or instruments to give power to the weak—to even the playing field.

The Obama-nation sees guns only from the victim's perspective. Why is that, I wonder? Could it be they know the victim mentality would change to a heroic mentality if the odds were changed in their favor if they had a means to defend themselves? This arouses the maternal guardian in me.

The question that arose after the Sandy Hook Elementary School tragedy of whether teachers and school administrators should be armed, I believe, and a few in close proximity to the issue think, the answer is academic.

Some in the industry took action while the federal talking heads discussed and debated the issue. The Buckeye Firearms Foundation reported, shortly after the incident, they were flooded with 650 applicants for a program that had only twenty-four openings available. Buckeye offered free attendance to educators into their Armed Teacher Training Program, which provided them with the necessary information to help them obtain a concealed carry permit. The cost of the program was $1,000. Buckeye, being a nonprofit organization, is run by volunteers and was able to offer the program through donations from other sponsors and fund-raising efforts.[13]

Applications for the program soon rose to more than nine hundred, and no one expected that trend to change. Nearly 20 percent of the applicants were principals and vice principals.

So while politicians on both sides of the aisle wage their debate on the ethics and the practicality of allowing firearms on school grounds or banning them from every American, teachers are clamoring for firearm training and concealed carry permits. Perhaps those are the people to whom we need to be listening. They are the ones closest to the issue.

Something else that needs addressing is the flags, stickers, or signs that are posted proclaiming that the school is a "no guns zone." Is that not risking children's lives and using them as bait for the criminally insane?

The duty to respect human life is paramount in a civilized society. Great anger or hatred toward someone else is the seed that can grow to produce the fruits of violence and murder. Again, guns are not what cause it; self-centered evil intentions are.

I hear about the crime rate in a big city, such as Chicago, and my first knee-jerk reaction is, "never want to go there." But is that the right reaction? Has God turned a blind eye to what is going on there, or has the salt of the earth, the light to the world, God's people, turned a blind eye? It is heartbreaking what is happening there. And what about Detroit?

Chicago is President Obama's adopted city due to his claims that Chicago is where he hails from, instead of Hawaii.

This is in a city with some of the toughest gun control laws in America. You cannot even purchase a handgun in Chicago. How do the police feel about the gun control laws? Chicago Police Superintendent Garry McCarthy was reported by Fox News to have said, "Aiming at assault weapons misses the mark when dealing with Chicago's gang violence." He added, "The weapon used is generally a handgun, and rarely is it purchased through legal channels."[14]

Most of the victims were shot with a handgun not an AR-15 or an "assault" rifle, which was the Obama-nation's targeted weapon. They were confusing everyone to further their antigun program. But does this change whether the gun is the culprit or the intentions of the one using the gun? That does not seem to ever be addressed. If it were the gun, why were there murders committed without them? Out of the 4,251, 3,371 were murdered with some kind of a firearm; for the remaining 880, the weapon was some other object. Objects that also are in existence for reasons other than committing murder, such as pocketknives, baseball bats, rope, gasoline, a screwdriver, or a pry bar.

Basically, an assault weapon can be anything. Less than 1 percent of the murders in Chicago, during this period, were committed with what the Chicago Police Department classifies as a "rifle," the classification for an AR-15.

Another bad idea that the Obama-nation supports is the United Nations' Arms Trade Treaty (ATT).[15] They tout it as a means to prevent the irresponsible sale, gift, or lease of weapons and ammunition across borders to hide the fact that it is a campaign of deception and deliberate misguidance for more control and interference for gun owners. Don't they mean criminal instead of irresponsible? There are already laws governing these transfers and transactions, and they are leaving out a huge element of this treaty. It will not only govern and control the transfer of weapons between countries but also between private individuals.

THE ABOMINATIONS OF THE OBAMA-NATION

House Resolution 814, introduced on November 16, 2012, by Rep. Mike Kelly (R-PA), made note of possible costly regulatory burdens on US businesses that import firearm parts and components due to it being up to the exporting state to decide what information is needed from the US businesses.

The resolution also exposed that the ATT places free democracies and totalitarian regimes on a basis of equality. It is a principle of sovereign equality imposing the same standards on all countries regardless of their political systems, whether it is a democracy or a dictatorship that professes the right of tyranny. To me, this is just another reason to disassociate ourselves with the United Nations.

The controversy is sure to continue due to the knowledge that there is a certain amount of responsibility that goes along with owning and using a firearm. Some folks have no confidence in their fellow citizens and some do. I have found that responsibility is not a bad thing to have, show, or expect from others, including our youths. I believe it builds character and puts things in the right perspective. But it is hard to expect others to be responsible when we, ourselves, are not. Still, why infringe on the rights of those who are responsible just because there are those who have evil intentions and are irresponsible? Does that not infringe on our right to life?

The ultimate legal authorities in this country are the sheriffs that are elected by the people in their prospective counties. The impact on our country could be immense if our county sheriffs turned a blind eye to the Constitution and the Bill of Rights, just as the Obama-nation has, and not enforce federal guidelines.[16]

In essence, it is the county sheriff's decision to abide by or refuse any federal guidelines. That means if a county sheriff thinks a federal or state law is unconstitutional or unlawful, he can refuse to enforce it. You've got to love James Madison for this contribution to the Constitution, and Supreme Court Justice Antonin Scalia for making the point known.

The perfect example, my favorite at least, and the epitome of the right to life and the protection and preservation of life was the story about the Georgia mom that shot the home intruder five times protecting her life and the lives of her two young boys.[17]

She probably would have fired more shots, but that was all the 38-caliber revolver held. The intruder used a crowbar to break in the front door. So, besides the fact that he had just broken into the house and she had a right to shoot him just for that, he was armed, too—with a crowbar.

She did all of this with the encouragement of a loving husband and the listening ears of a 911 emergency dispatcher, both of whom were on the phone during the event. He said he was proud of his wife, and so was I.

From stories like this, and their numbers are countless to be heard, common sense dictates that if the guns are taken out of the hands of responsible law-abiding mothers, fathers, sisters, brothers, and so on, there will be more rapes and more assaults and deaths. Stories like these are testimonies to the reason and rules that we live by to maintain the welfare for a free and moral society. This is the only kind of society worth living in. That is why I still want to be here in America and nowhere else.

Conclusion

It is my hope to stir a spirit of patriotism in us all with the understanding that this book is as much a revelation into who I am and how I evaluate the world around me as to the revealing of what I see as the obvious direction of the Obama-nation.

I tried to describe the political landscape from the vantage point of an average, everyday citizen with the insights that some may see as unique. Mine are insights into where the progressive's destructive ideology came from and where it wants to go. I believe it to be the adaptation of any or all of the ideological tools that can be used to bring about their desired end. It is an end that is not concrete or absolute and shifts as sand underfoot with prescribed cultural and social relative reality. Or should I say lack of reality? Their collaboration with those who are driven to exalt Islam through Shariah law is naive, at best, because they have their own agenda.

Our liberties are being redefined in order to neutralize their importance—whether they are our religious liberties, constitutional liberties, or our parental liberties to raise our children as we see fit and be the ultimate governor of our own exposures. The progressive movement, adopted by the Obama-nation, is openly and covertly navigating the advancement of secularism in America to reduce the autonomy of individuality and the institutions that are the backbone and strength that made this country so prosperous, morally upright, and unique, and the most generous country in the world.

One of their primary objectives is to limit the influence of faith in the public arena first and then dictate what doctrines are allowed to be ministered from the pulpit. Naming their initial targets directly is unnecessary. One just needs to be on the receiving end of it to know who it is with the bull's-eye on his or her back. In America, "religion" largely means Christianity. Those who deny or find it too hard to grasp are either part of the mechanism or are completely oblivious as to what is going on in this country due to complacency and self-absorption.

Today, the secular Obama-nation views orthodox Christians, fundamental Constitutionalists, and outspoken conservatives as troublesome, obstructive, outdated, negative, backward, and extremists. They want us to be seen in the same light of terrorists. In the eye of the Obama-nation, we are seen as lying, judgmental, antiscience, antigay and antiwomen, which equates to antiprogress as they see it. To move forward with their vision for social justice and their utopian empire, Christians and their biblical doctrine will either need to be changed, limited to private domains only, or removed altogether, especially in political realms.

Religious influence (i.e., Christian influence) is already being demonized in the affairs of state. Institutions of education and our courts of, now, relative law, are proudly following principles based on "public reason," which shifts with the winds of social events and perceptions that have no foundation in our Constitution. The Judeo-Christian ethics, moral principles, and values, through this line of reasoning, are being considered suspect, which is the progressives' means to usurp our Constitution, a document that I and many others would die—and have died—to protect.

Our Constitution protects our religious liberty in two ways. One is by prohibiting laws establishing a religion to prevent a dominant religion from using political power of majority rule to lay claim to its own doctrine, at the disadvantage of others, to form a government religion. The second way is by prohibiting laws that limit the free exercise of religion in public, not just in private.

The secular Obama-nation statists want to expand the prohibition of established religion to silence religious voices and discredit religiously motivated voters and limit the free exercise of their Christian ethics, moral principles, and values so that a new secular morality can prevail over American society without Christian reality holding it back.

Christianity provides the most secure guarantee of freedom. Our forefathers may or may not have been Christians, but all agreed in the principle that the law of God trumps the law of man and "should" have political implications. Our Declaration of Independence identifies our rights as being given by our Creator and cannot be overridden or taken away. Without this reality, we would be subject to the will of man and vulnerable to a system in which the state defines what is right and wrong, good or bad, which is the essence of tyranny. The progressive movement, now the Obama-nation, is the campaign of the will of man.

Christianity also provides the remarkable capacity for communities of faith to endure diversity and the ability to self-reflect and face our sin and wrongs that we do to God and to each other. It is the means in order to repent and be forgiven and to forgive others. It is the driving force to protect the vulnerable and weak and to fight to end discrimination, persecution, and violence even when these things rise up out of our own.

I do not fear the decline of Christianity. Christianity has proven itself enduring for over two thousand years. But I do fear for the survival of the 237-year-old original American Constitution, slightly younger Bill of Rights, and the principles laid out in the Declaration of Independence without which the authors knew none could survive.

George Washington devoted this country wholly to God on that faithful day so long ago. He enlisted America to be a representative of God's will within our borders and to be a shining city on the hill for the world to see. Would Washington's inscription still ring true today? Can we say that we are on the right side of history?

America has a job to do. We need to stand up for righteousness without fear of being called names or becoming unwelcome to some or unpopular. We need to remove ourselves and our children from their company and influence, like government schools and the debauchery they consider entertainment. Stop listening to their propaganda, contempt, and manipulation, especially when it comes to politics. We need to vote for representatives with Christian virtues and hold them accountable to the highest degree to reduce and minimize the corruption that comes with positions of power.

Make them understand: *right now is always the right time to do the right thing.*

Stop giving these descendents audience. Stop arguing and fighting them. Turn the other cheek, shake the dust from our feet, walk away, and don't look back. America already has in place what it needs to overcome calamity. We need to have faith in God and our founding documents to prove their sustainability and hold to their true meaning and intent. We just need to stop giving the Obama-nation hope that they can destroy them and the principles upon which they stand.

"Then if my people, who are called by my name, are sorry for what they have done, if they pray and obey me and stop their evil ways, I will hear them from heaven. I will forgive their sin, and I will heal their land" (2 Chronicles 7:14).[1]

May God bless a restored America.

A Desperate Prayer for My Country

By Betty Sue Prollock

Our dear Heavenly Father, hallowed is Your name, *Your kingdom come, Your will be done, on earth,* as it is in Heaven.

Dear Lord, I come to You as Your humble servant with a grateful heart to ask for Your divine Intervention and mercy, for we have fallen so short of Your joy, Your honor, and Your glory.

I give thanks for Your forgiveness of our sins, O Lord, both those that are seen and unseen. For forgiving us for being deceived or ignoring the signs of Your Great Revelation coming to pass before us. For forgiving our silence and cowardice. I pray we also have forgiveness for each other, and through our forgiveness and our repentance, we thank You for Your mercy and grace, O Lord.

I thank You for Your blessings of hope to encourage and embolden Your faithful to lead others to know You through Christ and champion Your principles and values here in America, in our personal lives, and around Your world to bring You joy.

I thank You for Your blessings of understanding and knowledge of Your truth through Your Word to rid us of confusion and discontent, calming our fears and bringing us into peace, unity, clarity, and focus, O Lord.

I thank You for Your blessings of wisdom and guidance to restore the original design of this nation based upon Your laws that are the foundation of our liberties and reason as it was meant to be.

I thank You for Your blessings of courage and strength to do Your will instead of our own by all those You have placed in authority so "we the people" can once again show our faith in You to have a secure and strong nation and bring You honor.

I thank You for Your deliverance from the ambassadors of evil that are the instruments of Your judgment, who prey upon our weakness and gullibility, who challenge the patience and temperance of Your faithful, who conspire against Your will, Your nature, and Your truth, making "we the people" pawns in their political games.

I thank You for Your divine protection for the unborn and born, alike, the young and innocent, the elderly, Your faithful, and for those in harm's way both abroad and here at home, and for Your divine healing hand to touch the sick, injured, and suffering.

I thank You for Your love that abounds within these United States of America by each one of us to one another here at home and around Your world to bring You glory.

To You belongs all our adoration and praise for all the many blessings "we the people" have been challenged with, granted, and have been allowed to prosper from and enjoy for so long, O Lord. Your infinite, unconditional love and mercy is undeniably complete, of which I am deeply grateful. You are the Alpha and the Omega, and the power and the glory forever and ever.

In Your Holy Son's name Jesus Christ, who is the Way, the Truth, and the Life, my Lord and Savior and the only Savior of Your world, do I ask these things of You, Dear Lord.

Amen

About the Author

Born in 1956, Betty Sue Prollock grew up in Baytown, Texas, in a strong Christian home. Her parents were faithful members of the local First Baptist Church, where her father served as deacon and her mother taught Sunday school. Betty Sue accepted Jesus Christ as her Savior at the tender age of seven.

Betty Sue graduated from high school in 1975 and attended Lee College. She married Brian in 1978 and moved with him as his career in the construction industry took the family to several states. She recently graduated with honors from Lanier Technical College in Georgia with a degree in residential construction management. They have two sons, Brian Jr., and Benjamin Levi. Betty Sue currently takes care of her elderly mother, who lives with her family in Cumming, Georgia. There, they are active members of First Redeemer Church, formerly pastored by Dr. Richard Lee and currently by Jeff Jackson.

The inspiration for this book came from the author's apathetic spiritual walk with Christ being revived along with a deep love for her country, combined with renewed dedication to family, a driving force, and natural-born instinct to protect and preserve. Her desires to break the chains of deception and expose the true beneficiary in all his subtleties are strongly evident in this book.

Betty Sue aspires to share the balance and harmony, knowledge and understanding of truth—the truth through God's reality, unaltered, as it should be, combined with the understanding that we can have compassion for our fellow man while still expecting accountability. She aspires to bring hope, unity, clarity, and focus back to God as a nation and leave this world a better place than how she found it.

Notes

Foreword

1. Joel B. Green, PhD, and Tremper Longman III, PhD (Gen. Eds.), *The Everyday Study Bible*, The Holy Bible, NCV. (USA: Word Publishing, 1996). Book of Ephesians, NT, Cpt. 6:11,14-18, 1,403.

Chapter 1: The Catalyst

1. George Washington's Speech, Inaugural Address, April 30, 1789, New York City (National Archives and Records Administration).
2. Green and Longman, *Everyday Study Bible*, OT, Proverbs 3:5, 708.

Chapter 2: Are We a Christian Nation?

1. Green and Longman, *Everyday Study Bible*, NT, John 18:37, 1,280.
2. Ibid., 1 John 3:8, 1,480.
3. Ibid., Ephesians 6:17, 1,403.
4. Thomas Jefferson, "Replies to Public Addresses," January 1, 1802, in A. A. Lipscomb and A. E. Bergh, eds., *The Writings of Thomas Jefferson*, vol. 16 (Washington, DC: Thomas Jefferson Memorial Association, 1907), 281-82.
5. Green and Longman, *Everyday Study Bible*, NT, Matthew 12:23, 1,136.
6. Committee of Five, including Thomas Jefferson, John Adams, and Benjamin Franklin, Declaration Of Independence, July 4, 1776.
7. Ibid.
8. Congress, Constitution of the United States, Preamble.
9. Fischer Ames, "The Bible as a School Textbook" Speech, *Works of Fisher Ames* (Boston: T. B. Wait & Co., 1809), 134-35.
10. Donald Lutz and Charles Hyneman, "The Relative Influence of European Writers on Late Eighteenth-Century American Political Thought," *The American Political Science Review* 78 (1984).
11. Amendments to the Constitution of the Unities States of America (Bill of Rights), Amendment 1, ratified December 15, 1791.
12. Green and Longman, *Everyday Study Bible*, OT, Deuteronomy 6:13, 207.
13. Ronald J. Pestritto and Charles and Lucia Shipley, *The Progressive Rejection of the Founding*, 617; David J. Bobb and Allen P. Kirby,

"Institutionalizing Progressivism: The New Deal and the Great Society," *The U.S. Constitution, A Reader*, Hillsdale College, 717-18.

14. George Washington, quote, Inaugural Address, April 30, 1789, New York City, (National Archives and Records Administration).
15. George Washington, quote, Thanksgiving Day Proclamation, October 3, 1789, New York City, (National Archives and Records Administration).
16. Thomas Jefferson, quote inscribed on the Northeast interior wall of the Jefferson Memorial, Washington, DC, 1774.
17. Green and Longman, *Everyday Study Bible*, OT, Psalm 140:4-8, 698.
18. Daniel Webster, speech reported in Edward Everett, ed., June 3, 1834, *The Works of Daniel Webster* (1851), vol. iv, 47.
19. Congress, The Constitution of the United States, Preamble.
20. Aristotle, *Nicomachean Ethics*, trans. Joe Sachs (Newbury, MA: Focus Publishing/R. Pullins, 2002) 1-12; Aristotle, *The Politics*, trans. Carnes Lord (Chicago: University of Chicago Press, 1984), 35-41.
21. Marcus Tullius Cicero, "On the Commonwealth," C. 54-51 BC, James E. G. Zetel, ed., *On the Commonwealth and on the Laws* (Cambridge: Cambridge University Press, 1999), 71-72.
22. Patrick Henry, "Give Me Liberty or Give Me Death" Speech, March 23, 1775, Henrico Parrish Church, Richmond, VA, Second Virginia Convention.
23. Lyndon B. Johnson, House Resolution 235, "The Restriction of Political Campaign Intervention by Section 501(c)(3) Tax-Exempt Organizations" 012-08-14; Robert A. Caro, *The Years of Lyndon Johnson Means of Ascent* 387 (1990), 2. *Id.* at 317 3. *Id.* at 316-17 4. traditionalvalues.org
24. Dr. Rickard G. Lee, gen. ed., *The American Patriot's Bible*, 2009, Holy Bible, NKJV. (Thomas Nelson, Nashville, TN, 1982).

Chapter 3: The Surrender of Sovereignty

1. un.org, official website.
2. A talk given by Ida Urso, PhD, "Let the Future Stand Revealed: Envisioning the World We Choose" speech, World Goodwill Symposium, October 28, 1995, New York City; Alice A. Bailey, *The Externalization of the Hierarchy*, 131.
3. Green and Longman, *Everyday Study Bible*, NT, Ephesians 6:12, 1,403.
4. Green and Longman, *Everyday Study Bible*, OT, Psalm 2:1-3, 610.
5. Judith Butler, "Excitable Speech: A Politics of the Performative," Rutledge, New York, 1997.

6. Secretary of State Hilary Clinton, Small Arms Treaty with UN, www. state.gov/t/index.htm, May 23, 2010.
7. www.un.org/en/preventgenocide/adviser/responsibility.shtml, 2005 UN Summit; James Simpson, Examiner.com, "The Responsibility to Protect Doctrine: A Pretext for Disarming Israel" article, January 16, 2013.
8. Background Guide, Executive Board of the United Nations Development Program (UNDP), UN-USA, December 13, 2007.
9. Glen Beck and Harriet Parke, *Agenda 21*, November 20 2012, Threshold Editions.
10. United Nations, *Treaties Series*, p. 3, depositary notifications C. N.147.1993.TREATIES-5, May 5, 1993, [amendments to article 43 (2)]1; and C. N.332.1995.TREATIES-7 of November 7, 1995 [amendment to article 43 (2)]; treaties.un.org/Pages/ViewDetails.aspx?mtdsg_no=IV-11&chapter=4&lang=en, Cpt. IV, Human Rights, (11.) *Convention on the Rights of the Child*, New York, November 20, 1989, Active September 2, 1990, Article 49(1), No. 27531.

Chapter 4: The New United States Constitution

1. James O. E. Norell, "The Movement to Torch The United States Constitution," con. ed., National Rifle Association, *America's 1st Freedom* magazine, May 2012 edition.
2. Green and Longman, *Everyday Study Bible*, NT, 1 Timothy 1:4-7, 1,428.
3. Alexis De Tocqueville, "God, Family, Country: Our Three Great Loyalties," quoted in *Ezra Taft Benson* (Salt Lake City: Deseret, 1975), 360.
4. Thomas Jefferson, letter from Thomas Jefferson to Thomas Cooper, November 29, 1802, transcription at the Library of Congress.

Chapter 5: Misinformation or Misdirection

1. Patrick Burke, "Stimulated Algae: Slime Blooms in Reflecting Pool After Feds Spend $34 M to 'Improve Quality and Appearance of the Water,'" CNSNEWS.com, September 28, 2012.
2. Alexander Hamilton, "No. 71: The Duration in Office of the Executive," March 18, 1788, Clinton Rossiter, ed., *The Federalist Papers* (New York: Mentor, 1999), 429-34, Par. 2.
3. Bob Unruh, "Christianity gets flayed at home of Liberty Bell: You won't believe what tour guides say about Founding Fathers' beliefs," *Faith Under Fire*, World Net Daily Exclusive, September 19, 2010.

4. Rep. J. Randy Forbes, national motto letter to president, www.forbes.house.gov; Stephen Dinan, "Obama Muffed U.S. Motto," *Washington Times,* December 6, 2010.
5. Ann-Marie Murrell, "Black Pastor Sues Obama, Democratic Party for Racism," *Patriot Update*; Frances Rice, "Blacks Sue Obama And Democrats for Racial Discrimination," September 25, 2011.
6. Green and Longman, *Everyday Study Bible,* NT, Romans 1:24-25, 1,340.
7. Terence P. Jeffrey, "A Majority of Democrats Seldom or Never Go to Church, Says Gallup," CNS News, November 7, 2011.
8. Green and Longman, *Everyday Study Bible,* NT, Ephesians 6:16, 1,403.
9. *Zorach v. Clauson*, 343 U.S. 306 (1952); Frank J. Sorauf, "Zorach v. Clauson: The Impact of a Supreme Court Decision," *American Political Science Review* 53, no. 3 (1959) 777-91.

Chapter 6: The Animus to Christianity

1. Office of the Press Secretary, The White House, Weekly Address: "On Thanksgiving, Grateful for the Men and Women Who Defend Our Country," November 24, 2011; Scott Baker, "Obama Doesn't Mention 'God' in Thanksgiving Message—Problem?" *The Blaze*, November 24, 2011.
2. Green and Longman, *Everyday Study Bible,* OT, Psalm 117, 685.
3. Green and Longman, *Everyday Study Bible,* NT, Romans 1:21, 1,340.
4. Barack Obama, 2012 National Day of Prayer Breakfast speech transcript, *Washington Post,* Washington DC, February 2, 2012.
5. US Senator Barack Obama, keynote address: "Our Past, Our Future & Vision for America, Call to Renewal," www.obamaspeeches.com, June 28, 2006; David Espo, "Obama: Democrats Must Court Evangelicals," Associated Press, June 28, 2006.
6. Barack Obama, remarks at the Congressional Hispanic Caucus Institute's 33rd Annual Awards Gala, Washington Convention Center, Office of the Press Secretary, The White House, Washington DC, September 15, 2010.
7. Jason Lee, "Barack Obama, George Soros and the Religious Left," *American Thinker,* June 12, 2011; Aaron Klein, "Obama pastor: Occupiers on Wall Street like Jesus, Suggests church members have 'potluck' at protests," *WND,* October 9, 2011.

Chapter 7: The National Council of Churches

1. Penny Starr, "National Cathedral Leader: 'Homophobia' a Sin; Same-Sex Marriages Will Be Performed," CNS News, October 7, 2013; pecf. cathedral.org; "Historic Washington National Cathedral to Perform Same Sex Weddings," *Beginning and End*, February 27, 2013.
2. Green and Longman, *Everyday Study Bible*, NT, 2 Peter 2:1, 1,474.
3. Ibid., Acts 20:28, 1,322.
4. Ibid., Matthew 16:18, 1,144.
5. Linda Kimball, "Cultural Marxism," *American Thinker*, February 15, 2007; Pamela Geller, "Muslims Attack Christianity at Trinity University: Creeping Sharia: American Dhimmitude," *Daily Caller*, March 29, 2010; Andy and Berit Kjos, "From Marx to Lenin, Gramsci and Alinsky," www.crossroad.to/Quotes/communism/marx-gramsci.htm.
6. Green and Longman, *Everyday Study Bible*, NT, Acts 20:29-30, 1,322.
7. Charles Gregg Singer, *Unholy Alliance: The Definitive History of the National Council of Churches and Its Leftist Policies—from 1908 to the Present* (Arlington House, New York City, NY, 1975).
8. Robert Candler, *Shadow World: Resurgent Russia, the Global New Left, and Radical Islam* (Regnery, Washington, DC, August 5, 2008), 313.
9. Ibid.

Chapter 8: Liberation Theology or Ideology?

1. Green and Longman, *Everyday Study Bible*, NT, John 10:14-15, 1,268.
2. Ibid., John 10:9, 1,268.
3. Green and Longman, *Everyday Study Bible*, NT, Galatians 5:19-21, 1,395.
4. Kyle-Anne Shiver, Obama, "Black Liberation Theology, and Karl Marx," *American Thinker*, May 28, 2008; http://www. newworldencyclopedia.org/entry/Liberation_theology; Glenn Beck and John Kenneth Blackwell, "Black Liberation Theology Interview," www.glennbeck.com/content/articles/article/196/7574, March 20, 2008.
5. Joe Holley, "Civil Rights Leader James Forman Dies," *Washington Post*, January 11, 2005.
6. Martin Luther King, Jr., Bus Boycott speech, Montgomery, AL, December 31, 1955, en.wikipedia.org.

7. Trevor Loudon and Rodney R. Stubbs, *Barack Obama and the Enemies Within* (CreateSpace Independent Publishing, Pacific Freedom Foundation, Las Vegas, NV, October 19, 2011), 524.

8. Abraham Lincoln, "A House Divided" speech, en.wikipedia.org.

9. Lester J. Cappon, ed., *The Adams-Jefferson Letters*, vol. 2, John Adams in a letter to Thomas Jefferson, June 28, 1813 (Chapel Hill, NC: University of North Carolina Press, 1959), 339-40.

10. Green and Longman, *Everyday Study Bible,* OT, Psalm 23, 623-4.

The Guided Tour of Obama's book: *Dreams from My Father*

1. Green and Longman, *Everyday Study Bible,* NT, Matthew 5:43-44, 1,126.

Chapter 9: His Book: *Preface to the 2004 Edition*

1. Green and Longman, *Everyday Study Bible,* NT, Matthew 22:36-39, 1,156.

2. Ibid., Matthew 15:14, 1,143.

3. Ibid., Matthew 23:16-22, 1,157.

4. Ibid., Matthew 16:26, 1,144.

5. Ibid., Romans 12:2, 1,352.

6. Andrew Walden, "Obama's Other Controversial Church," *American Thinker,* June 14, 2009.

7. George Sutherland, "Principle or Expedient?" *Constitutional Review,* vol. 5 (October 1921), 18.

8. Green and Longman, *Everyday Study Bible,* NT, 2 Corinthians 4:16-18, 1,381.

9. Stokely Carmichael, "Black Power" speech. Ref. 22, accessed 17 March 2007, Wikipedia.

10. Green and Longman, *Everyday Study Bible,* OT, Ezekiel 18:23.

11. Ibid., Matthew 13:3-15, 1,137-38.

12. John Locke, *Second Essay Concerning Civil Government,* 56, par. 135.

13. Green and Longman, *Everyday Study Bible,* OT, Proverbs 1:7, 707.

14. Sir William Blackstone, *Commentaries on the Laws of England,* 1:54, 56, 63.

15. Dr. Rickard G. Lee, gen. ed., *The American Patriot's Bible,* NT, Galatians 5:22-23, 1,335.

16. Green and Longman, *Everyday Study Bible,* NT, 2 Corinthians 1:9, 1,379.

17. Ibid., John 1:1-5, 1,251.
18. Ibid., John 3:16-17, 1,256.

My Conclusion to His Book

1. Green and Longman, *Everyday Study Bible*, OT, Psalm 37:7-8, 630.
2. Green and Longman, *Everyday Study Bible*, NT, Matthew 5:39-40, 1,126.

Chapter 10: The Obama Brand

1. David A. Patten, "Trump: New Facts Emerging on Obama Birth Certificate," *Newsmax*, March 28, 2011; Bob Unruh, "Trump: Obama snub proves foreign birth 'This may go down as the greatest con in the history of American politics,'" *WND Exclusive*, November 1, 2012; Alan Silverleib, "Obama releases original long-form birth certificate," *CNN*, April 27, 2011.
2. Andrew Mytelka, "Obama Says Police 'Acted Stupidly' in Arresting Harvard Professor," *The Chronicle*, Washington, July 22, 2009; "'Scofflaw' Obama has history with 'stupid' Cambridge police: Condemns action of officer at department that ticketed prez 17 times while a student," *WorldNetDaily*, July 24, 2009; Dana Milbank, "Washington Sketch: Beer Summit Wasn't One for the Guinness Book," *Washington Post*, July, 31, 2009.
3. Jack Shafer, "What Do Herbert and Marion Sandler Want?: Investigating the funders of ProPublica, the new investigative journalism outfit," *The Fray, Slate, The Washington Post*, October 2007; Aaron Klein, "NBC newsrooms get fresh leftist invasion: Look who's providing major funds to National Broadcasting Company," *WND Exclusive*, December 6, 2011.
4. Barack Obama, Obama's speech at the Nuclear Security Summit, Council on Foreign Relations, Washington, DC, April 13, 2010.
5. Green and Longman, *Everyday Study Bible*, NT, Matthew 7:15-19, 1,128.
6. Ibid., Galatians 5:19-21, 1,395.
7. Barack Obama, full test of President Obama's economic speech in Osawatomie, Kansas, *Washington Post*, December 6, 2011.
8. Christina Hartman, "Obama Under Fire for Not Saying 'God' in Thanksgiving Speech," *Newsy*, November 25, 2011; da Tagliare, "Obama's Thanksgiving Address Fails to Mention God," *Godfather Politics*, November 28, 2011.

9. Barack Obama, remarks by the president at a campaign event, The White House, Office of the Press Secretary, W Hotel, San Francisco, California, October 26, 2011; Madeleine Morgenstern, "Obama Admits: 'Not as Trendy' to be a Supporter as it was in 2008," *The Blaze*, October 26, 2011.

10. John McCormack, "Obama: Small-Town Midwesterners 'Bitter,' American Businessmen 'A Little Bit Lazy,' America 'A Little Soft,'" *Weekly Standard,* November 17, 2011.

11. Pamela Geller, Obama's Republican Derangement Syndrome, Resource: "Obama For America," at theWhite House 2012, *Atlas Shrugs*, December 14, 2011.

12. Barack Obama, *text* of President Obama's US policy in Middle East and North Africa speech, *New York Time*, Washington, DC, released by the White House, May 19, 2011.

13. Green and Longman, *Everyday Study Bible,* OT, Genesis 12:3, 16-17.

14. "Los Angeles Times Sweeps Obama Tape under the Rug," *FoxNews*, October 28, 2008; Aaron Klein, "L.A. Still Conceals Obama Terror Video: Includes glowing testimonial for proof who excuses violence," *WND Exclusive*, September 30, 2009.

15. "Obama 'Bow' to Saudis: CNN Reporter Asks White House To Clarify," *Huffington Post,* May 10, 2009.

16. Angela Charlton, "Sarkozy overheard telling Obama Netanyahu's a liar," Associated Press, November 8, 2011.

17. "Solutions for America: Reining in Runaway Spending and Deficits," *Heritage Foundation*, August 17, 2010.

18. Green and Longman, *Everyday Study Bible,* OT, Deuteronomy 28:44, 228.

19. Ibid., Isaiah 1:22-23, 774.

20. Ibid., Malachi 3:5, 1,109.

21. David Jackson, "Obama: God wants us to put people back to work," *USA TODAY*, November 2, 2011; Kimberly Schwandt, "Obama: 'In God We Trust' Vote Not Creating Jobs," FoxNews, November 2, 2011.

22. Green and Longman, *Everyday Study Bible,* NT, 2 Thessalonians 3:7-10, 1,425.

23. Jeffrey H. Anderson, "Obama Misquotes Declaration of Independence, Again," *Weekly Standard*, October 20, 2010; Sterling Beard, "Obama Cuts 'Under God' Out of Gettysburg Address," *National Review*, November 19, 2013.

24. Barack Obama, Obama's 2006 speech on faith and politics, text of Barack Obama's keynote speech, Call to Renewal's Building a

Covenant for New America conference in Washington, DC, *New York Times*, June 28, 2006.

25. Green and Longman, *Everyday Study Bible*, OT, Isaiah 52:5-6, 835.

26. Green and Longman, *Everyday Study Bible*, NT, John 14:21, 1,275.

27. Green and Longman, *Everyday Study Bible*, OT, Proverbs 28.5, 738.

28. Becket Adams, "Million Dollar Question to Obama: 'Do You Take Any Personal Responsibility For Your Administration Creating Current Economic Conditions?'" *The Blaze*, December 14, 2011.

29. Mike Brownfield, "Infographic: Weak Job Growth in the Obama Economy," *The Foundry, Heritage Network*, December 5, 2011.

30. "The 'Empathy' Nominee: Is Sonia Sotomayor Judically Superior to 'A White Male'?" *Wall Street Journal*, May 27, 2009.

31. Keith Laing, "SC Gov. Haley: President Obama Made NLRB-Boeing Complaint a Political Issue," *The Hill*, June 16, 2011.

32. Green and Longman, *Everyday Study Bible*, OT, Psalm 7:8-9, 614.

33. Ibid., Proverbs 11:6, 717.

34. Barack Obama, FULL TEXT, VIDEO: "Obama Michigan Graduation Speech," *Huffington Post*, May, 20, 2010.

35. Green and Longman, *Everyday Study Bible*, NT, 2 Peter 2:2-3, 1,474.

36. Ibid., 1 Peter 2:16, 1,469.

37. Elise Viebeck, "Republican Rep. Chris Smith calls Obama the 'abortion president,'" *The Hill*, January 22, 2013.

38. Green and Longman, *Everyday Study Bible*, OT, Proverbs 26:4-5, 736.

39. Jeffrey T. Kuhner, "Pres. of the Edmund Burke Institute, Obama's Homosexual America," *Washington Times*, May 10, 2012.

40. Green and Longman, *Everyday Study Bible*, OT, Leviticus 18:22, 141.

41. Bob Unruh, "Obama offers plan for U.S. to be Global LGBT Sex Cop: Wants to import homosexuals with special asylum privileges," *WND Exclusive*, December 7, 2011.

42. Bob Unruh, "Obama effectively admits DOMA constitutional: DOJ brief submitted for coming court battle over same-sex marriage," *WND Exclusive*, February 27, 2013; Peter Baker, "For Obama, Tricky Balancing Act in Enforcing Defense of Marriage Act," *New York Times*, March 28, 2013.

43. Green and Longman, *Everyday Study Bible*, NT, Romans 8:5-8, 1,345.

44. Fred Dardick, "Firing Inspector General Gerald Walpin for investigating sexual predator and Obama friend Sacramento Mayor Kevin Johnson," *Conservative Spotlight*, September 16, 2012; Dotcomabc, "Inspector General Fired by President Obama Files Lawsuit to Be Reinstated," *ABC News*, July 19, 2009; Ed O'Keefe,

"Watchdog fired by Obama loses appeals case article," *Washington Post*, January 4, 2011.

45. John Wesley, *Wesley the Man*, University of Manchester, John Rylands Library, Exhibitions, "John Wesley (1703-1791): Life, Legend and Legacy."

46. Green and Longman, *Everyday Study Bible*, OT, 1 Chronicles 29:12, 482.

47. Gary DeMar, "Obama Lied: Buffet and His Secretary Pay the Same Tax Rate," *Godfather Politics*, January 25, 2012.

48. Nicholas Ballasy, "Obama says he'll be taking 'executive actions' without Congress on 'regular basis' to 'heal the economy,'" *Dailey Caller*, October 24, 2011.

49. Allahpundit, "Good News: State Dep't refuses to condemn Iranian crackdown," *Hot Air*, June 15, 2009; David Crawford, "How Obama Killed the Iranian Election Protests," Summer 2009, *The Under Current*, July 17, 2009.

50. Jerry Markon and Michael D. Shear, "Justice Department sues Arizona over immigration law: Lawsuit filed to block Arizona immigration law," *Washington Post*, July 7, 2010.

51. Stephen Dinan, "Obama adds to list of illegal immigrants not to deport: Parents," *Washington Times*, August 23, 2013.

52. Walid Shoebat, "Egypt's BEARD DAY: Friday Demonstrations In Support of Bearded Officers," *Shoebat Foundation*, September 14, 2012; Bruce Thornton, "A Lovely Little NATO Intervention," *Front Page Magazine*, August 23, 2011.

Chapter 11: Whetting Worldly Appetites

1. Nobelprize.org, official website, "The Nobel Peace Prize for 2009," Barack H. Obama, Oslo, October 9, 2009; Peter Beinart, "Obama's Nobel Farce," *Daily Beast*, October 9, 2009; Jon Boone in Kabul, Rory McCarthy in Jerusalem, Martin Chulov and Enas Ibrahim in Baghdad, "Barack Obama's Nobel prize greeted with cynicism, surprise and optimism: Residents of Kabul, Baghdad and Jerusalem voice reservations at US president's award," *Guardian*, October 9, 2009.

2. Woodrow Wilson, "Socialism and Democracy," August 22, 1887, Hillsdale College Politics Faculty, ed., *The U.S. Constitution A Reader*, Part X: The Progressive Rejection of the Founding, 646; Woodrow Wilson, "Socialism and Democracy," August 22, 1887, in Arthur S. Link, ed., *The Papers of Woodrow Wilson*, vol. 5 (Princeton University Press, Princeton, NJ, 1966-1993), 559-62.

3. Erik Thompson, "Bruce Springsteen 'Working On A Dream' Review," Album Reviews, *Culture Bully*, January 26, 2009.
4. Kevin McCullough, "His Classroom's Marchin' On!," *Fox News*, September 24, 2009; "McNorman Children Indoctrination Song for Dear Leader In South Hersey Update," under uncategorized, *Word Press*, September 24, 2009.
5. Michael Stone, "Obama song: School children praise Pres" (Viral Video, lyrics) *Portland Progressive Examiner*, September 24, 2009.
6. Todd Starnes, "Artwork Likens Obama to Jesus," *Fox News and Commentary*, Fox News Radio, September 4, 2012.
7. Green and Longman, *Everyday Study Bible*, OT, Ezekiel 1:14, 943.
8. Ibid., OT, Daniel 10:6, 1,015.
9. Green and Longman, *Everyday Study Bible*, NT, Matthew 24:27, 1,159.
10. Ibid., NT, Luke 10:18, 1,221.
11. Ibid., 2 Peter 2:1-3, 1,474.

Chapter 12: Islamic Modus Operandi

1. Green and Longman, *Everyday Study Bible*, OT, Genesis 16:11-12, 22.
2. "Dwight D. Eisenhower Delivers the Commencement Address at Pennsylvania State University Park, Pennsylvania, 06/11/1955," *National Archives*, OPA—Online Public Access, research.achives.gov/description/66337974.
3. "Search for Common Ground," US-Muslim Engagement Project, a collaboration of the Consensus Building Institute Convergence, and IRSS, An Initiative of Search for Common Ground and the Consensus Building Institute, established in 2009, development in 2006; Pamela Geller, "Blueprint for US Surrender To Islam: The US Muslim Engagement," *Atlas Shrugs*, March 16, 2009.
4. Stephen Coughlin, "Analysis of Muslim Brotherhood's General Strategic Goals for North American Memorandum," *The Investigative Project of Terrorism*, September 7, 2007.
5. Iseabail MacLeod and Mary Pauson, eds., *Webster's New Dictionary* (Windsor Court, New York, NY USA, Geddes & Grosset, New Lanark, Scotland, 1989), 726.
6. Green and Longman, *Everyday Study Bible*, NT, 2 Corinthians 10:5, 1,384.
7. Robert Spencer, *The Complete Infidel's Guide to the Koran* (Washington, DC: Regnery Publishing, 2009), Cpt. 4, 63.
8. Spencer, *Complete Infidel's Guide to the Koran*, Cpt. 10, 202; Walid Shoebat and Joel Richardson, *God's War on Terror: Islam, Prophecy*

and the Bible (Top Executive Media, Booksxyz, Lafayette, LA 2008), Cpt. 16, 70-78.

9.   Shoebat and Richardson, *God's War on Terror*, Cpt. 16, 74.

10. Spencer, *Complete Infidel's Guide to the Koran*, Cpt. 6, 105-7; Robert Spencer, "Blogging the Qur'an": Sura 13, "had Allah willed, He could have guided all mankind" (v. 31), "those whom Allah leaves to stray, no one can guide" (v. 33), and other passages that state that one's belief or unbelief is up to Allah (10:99-100), *The Thunder*, January 28, 2008.

11. Green and Longman, *Everyday Study Bible*, NT, Philippians 2:12-13, 1,407.

12. Kenda Creasy Dean, *Almost Christian: What the Faith of Our Teenagers Is Telling the American Church* (New York: Oxford University Press, 2010), Cpt. 1, 7.

13. Barbara A. Lewis, *The Teen Guide to Global Action: How to Connect with Others (Near & Far) to Create Social Change* Minneapolis, MN: Free Spirit Publishing, 2008).

14. Shoebat and Richardson, *God's War on Terror*, Preface, iii.

15. Bob Unruh, "'Superb' officer rebranded 'objectionable' after Muslims complain; Law firm defending instructor after Islam material purged," *WND Exclusive*, October 3, 2012.

16. Michael Carl, "Morsi denial of Copt persecution just Shariah-speak, 'A classic example of the Islamic inversion of reality,'" *WND*, September 3, 2012.

17. Fox News, "National Security Hawks Call for Brennan's Resignation," *FoxNews.com*, September 29, 2010.

Chapter 13: The American Muslim Brotherhood and CAIR

1.   Green and Longman, *Everyday Study Bible*, NT, Luke 12:54-56, 1,228.

2.   Michael Carl, "Decorated General: Shariah is here now! Tells audience influence has penetrated 'deepest halls of our government,'" *WND Exclusive*, July 14, 2012.

3.   Kevin A. Lehmann, "Supreme Court Justice—Elena Kagan—is Pro Sharia Law," *The United West*, July 5, 2011.

4.   Frank Gaffney, The Muslim Brotherhood in America: a course in 10 Parts, Center for Security Policy, muslimbrotherhoodinamerican.com.

5.   Art Moore, "U.S. Muslim Lobby Fights Measure to Protect Jews: California resolution calls on universities to combat anti-Semitism," *WND Exclusive*, September 7, 2012.

6.   WorldNetDaily, "CAIR Tells Muslims How To Limit TSA Inspection: 'They SHOULD NOT subject you to a full-body or partial-body pat-down,'" *World Net Daily Exclusive,* November 12, 2010.

7.   Howard Portnoy, "Georgia middle schoolers taught 'positives' of Sharia law," *Hot Air,* September 26, 2011; Lindsay Field, "School's curriculum on Mideast adjusted after parent protests," *Marietta Daily Journal,* Marietta, Georgia, September 22, 2011.

8.   Drew Zahn, "Shhhh! CAIR wants speaker silenced at U.S. Law School: Group Claims Former Muslim's Criticism of Islam 'Reminiscent of Nazi Germany,' Homeland In Security," *WND Exclusive,* October 2, 2011.

9.   Bob Unruh, "Advertisers Fleeing Muslim 'Propaganda': Sears, Wal-Mart, Home Depot, others drop support for program, Stealth Jihad," *WND Exclusive,* November 22, 2011.

10. WND, "Has Major Media Company Gone Completely Bonkers?: New Your-based news giant becomes best buddies with controversial figure," *WND Exclusive,* October 21, 2011.

11. Green and Longman, *Everyday Study Bible,* NT, Hebrews 6:4-6, 1,450.

12. Art Moore, "Another Huma Link to Muslim Brotherhood: Hillary's top aide was executive board member of front group," *WND Exclusive,* August 19, 2012.

13. Peter Brown, "Radical Islam Joins the DNC," *The Western Center For Journalism: Informing And Equipping Americans Who Love Freedom,* August 22, 2012; Hilary Trenda, "Muslim Jumah ends with disappointing attendance," *Charlotte Observer,* September 2, 2012.

14. Robert Spencer, "Shock horror: Muslim leader condemns Myrick anti-jihad plan," *Jihad Watch,* April 29, 2008.

15. Green and Longman, *Everyday Study Bible,* NT, Romans 1:21, 1,340.

16. Green and Longman, *Everyday Study Bible,* NT, 2 Thessalonians 2:3-4, 1,424.

Chapter 14: Islam in American Courts

1.   Green and Longman, *Everyday Study Bible,* NT, Romans 13:1, 1,353.

2.   "Not Your Father's America, Look who's Deciding American Court Cases: You knew it was coming, now it has finally arrived," *WND Exclusive,* October 25, 2011; David Reaboi with The Center for Security Policy, "Shariah Law and American State Courts: An Assessment of State Appellate Court Cases," Version 1.4, June 21, 2011; Gary DeMar, "Sharia Law Deciding American Court Cases," godfatherpolitics.com, December 10, 2011.

3. George Washington, "Farewell Address," September 19, 1796, in W. B. Allen, ed., *George Washington: A Collection* (Indianapolis, IN: Liberty Fund, 1988), 512-17; Library of Liberty[http://app.libraryof liberty. org] hosted by Liberty Fund; The Hillsdale College Politics Faculty, ed., "Farwell Address: George Washington," *The U. S. Constitution: A Reader*, III, 144.

4. Fox News, "Kansas lawmakers pass anti-Islamic law measure," John Hanna, Associated Press, Topeka, KS, May 11, 2012; *New York Daily News*, "Kansas Senate passes law banning Sharia, other foreign laws from state courts," John Hanna, Associated Press, Topeka KS, May 11, 2012; *USA Today*, "Kansas governor signs measure blocking Islamic Law," John Hanna, Associated Press, Topeka, KS, May 11, 2012.

5. *New York Times*, "Founder of Muslim TV Station Is Guilty of Beheading Wife," Associated Press, Buffalo, NY, February 7, 2011.

6. Green and Longman, *Everyday Study Bible*, OT, Deuteronomy 32:4.

7. Green and Longman, *Everyday Study Bible*, OT, Psalm 19:7-8.

Chapter 15: American Financial Shariah Compliance

1. Office of the Press Secretary, White House Appoints 2010-2011 Class of White House Fellows, The White House, Washington, DC, June 22, 2010; Chelsea Schilling, "White House Welcomes Shariah Finance Specialist: Obama selects Muslim expert in Islamic Transactions as fellow," *World Net Daily*, Homeland Insecurity Exclusive, June, 25, 2010; "Practical Law, Sukuk al mudaraba," *A Thomson Reuters Legal Solution*, UK; Sukuk al musharaka, *A Thomson Reuters Legal Solution*, UK.

2. Green and Longman, *Everyday Study Bible*, NT, Luke 12:2-3, 1,226.

3. David McPherson, "Movement to Scrap 401(k)s Gains Traction," *ABC News*, October 28, 2008; Jeffrey Brown, "Reasons to be Wary of State-Run Retirement Plans," *Forbes*, Washington DC, February 10, 2014.

4. WND Exclusive, "Has Major Media Company Gone Completely Bonkers?: New York-based news giant becomes best buddies with controversial figure," *WND*, October, 21, 2011; Bob Unruh, "Court: Marine Can't Challenge Shariah: But judges admit tax funds used 'for arguable religious purposes,'" *WND* Exclusive, June 1, 2012.

5. Green and Longman, *Everyday Study Bible*, OT, Proverbs 13:3, 719.

6. American Freedom Law Center, *Murray v. United States Department of Treasury*, americanfreedomlawcenter.org., Case: *Murray v. United States Department of Treasury, et al.*

7. Spencer, *Complete Infidel's Guide to the Koran*, Cpt. 7, 115.

8. Chelsea Schilling, "U.S. Treasury teaches 'Islamic Finance 101': Advisers, scholars to promote controversial Shariah finding," *World Net Daily*, November 5, 2008.

9. Green and Longman, *Everyday Study Bible*, OT, Deuteronomy 28:7, 227.

Chapter 16: The Truth about Homosexuality

1. Green and Longman, *Everyday Study Bible*, NT, Romans 12:9-10, 1,353.
2. Ibid., Matthew 15:19-20, 1,143.
3. Green and Longman, *Everyday Study Bible*, OT, Malachi 2:15, 1,109.
4. Ibid., Leviticus 18:22, 141.
5. Ibid., Proverbs 25:28, 736.
6. Anonymous, *The Queen James Bible*, published by Queen James, 2012.
7. Green and Longman, *Everyday Study Bible*, NT, Revelation 22:18-19, 1,515.
8. Ibid., Matthew 19:4-6, 1,147.
9. Ibid., Romans 1:24-27, 1,340.
10. Ibid., Romans 1:32, 1,340.
11. Jerome R. Corsi, "Obama didn't join Wright's church to follow Jesus: Members: 'It was a political decision, not a religious one,'" *WND* Exclusive, third of a series of articles WND has developed by months of confidential in-person interviews with members of Trinity United Church in Chicago, October 8, 2012.
12. Green and Longman, *Everyday Study Bible*, NT, 2 Thessalonians 2:10-12, 1,424.
13. David Gibson, "Obama and Gay Marriage: The Golden Rule Rules," Religion News Service article, *USA TODAY*, updated May 10, 2011.
14. Thomas.loc.gov, Bill Text 104th Congress (1995-1996) H.R.3396.ENR, *The library of Congress*.
15. Green and Longman, *Everyday Study Bible*, OT, Genesis 1:24, 5.
16. Newsmax, "Suspect in FRC Shooting Was Volunteer at Gay, Lesbian Group," Associated Press, August 16, 2012.
17. Bob Unruh, "Homosexual Activist Unleashes Another Rant Against Christians: 'Every dead gay kid is victory for FRC,'" *WND* Exclusive, October 2, 2012; Brody Levesque, "Gay Activist Unloads On FRC Head Perkins and Congresswoman Michelle Bachmann," *BN&S News and Commentary*, Winona, MN, October 2, 2012.

18. Coleen Curry, "Anti-Bullying Campaign Called Gay Indoctrination By Conservative Group," *ABC news* via *Good Morning America,* October 15, 2012.

19. Glenn Beck, "Saul Alinsky's 12 Rules for Radicals," *Best of Beck;* James Taranto, "Rules for Presidents: Obama tries to fight the system. One wonders when it'll dawn on him that he is the system," *The Wall Street Journal,* updated October 23, 2009.

20. Green and Longman, *Everyday Study Bible,* OT, Psalm 5:9-10, 613.

21. Philip Hodges, "Liberal Media Fabricate Another 'Scandal,'" *Godfather Politics,* July 30, 2012.

22. Green and Longman, *Everyday Study Bible,* NT, Romans 8:28-29, 1,346.

23. United States Court of Appeals, No. 09-11237—George C. Steeh, District Judge, 10-2100/2145 *Ward v. Polite et al.* Opinion, Eastern District of Michigan at Detroit, October 4, 2011; Mark E. Oppenheimer, "A Counselor's Convictions Put Her Profession on Trial," *New York Times,* February 3, 2012.

24. Linda Harvey, "Banned Books Week: Smoke Screen of Hypocrisy," *WND* Exclusive, September 23, 2005; "Is Library Association's 'Banned Book Week' Really 'Gay' Promotion," *WND* Exclusive, September 25, 2011.

25. Fred Lucas, "Fiscal Commission Calls for Elimination of Safe Schools Czar's Office," *CNS News,* November 10, 2010.

26. Green and Longman, *Everyday Study Bible,* OT, Proverbs 20:7, 728.

27. Office of the Press Secretary, Presidential Memorandum—International Initiatives to Advance the Human Rights of Lesbian, Gay, Bisexual, and Transgender Persons," The White House, Washington DC, December 6, 2011; WND, "What You Do In Bedroom Private? Not To Obama," *WND* Exclusive, December 11, 2011.

28. Stanton L. Jones and Mark A. Yarhouse, *Homosexuality: The Use of Scientific Research in the Church's Moral Debate* (Downers Grove, IL: Inter Varsity Press, 2000); WND, "'Groundbreaking' Study Shows 'Gays' Can Change: Contradicts belief altering orientation causes depression, anxiety, self-destructive behavior," *WND* Exclusive, September 15, 2007.

29. Green and Longman, *Everyday Study Bible,* NT, Romans 1:18-20, 1,339-40.

30. Matt Staver, "Hate Crimes Bill Protects Cross-Dressers and Pedophiles by Not Veterans or Grandmas," *Liberty Counsel,* April 28, 2009; Chelsea Schilling, "Obama Signs Hate-Crimes Bill Into Law: 'It's a very sad day for American and for religious liberties,'" *World Net Daily* Exclusive, October 28, 2009.

31. Alissa Tabirian, "Child Trauma Expert: Pro-Pedophilia Groups Are 'Grooming' Public to Accept Adult-Child Sex," *CNS NEWS*, October 16, 2013; "The History of Psychiatry and Homosexuality, the Declassification of Homosexuality," by the American Psychiatric Association (APA), *LGBT Mental Health Syllabus*.
32. Bob Unruh, "Psychiatrists Seek to Destigmatize Adult-Child Sex: Conference concludes better to 'focus on the needs' of pedophile than worry about protect children," *World Net Daily*, August 22, 2011.
33. Rena M. Lindevaldsen, *The Lisa Miller Story: Only One Mommy, A Woman's Battle for her Life, Her Daughter, and Her Freedom* (Orlando, FL: New Revolution, 2011).
34. Green and Longman, *Everyday Study Bible*, OT, 2 Chronicles 7:14, 488.
35. Bob Unruh, "Cross-dressing Cafeteria Worker Turns Stomachs of Parents, Kids: Exposed bra straps 'would not be permissible for students,'" *WND* Exclusive, September 23, 2011.
36. Thomas More Law Center news release, "Student Sues School District and Teacher Over Punishment Received After He Expressed His Religious Belief Opposing Homosexuality," *Alliance Alert: Alliance Defending Freedom*, December 15, 2011, *Tinker v. Des Moines Indep. Cmty. Sch. Dist.*, 393 U.S. 503, 506 (1969).
37. Office of the Press Secretary, Executive Order 13585—Establishing a Coordinated Government-wide Initiative to Promote Diversity and Inclusion in the Federal Workforce, The White House, Washington DC, August 18, 2011.
38. Green and Longman, *Everyday Study Bible*, NT, Romans 1:28-32, 1,340.

Chapter 17: The Antisanctity of Life Delusion

1. Green and Longman, *Everyday Study Bible*, OT, Psalm 139:13-16, 697.
2. Stephen Adams, medical correspondent, "Killing Babies No Different From Abortion, Experts Say," *The Telegraph*, UK, February 29, 2012.
3. Rodney Stark, The *Rise Of Christianity: How the Obscure, Marginal Jesus Movement Became the Dominant Religious Force in the Western World in a Few Centuries* (Princeton University Press, Princeton, NJ, 1996), 3.
4. Green and Longman, *Everyday Study Bible*, NT, Galatians 6:7-8, 1,396.
5. Terence P. Jeffrey, "Planned Parenthood Did One Abortion Every 95 Seconds—As Many in One Year as Live in Cincinnati," *CNS News*, April 8, 2011.

6. Rita Diller, "Planned Parenthood's Missing Millions: New GAO report reveals disturbing financial discrepancies," *Washington Times*, June 18, 2010.

7. David Green, "Column: Christian Companies Can't Bow To Sinful Mandate," *USA Today*, September 12, 2012.

8. Jack Kenny, "Obama Administration's War on Religion," *New American*, December 2012.

9. Chuck Donovan, "Conscience Regulations: HHS Stops (Just) Short of Rescission," *The Foundry*, Heritage Foundation, February 18, 2011.

10. Fred Lucas, "Obama Defends Roe v. Wade As Way for 'Our Daughters' to Have Same Chance As Sons to 'Fulfill Their Dreams,'" *CNS NEWS*, January 23, 2012.

11. Lydia Saad, "The New Normal on Abortion: Americans More 'Pro-Life'": "For second year straight, 'pro-life' and 'pro-choice' closely matched," *Gallup,* May 20, 2010.

12. Karl Marx and Friedrich Engels, *"Communist Manifesto" Essay, Sec. 2, "Abolition of the family! Even the most radical flare up at this infamous proposal of the Communist,"* New York Daily Tribune, 1850-1859

13. Green and Longman, *Everyday Study Bible*, OT, Exodus 20:12, 92.

14. Jack Cashill, "How Sebelius Subverted the Tiller Abortion Trial," *WND Commentary,* April 2, 2009.

15. John C. Willke, MD; Barbara H. Willke RN; John Jefferson Davis, PhD; David C. Reardon, PhD; Abort73.com; Eternal Perspective Ministries; Abolish Human Abortion; Life Issues Institute; BlackGenocide.org; Heritage House '76 Inc.; and The Center for Bio-Ethical Reform, *Abortion Facts*, "Partial Birth Abortion," 2014; Richard Willing, "Federal Abortion Ban Gets 3rd Rejection," *USA TODAY*, September 8, 2004, updated September 9, 2004.

16. J. D. Mullane, "What I Saw At The Gosnell Trial," *Buck County Courier Times*, April 15, 2013.

17. Green and Longman, *Everyday Study Bible,* NT, 1 Thessalonians 4:3-8, 1,421.

18. Green and Longman, *Everyday Study Bible,* OT, Genesis 9:5-6, 14.

Chapter 18: The Right of Self-Preservation

1. Bob Unruh, "'Vast Majority' Support Voter ID Procedures," WND/ WENZEL POLLS series for *WND,* Wenzel Strategies, Columbus, OH, September 13, 2012.
2. Philip Hodges, "Eric Holder Said Gun Owners Should 'Cower' Like Smokers," *Godfather Politics,* January 14, 2013.
3. Jana Winter, "Ex-Burglars Say Newspaper's Gun Map Would've Made the Job Easier, Safer," *Fox News,* January 6, 2013.
4. Michael E. Hammond, "HAMMOND: Obama's Gun-Control Dictate on 'Mental Health' Threatens Veterans' Rights," *Washington Times,* January 7, 2014.
5. Green and Longman, *Everyday Study Bible,* OT, Jeremiah 29:7, 893.
6. Tim Brown, "Exposing The left's Demonizing Of The Modern Musket: Real Numbers Of Violent Crime In The U.S.," *Freedom Outpost,* January 2, 2013.
7. Larry Klayman, Freedom Watch director, "Obama, Biden and Gun Control Task Force Sued," *Freedom Watch USA,* January 15, 2013.
8. Fred Lucas, "Biden Compares Gun Control to Car Air Bags: 'We're Saving Lives,'" *CNS NEWS,* January 10, 2013.
9. "American Memory, Lexington and Concord, The Minute man, Concord, Massachusetts," Library of Congress, 1900.
10. Aaron Klein, "Revealed: Obama's Likely Executive Orders on Guns; Group with enormous influence on White House issues specific plans," *WND* Exclusive, January 15, 2013.
11. Michael Maharrey, "The Constitution Doesn't Create Rights," Tenth Amendment Center, November 5, 2013.
12. Taylor Rose, "Constitution 'No Impediment' To Obama; America's reaction to sweeping gun control agenda," *WND* Exclusive, January 16, 2013.
13. Buckeye Firearms Association, "Armed Teachers: Over 600 Have Applied for Training," January 2, 2013.
14. Mike Tobin, "Chicago Has Tough Gun Laws, But Leads Nation In Gun Violence," *Fox News,* January 4, 2013.
15. Ted R. Bromund, PhD, "The Truth About the Arms Trade Treaty," *The Foundry,* Heritage Foundation, February 8, 2013.
16. 1997 court case *Printz v. United States,* and Judge Ellis Gregory Jr., 21st Judicial Circuit argument, 1991 case *Gregory v. Ashcroft,* 501 U.S. 452.
17. Christian Boone, "Cops: Mother Of Two Surprises Intruder With Five Gunshots," *Atlanta Journal-Constitution,* January 4, 2013.

Conclusion

1. Green and Longman, *Everyday Study Bible,* OT, 2 Chronicles 7:14, 488.

Arabic Glossary

1. Green and Longman, *Everyday Study Bible,* OT, Psalm 119: 105-6, 688.
2. Green and Longman, *Everyday Study Bible,* NT, Matthew 5:18, 1,125.

Arabic Glossary

The Quran

It is perhaps a common misunderstanding of the law of God to think that it was imposed upon the Jewish people in order for them to become God's chosen people. This is not the case. God chose the Jewish people first among all the nations, beginning with Abram and culminated in the Exodus. God did not say to Abram that he had to obey before he would call on him; nor did God tell them when they were in Egypt that they first had to prove themselves faithful before He would bring them out of slavery.

To put it another way, God did not say, "These are the things you have to do if you want to become my people." Rather He said, "I have made you my people, now these are the things I want you to do." The law of God was a gift to His people to teach them how they might obey God and fully enjoy His blessings.

"Your word is like a lamp for my feet and a light for my path. I will do what I have promised and obey your fair laws" (Psalm 119:105-106).[1]

"I tell you the truth, nothing will disappear from the law until heaven and earth are gone. Not even the smallest letter or the smallest part of a letter will be lost until everything has happened" (Matthew 5:18).[2]

Even if you do not read the Bible much or at all, and you have grown up in America, you probably would have been exposed to Christian traditions, expressions, and God-based sense of reality in some way. The reason for this dictionary is to expose you to a different reality that is intruding on our reality. A very different way of thinking and determining right and wrong.

These are a few Arabic words that might help your understanding of how Muslims think and what they consider acceptable or heresy. I know you may be inclined to just skip over this part due to the sheer anticipation of boredom that would accompany the idea of reading a dictionary. But I urge you to do just that. Remember, this is not an American-based dictionary. This is from a totally different culture. The words will be foreign to you and probably will not stick in your mind for long. It is the definitions that will stick. Along with knowing that Muslims actually have a word that has that meaning, that is what will stick.

Abdullah—Slave of Allah.

Abrogate—Cause to be forgotten; substitute something different or similar; to cancel out a Quranic verse by a later, contradictory verse; a concept acknowledged by mainstream Islamic tradition.

Ahmad—The Most Praised One.

Akharah—Islamic accountability; judgment day.

Akher—"Last," one of Muhammad's nicknames.

Al-Aqsa—Mosque located on the Temple Mount in Jerusalem; originally thought to have been in Mecca.

Al-Hadi—"The Guide," one of Muhammad's nicknames.

Al-Hanifiyyah—The Upright Way; the religion with Allah.

Al-Hatim or Al-Hijr—An area in Mecca opposite the Ka'bah (burial place of Hagar and Ishmael).

Al-Ikhwan—Muslim Brotherhood.

Al-Insan Al-Kamel—"The Perfect Man," one of Muhammad's nicknames.

Al-istita'a—One who possesses in full the capacity to act through free will; believed by Allah to be heresy.

Al-Khadir—Also Al-Khidr or Khidr; the green man; green symbolizing freshness of knowledge; Islamic and pre-Islamic lore; is associated with the "Water of Life" or the fountain of "Eternal Youth"; is referred to as the Mentor of Moses in the Quran, Hadith, and SufTafsirs.

Al-Maqam-Al-Mahmud—"The Glorious One," one of Muhammad's nicknames.

Al-mashi'a—Free will; believed by Allah to be heresy.

Al-Masih—Christ; a proper name, not a title; derived from the Arabic verb Massaha, which means to anoint someone with oil for healing instead of meaning "anointed one" as interpreted in Hebrew.

Al-Masih Ad-Dajjal—The Muslim False Messiah; the Christian's Jesus, Son of God.

Al-Mustafa Al-Mukhtar—"The Chosen One," one of Muhammad's nicknames.

Al-qudra—Effective power; believed by Allah to be heresy.

Al-rasul Al-A'tham—"The Greatest of All sent by Allah," one of Muhammad's nicknames.

Al-Siraj Al-Muneer—"The Luminous One, The Glowing Lamp," one of Muhammad's nicknames.

Al-Tawbah—Also Surat-at-Tauba; Surah Bara'at; the Koran's 9th sura (chapter): Then fight and slay the pagans wherever you find them and seize them, and besiege them and lie in wait for them in each and every ambush. Verse 9:5 Famous "Verse of the Sword" says "Then, when the sacred months have passed, slay the idolaters wherever ye find them, and take them (captive), and besiege then, and prepare for them each ambush. But if they repent and establish worship and pay the poor-due, then leave their way free. Lo! Allah is Forgiving, Merciful."

Allah—In Arabic "the God"; the god of Islam.

Amir—"The Prince," one of Muhammad's nicknames.

Amirul Mu'minin—Leader of the Believers; one of the titles of the caliph; the leader of the Sunni Muslims from the seventh century until 1924; during jihad has the choice of distributing captives among the Mujahidin (jihad warriors), in which event they will become the property of these Mujahidin.

As-Sakinah—Tranquility or peace and reassurance along with angels; adaptation of the Hebrew Shekinah, which refers in Jewish tradition to God's presence in the world.

Ash-shaikh—Married men.

Ash-shaikhah—Married women.

Asr—Afternoon prayer.

Assalaamu alaykum—"Peace be upon you"; the greeting that a Muslim extends to a fellow Muslim only; "peace be upon those who are rightly guiked" is the greeting that they say to non-Muslims.

Awal—"First," one of Muhammad's nicknames.

Awal-Khalq-illah—"The first of Creation," one of Muhammad's nicknames.

Ayah—(also Aya) Verse in the Koran.

Ayat—Verse in the Koran; "signs of/from Allah" which only the Koran has.

Baitul Muqaddas—Holy House; a mosque or temple in Jerusalem.

Bismilah—The Sura of Punishment; also referred to as Repentance; is security, this sura was revealed to remove security by the sword; contains the Verse of the Sword, "slay the idolaters wherever you find them."

Bismillah ar-Rahman ar-Rahim—In the name of Allah, the compassionate, the merciful.

Buraq—An animal described by Muhammad as "half mule, half donkey, with wings on its sides with which it propelled its feet" of which Muhammad rode into heaven with Gabriel in a dream.

Caliph—Islamic emperor.

Caliphate—Islamic empire; world or regional domination.

"Companions of the Fire"—The damned; disbelievers in hell.

"Companions of the Garden"—Believers who Allah blesses.

Dar al-harb—House of War; non-Muslim world.

Dar al-Islam—House of Islam; the Islamic world.

Da'wa—Islamic proselytizing; missionary activity promoting Islam and Shariah law.

Dhimmis (Dhimmah)—Subject Jews and Christian people who submit to the role of Islamic law; protected people as long as they submit to Islam or Shariah law; covenant of protection from Allah; People of the Book who are made to "feel themselves subdued" but are allowed to practice their religion but do not enjoy equal rights with Muslims; atonement for rejecting Allah; posture of lowering themselves during the collection of the jizya (the non-Muslim poll tax); Muslims are not allowed to honor them or elevate them above Muslims, for they are miserable, disgraced and humiliated.

Din—The straight religion; includes forms of all other religions.

Diyah—Blood money; a payment to compensate for the loss of a person's life; the payment for killing a woman, which is half of what is paid for killing a man; payment for killing a Jew Christian is one-third of what is paid for killing a male Muslim.

Eidal-Adha—The Koranic version of the story of Abraham and Isaac (in the Koran it was Ishmael) that holds up hatred as exemplary, while belittling the virtue of forgiveness for nonbelievers of Islam.

Fasaad—Jews that they believe strive to do mischief on earth.

Fatiha—Opening; first sura (chapter) of the Koran; most common prayer in Islam: (Allah) "Lord of the Worlds" who alone is to be worshiped and asked for help, the merciful judge of every soul on the Last Day. Show us the straight path (Islam), the path of those whom Thou hast favored; not the path (disbelief) of those who earn Thine anger (Jews) nor of those who go astray (Christians); recited seventeen times a day within Islam's five requisite prayers a day.

Feast of Eid al-Adha—Commemoration of the end of the pilgrimage to Mecca, the Hiff, and Abraham's willingness to sacrifice his son.

Fida'e—From the source word Fiduah meaning sacrificial lamb; suicide martyr; best way for one to assure Islamic salvation.

Fitnah—Mischief.

Fuqahd'—All Islamic jurists.

Gharan—Peril, risk or hazard insurance; the avoidance of excessive uncertainty which is consider gambling and is forbidden.

Gharqad—Tree of the Jews.

Hadd—The prescribed punishment for fornication, which is stoning; not seen to be necessary for men but only for women; an added commentary in the Koran (4:16) that refers to men who commit fornication or sodomy.

Hadith—Sayings of Muhammad; traditions, words, actions, deeds and related matters of Muhammad; a verbose and detailed collection along with the Quran, being oblique and allusive, is the foundation for Islamic legal reasoning; elucidates the Quran in many particulars where Muhammad is at the center of both and the standard by which all behavior is measured.

Hafiz—One who memorized the entire Quran.

Halal—Lawful food preparation that is compliant to Shariah law that curtails the animal to be killed while the butcher facing Mecca (the black stone) and either cries "Allah Akbar" or has a tape playing that is repeatedly saying the words while processing the meat.

Hanif—Indicates one (as in Abraham) who held the original monotheistic religion that was later (so called) corrupted to create Judaism and Christianity; a person of pure natural belief and who inclines from all other religions to the Straight Din(religion); a Muslim and affirmer of the Divine Unity.

Haram or hima—Two meanings; any act that is forbidden by Allah; geographical environmental protected areas; the sacred precincts of Mecca.

Hawwa—Eve, as in Adam and Eve.

Hijab—Headscarf worn by Muslim women.

Himas—Islamic environmental laws; covers forests and wildlife.

Ikhwani—The Ikhwan (Arabic for *brothers*) was an Islamic religious militia, which formed the main military force of the Arabian ruler Ibn Saud and played a key role in establishing him as ruler of most of the Arabian Peninsula, in his new state of Saudi Arabia. According to Wilfred Thesiger, this militant religious brotherhood declared that they were dedicated to the purification and the unification of Islam.

Iman—Faith.

Infidel—Anyone who refuses to submit to Allah, having no associates, as the one true god and to recognize Muhammad as his prophet.

Injil—What Muslims identify as the Gospel in the Quran; an original Gospel, which was promulgated by Jesus as the Torah was promulgated by Moses and the Qur'an by Muhammad al Mustafa.

Isa—Jesus in Arabic; son of Maryam; not the son of God that is referred in the Christian New Testament Bible.

Isra'iliyat—Jews; of or from Jews.

Jaahiliyyah—Barbarism.

Jahannum—Hell.

Jahiliyya—The pre-Islamic period of ignorance; the society of unbelievers.

Jasad—Dead body not necessarily human but can be.

Jazia—Also jizya; a tax that the Koran (9:29) specifies must be levied on Jews, Christians, and some other non-Muslim faiths as a sign of their subjugation under the Islamic social order.

Jews—Apes and pigs; People of the Book (Jews and Christians); lovers of lies.

Jihad—Means "struggle" in Arabic; to "strive with might and main in the cause of Allah" (Jihad fi sabil Allah) refers to jihad warfare; fighting to extend the boundaries of the Islamic world called the House of Islam (dar al-Islam), at the expense of the non-Muslim world, called the House of War (dar al-harb); a Koranic declaration that those who "strive in the way of Allah . . . have hope of Allah's mercy" is a call to jihad and a promise of reward for those who answer the call; "Strive" here is jahadu, which is a verbal form of the noun jihad, and in Islamic theology "jihad for the sake of Allah" or "jihad in the way of Allah" always refers to jihad warfare; has been used in other connotations to refer to internal or spiritual struggle but are not the original context for its meaning; Islamic offensive warfare; Holy War.

Jinns—A kind of invisible or visible spirit that can pose as what or whoever it wants to that the Koran associates with Satan.

Jizya—Non-Muslim poll tax; the alternative to converting to Islam, but if refused, Muslims are directed to go to war with; only those People of the Book qualify; seen as lowering themselves to Muslims; is believed to be collected or taken in a manner of belittlement and humiliation.

Jum'ah—Friday prayer: is a congregational prayer held every Friday, just after noon in the place of dhuhr; it is half the zuhr (dhuhr) prayer, for convenience, preceded by a sermon as a technical replacement.

Ka'aba—The Meccan shrine to which every Muslim, if able, is obligated to make at least one pilgrimage; was a pagan Arab shrine and a center of pilgrimage long before Muhammad began preaching Islam; is claimed to have been constructed by Abraham and his son Ishmael.

Ka'bah—Burial place of Hagar and Ishmael.

Kafir—An individual unbeliever.

Khalifa—Islamic trusteeship; the vicar of Allah on earth and the supreme ruler of the Muslim Umma (Islamic community).

Khatimun-Nabiyeen—"The Seal of Prophets," one of Muhammad's nicknames.

Khutba—Religious talk; preaching.

Kitman—Lying by omission. An example would be when Muslim apologists quote only a fragment of verse 5:32 (that if anyone kills *"it shall be as if he had killed all mankind"*) while neglecting to mention that the rest of the verse (and the next) mandate murder in undefined cases of "corruption" and "mischief."

Kufaar—A group of unbelievers.

Kuffar—Disbelievers; infidels; those who reject Islam.

Kufr—Disbelief.

Madrassas—An Islamic religious school; school of choice by the Taliban; Saudi financed are causing an explosive growth of these schools worldwide; not so much concerned about scholarship as making war on infidels; teaches Wahhabism.

Mahdi—"The Guided One/Deliverer," one of Muhammad's nicknames.

Maisir—An increase in capital without any services provided such as interest on loans; considered gambling and a sin; it is prohibited by the Quran.

Makkah—Conquest.

Mauritanian—A slave that is born and bred as a slave, a slave whose parents and grandparents before him were slaves, does not need chains; raised as a domesticated animal.

Mecca—Islam's holy city.

Mozarab—Christian dhimmis.

Mu'tazilites—Separated Ones; Muslims who have withdrawn; those who tried to develop a method of Quranic interpretation that was freer from the literal meaning of the text.

Mudaraba—Profit sharing from a Shariah-compliant contractual investment.

Mudareb—Managing trustee of a Shariah-compliant contractual investment.

Muhammad—Prophet of Allah; a warner; a bearer of good tidings; "The Praised One."

Mujahidin—Jihad warriors.

Munji—"Savior," one of Muhammad's nicknames.

Muruna—The practice of defying the Muslim faith for the purpose of gaining the trust of one's enemy.

Mushaf—The complete copy of the Quran.

Mushrikun—Polytheists; those who commit the cardinal sin of shirk—associating partners with Allah as in God the Father, Jesus His Son and the Holy Spirit; they see Christians as pagans.

Muslim(s)—Follower of Allah, the prophet Muhammad, and the Quran.

Nikah mut'a—Temporary marriage: of which the duration is specified at is beginning, and after it ends the couple part without further ado.

"People of the Book"—Mostly Jews, but includes Christians.

Periklytos—Paraclete; counselor; Islamic apologists claim is a corruption of periklytos, which means "famous," "renowned," or "praised one"; like when Jesus referred to "Counselor" in John 14:16—17, which is very unlikely.

Qibla—Direction for prayer; toward Mecca and the sacred Mosque.

Qisas—Retaliation for murder; equal recompense to be given for a life or a victim.

Quraish—Mohammad's tribe.

Qur'an—Also Koran; Islamic holy book; not arranged chronologically or by subject matter, but by the length of the chapter (sura); contains 114 chapters that survived, the original book and number of suras are unknown, the first chapter being sura 96 and the last chapter being sura 110; the recitations Mohammad received (of his own proclamation to have received) claims they came from the angel Gabriel transmitting the direct words of Allah, beginning in 610 AD; perfect copy of the "Mother of the Book"; Signs of Allah.

Qurra—Those who know the Quran by heart.

Rab al Maal—The investor associated with a Shariah-compliant contractual investment.

Rahmatan-lil-A'alameen—"Mercy to All Mankind," one of Muhammad's nicknames.

Reliance of the Traveller ('Umdat al-Salik)—A Classic Manual of Islamic Sacred Law (Shari'ah), trans. Nuh Ha Mim Keller (Beltsville, MD: Amana Publications, 1999), Ahmed ibn Naqib al-Misri.

Riba—Accumulating interest; forbidden in Islamic economic jurisprudence fiqht and considered as a major sin; considered unjust gains in trade or business; considers it exploitation. There are two types of riba discussed by Islamic jurists: an increase in capital without any services provided and speculation.

Sahih Burhari—The most sound or reliable hadiths (sayings and activities of Mohammad) found in the Sunnah.

Salaf—Many scholars of the predecessors.

Salat—Islamic prayer that can only be performed by Muslims.

Satan—The father of the jinn (invisible spirits) and who was among the angels.

Sayyid Walad Adam—"The Leader of the Sons of Adam," one of Muhammad's nicknames.

Shahada—The first part of the Islamic declaration of faith, "There is no god except Allah."

Shahadah—Martyrdom; the theological underpinning of both jihadism and suicide bombings; grounded in traditional and authoritative Shariah law.

Shaheed—Islamic martyr; one who atones for sin, even his own; assurance of salvation and entry into Paradise; can be an intercessor for seventy members of his/her family.

Shafi—"Healer"; one of Muhammad's nicknames.

Shaqqa—"Split" in Arabic; also plowing or digging the earth.

Shariah—Also Shar'iah; Islamic sacred law.

Shaytan—Devils.

Shi'a—Shi'ite; a following or sect; "Party" of 'Ali (Mohammad's son-in-law) who they believe was designated by Mohammad to succeed him as leader of the umma of Islam; one of the two primary branches of Islam (the other being of the majority Sunni).

Shirk—Worshipping gods other than Allah; the cardinal sin in Islam; the association of partners with Allah (i.e., Jesus being the Son of God).

Sic—What Muslims consider a wrongful action or war against Islam, also "shaqqa" or split, plowing or digging the earth; allegations that the Koran teaches violence and religious hatred.

Six Bounties of martyrdom—

1. He will be forgiven with the first drop of his blood that is spilt.
2. He will see his place in Paradise (at the time of death).
3. He will be saved from the "Great Horror" (on the Day of Judgment).
4. A Crown of Dignity will be placed on his head, which contains many conundrums, each one being more precious than this life and all that it contains.
5. He will have seventy-two women (virgins) of Paradise.
6. He will be allowed to intercede for seventy of his family members (who would have otherwise gone to hell).

Sunna—The "trodden path"; "the way"; "example"; "habitual practice"; refers to the example or path of the Prophet Muhammad and his followers.

Sunnah—Way of the Messenger of Allah; a voluminous collection of accounts of the Islamic prophet's sayings and activities, as recounted by his followers; was subject to forgery and fabrication.

Sunni—The followers of Sunni Islam; one of the two major branches of Islam (the other is Shi'a); they are the majority in most Islamic countries outside of Iran, Iraq, Yemen, and Bahrain.

Sura—Chapter in the Quran.

Tafsir al-Jalalayn—a Koran commentary highly regarded by Muslims.

Taghut—Anything worshipped other than Allah.

Talaq—Divorce; a man can only divorce his wife two times, if they divorce a third time they cannot remarry again until after she has married another husband and he has divorced her; leads to temporary marriages.

Taqiyya—Saying something that isn't true; a developed doctrine of deception; exclusively Shi'ite.

Tawheed—Islamic unity; Islamic Unitarianism that Allah is a "single one" that is set in contrast with the Christian Trinity.

Tawrah—Torah; Jewish Scripture; First five books of the Bible written by Moses.

"Those whom your right hands possess"—Term or phase repeatedly used in the Koran referring to slave girls; women captured during jihad to be used for whatever the "possessor" wills; includes the offspring of slaves, before or after enslavement; positive traditional Muslim behavior and ideology according to the Koran.

Tilth—Field; as in what a woman is likened to.

Tree of Zaqqum—Tree from which the food the damned will eat that Allah created as a torment for wrong-doers; springs up "in the heart of hell" and bears fruits that resembles "the heads of devils."

Umm al-Kitab—The "Mother of the Book," which has resided forever with AllahUmmah—the Muslim community of believers; a concept where loyalty that trumps family and other societal ties.

Umma—Islamic community; derived from the Arabic word umm ("mother"); used as the unity of Muslims.

Vis-a-vis—State of subjugation for the People of the Book; meant to enforce upon them a constant sense of degradation due to their rejection of Muhammad and Islam; meant to be humiliating and degrading.

Waaf—A religious endowment; a bestowal from Allah.

Wahhabism—The fundamental teachings of Islam that is taught in Madrassas or Islamic schools.

Waidriboohunna—The punishment of Muslim women; abuse; taught by the Koran for men to warn their wife and send her to sleep in separate beds and to go away from them; the different interpretations are:

Pickthall: to scourge them (the wife)

Yusuf Ali: (and last) beat them lightly

Al-Hilali/Khan: (and last) beat them (lightly, if it is useful)

Shakir: and beat them

Sher Ali: and chastise them

Khalifa: then you may (as a last alternative) beat them

Arberry: and beat them

Rodwell: and scourge them

Sale: and chastise them

Asad: then beat them

Dawood: and beat them.

Wali—A Muslim saint.

Waqf—A religious endowment; a bestowal from Allah in which the land of Palestine is considered by Islam (Hamas)

Zakat—Charity which only Muslims pay; the poor-tax.